Ida Craddock (1857–1902)

Sexual Outlaw, Erotic Mystic

The Essential Ida Craddock

Weiser Books

This edition first published in 2010 by Weiser Books,
an imprint of Red Wheel/Weiser, LLC

With offices at:
65 Parker Street, Suite 7
Newburyport, MA 01950
www.redwheelweiser.com

ISBN: 978-1-57863-476-7

Library of Congress Cataloging-in-Publication Data available on request

Cover design by Kathryn Sky-Peck
Text design by Jane Hagaman
Typeset in Cochin and Caslon Antique.
Cover photograph courtesy of Southern Illinois University, Carbondale.

Printed in the United States of America
IBI

Dedication

For my wife, Lita-Luise,
and all courageous women who
refuse to compromise their beliefs

Contents

Acknowledgments

This book has been over ten years in the making. It evolved from a research project I embarked upon in 1998 with my close friend and spiritual brother, Erik Freeman. On our original quest, we were favored with the generous hospitality and historical insights of Martin P. Starr in Chicago. The result of that trip was a paper I presented in 1999 at the second national conference of Ordo Templi Orientis in Portland, Oregon, later published as "Ida Craddock: Sexual Mystic and Martyr for Freedom" in the anthology *Book of Lies: The Disinformation Guide to Magick and the Occult* (2003). We also made many of Craddock's works available online at *www.idacraddock.org*, with the assistance of Sharon Sheinker and the sponsorship of the O.T.O.

The primary repository for Ida Craddock's works is the Special Collections Research Center at the Morris Library, Southern Illinois University, Carbondale. I am indebted to the SCRC for its kind permission to publish items from its collection, and particularly to its director, Pamela Hackbart-Dean, and staff members Mark Choate, Judy Simpson, and Darla Loftus, for their assistance in making this book a reality.

Materials were also kindly made available by the Spencer Research Library at the University of Kansas, the New York Academy of Medicine, the New York Public Library, and the Wisconsin Historical Society. Permission to quote from *The Truth Seeker* was furnished by the Truth Seeker Company. Permission to reprint Aleister Crowley's review from *The Equinox* was furnished by Ordo Templi Orientis.

I would also like to thank William Breeze for invaluable research assistance and editorial advice, and Richard Kaczynski for additional research help. Erik Freeman has also continued to inspire and challenge me to do my best throughout the writing of this book. I am grateful to my editor at Red Wheel/Weiser, Amber Guetebier, for guiding me through the perilous process of publishing my first book, and to Lon Milo Duquette and James Wasserman for their confidence in recommending me to undertake this project.

Finally, I would like to thank my father, Vere Claiborne Chappell, for instilling in me a sense of discipline and the importance of good grammar, and most of all my wife, Lita-Luise Chappell, who not only provided research assistance, but also unwavering support and understanding throughout this journey.

Foreword

"It has been my high privilege to have some practical experience as the earthly wife of an angel from the unseen world." So begins Ida Craddock's 1894 book *Heavenly Bridegrooms*, of which the magician, Aleister Crowley, declared, "No Magick library is complete without it."

Ida Craddock daringly sought to bring her understanding of the sacred symbolism and divine purpose of humanity's most elemental creative impulse—sex—to the public eye. For a 19th-century woman in America during the reign of morality czar Anthony Comstock, this was worse than lunacy, especially when she applied her wicked sense of humor to the ludicrousness of such situations as Comstock's attack on the Egyptian belly dancers at the Chicago World's Fair. Craddock wrote in her first article for the public, "It was easy to tell who among the spectators were unduly agitated by the sight of the *Danse du Ventre*, since these [persons] usually ejaculated 'disgusting,' and precipitately fled." Few readers would have missed her allusions to premature ejaculation by supposed sexual purists who lacked the refined sexual control advocated by Craddock, but she made a vicious enemy of Comstock.

Sexual surgery on women—to curb rebelliousness, sexual excess, and masturbation—reached its height in the United States during Craddock's lifetime. It was routinely performed to "cure" female insanity and rehabilitate prisoners. Female castration was thought to make a woman more tractable, orderly, predictable, and cleanly. Among middle-class women, whose ideal was a passionless sexual restraint, physical response was perceived as coarse, common, and immodest.[1] Craddock evidenced knowledge of

[1] See G. J. Barker-Benfield, *The Horrors of the Half-Known Life: Male Attitudes Toward Women and Sexuality in Nineteenth-Century America* (New York: Routledge, 2000).

explicit sexual practices that would "pass unquestioned if coming from a scientist" but, from an unmarried woman with no "illicit experience," was considered proof she must be insane. No wonder Craddock fled to England when her mother tried to have her committed to an asylum. Can we fail to feel for her when, after being hounded by Comstock for nine years, she chose suicide, in a deliberate act of martyrdom, rather than serve a long prison sentence? Be sure to read "Ida's Last Letter to the Public" to discover the gross iniquities of the case.

In 1994, my biography of three original female members of the 19th-century magical organization, the Hermetic Order of the Golden Dawn, was published with the subtitle "Rebels and Priestesses." Thus, it seems fitting that I was asked to write the foreword to this book about an "outlaw and mystic" from the same period and a similar occult background. I wanted to know what motivated and enabled these women to walk the borderland between society and spirit with such clarity and self-determination, and to understand how they succeeded and how they failed. The Golden Dawn had its own brush with the magical aspects of the "sex issue" and skirted it by suspending a couple of members and reserving such matters for only the highest levels of the Inner Order, which few ever attained.

Ida Craddock advocated a form of Western tantra rooted in the practices of several turn-of-the-century American spiritual communities. Through pamphlets and an extensive private clientele, she recommended that a married couple "enter into harmonious relations with the ideal, generous and pure" through controlled relations (including the restriction of seminal emissions during orgasm) that she described in exacting detail. As an additional benefit, all children would be the result of deliberate choice, not accidents. In a field dominated in both the East and West by males, misogyny, and secrecy, Craddock spoke and counseled frankly from a woman's perspective about what constituted sacred sex.

Perhaps the most controversial element of her life was her public declaration of having married, in October 1892, a spiritual, angelic husband who had left the physical plane many years before. Anticipating the reaction of others, Craddock wrote that her psychical experience could be either fact or hallucination, but claimed that the majority of her sexually explicit knowledge was a result of that union.

With the advent of Spiritualism in 1848, a path had opened to one of the few socially accepted expressions of women's power—access to the spirit world. As a research assistant to W. T. Stead (editor of the metaphysical magazine *Borderland*), and through her studies with the Theosophical Society, the Society for Psychical Research, Christian Science, New Thought, and of teachings like that of the Oneida Community, Craddock's knowledge of the occult was deep. She must have believed herself to be on the cutting edge of a new era in which the powers of mind and direct access to the angelic world would be recognized, even esteemed, by the more forward-thinking members of society. Instead, like the women who dared to teach birth control, she was hounded, institutionalized, and eventually sentenced to prison for passing on her knowledge. Some of her material would be adapted, without acknowledgment, into a mid-20th-century work on sex magic. Yet her writings would surely have been lost except for a lawyer with a special interest in free speech and in the origins of religion in sexuality. Nevertheless, even Theodore Schroeder characterized her experiences (just as she had predicted) as "erotic hallucinations," thus psychologizing them.

Through much of this book, biographer Vere Chappell lets Craddock speak for herself, allowing us to evaluate her accounts in our own ways. He also provides an excellent bibliography, emphasizing works on the confluence of occultism and sexuality.

While not everyone will share her conviction that sexual relations should be reserved for marriage, many will be fascinated by Craddock's recommendations regarding the spiritual side of sexuality and her clear and sensible prenuptial and marital advice. Furthermore, she was a rigorously honest and articulate recorder of a whole class of human experience that modern science has yet to examine with any kind of true open-mindedness. Reprinted here are Craddock's extensively researched myths and accounts of sex along the borderlands between worlds—rich fodder for any writer of otherworldly romance. Even today, few have come forward as overtly as Egyptologist Dorothy Eady (alias Om Sety, 1904-1981), who spoke openly of her ongoing marriage and sexual relations with a long dead pharaoh.

We may want to consider Craddock in light of modern communications and interactions, not only with the dead, but with extra-terrestrials, disincarnate beings, daimons, and ascended masters. These have been related by intelligent, psychologically high-functioning individuals well regarded in their professional fields, who attest to the reality, though not the provability, of their own experiences. Are these all hallucinations, insanity, or mere constructs of the human psyche? Or is there a distinct reality that exists along the borderlands of our everyday existence?

Ida Craddock believed that spirit bridegrooms and brides are much more frequent than is generally supposed. So, whether this book encourages people to discuss their own encounters more openly or to explore the considerable material now available on sacred sexuality, Ida Craddock, through the grace of Vere Chappell and in adherence to the laws protecting freedom of speech, is again teaching "the fundamental principles of sex morality on the Borderland." You have in your hands a book that can provide you with a map to that territory and a description of what Craddock found to be its greatest perils and safeguards.

Mary K. Greer,
author of *Women of the Golden Dawn: Rebels and Priestesses*

Editorial Conventions

This book is an anthology of works by Ida Craddock, embedded in a biography. Therefore, the editorial context varies depending on whether the text is mine or Craddock's. When I include quotes in the biographical text of each chapter, my omissions are denoted by ellipses. When ellipses appear in quotes within Craddock's works, they are hers.

In editing Craddock's works, I have silently corrected obvious grammatical and typographical errors, updated archaic spelling, modernized foreign language transliterations, and rendered consistent punctuation and visual style, taking care not to alter the original meaning of the text. My editorial interpolations are enclosed in square brackets, while those found in Craddock's original texts are enclosed in curly braces. All footnotes are my own unless otherwise noted.

I have used the following abbreviations to denote the sourcing of some materials:

ANCL	Ante-Nicene Christian Library
ICC	Ida C. Craddock
SCRC	Special Collections Research Center, Southern Illinois University, Carbondale
TS	Theodore Schroeder

Introduction

The sexual outlaw sat alone in her room, considering her options. She had already been arrested in Philadelphia, Chicago, and Washington, DC. Here in New York, she had endured three months in the workhouse on Blackwell's Island, an ordeal that almost killed her. Now, at forty-five years old, she had been convicted once again. The next morning, she was due to appear in court to face sentencing for her crime. But she wasn't about to let that happen. Her things were all packed—her books, some clothes, and her most valuable possession: a well-used Remington typewriter. She could always leave, making her way to California, or perhaps back to London where she had escaped once before, safely out of the reach of the agents of the American Inquisition, who would not rest until she was silenced for good. She had been a fugitive before; she knew how to elude the police, the private detectives, and the men from the asylum. But what good would it do?

She thought about the offenses for which she had been convicted. She was a danger to public morals, they said. A threat to the nation's youth. Not in her right mind. But they didn't understand. She had a gospel to preach—a message of beauty, joy, and spiritual enlightenment. So much pain and suffering could be eased, so much ignorance and bitterness could be avoided, if only she were allowed to share her teachings with the world. The world badly needed them, of that there was no doubt.

She looked at her image in the mirror: her long blond hair primly done up in a bun; her alabaster complexion, determined brow, and clear blue eyes. She was certain that her motives were pure. She stood for moral correctness, right living, and clear thinking—never hedonistic indulgence or uncontrolled passion. Hundreds had benefited from her instruction. She had been praised by doctors and clergymen alike, all of whom attested to the value of her writings. But because her subject was sex—only within marriage, of course—she was accused of being obscene, lascivious, lewd, and dirty, if not insane.

She knew what she had to do. They must not be allowed to silence her. Her precious manuscripts had already been sent away for safekeeping, where no one—not even her mother—would be able to find and destroy them. Someday, when the American public was ready, they would be published. But, in the meantime, she would make her case to the people, and ensure that her side of the story would be told. For the last time, she rolled a sheet of paper into her trusty Remington and began to type.

As the morning dawned, Ida Craddock carefully disconnected the hose from her gas stove and opened the jet. Lying back on her bed, she took the razor she had prepared and drew it across her wrist, just to be sure. As her awareness began to fade, she was not afraid, for she could already see her spirit companions gathering to meet her on the other side of the Borderland. Soon she would be free.

American Spirituality at the Turn of the Century

America in the late 19th century was undergoing a period of rapid social change. The country was buffeted by a series of interrelated movements advancing new religious, sexual, and political ideas. Some were more popular than others, and many were more widely known for their radicalism than for their mainstream appeal; but all had an impact on the collective public psyche, setting the stage for yet more dramatic changes to follow at the turn of the century.

Spiritually, America was in the midst of the Third Great Awakening, a period of intense religious activity.[2] With it came a renewed enthusiasm for evangelical Protestantism and moral reform, which in turn spawned "social purity" initiatives and "clean living" organizations like the Young Men's Christian Association (YMCA) and the Women's Christian Temperance Union (WCTU). Both groups had active political agendas that

2 Historians have denoted several periods of American religious revival as "Great Awakenings." The First Great Awakening, circa 1730–60, was characterized by a rise in Congregationalism. The Second Great Awakening occurred around 1800–1840 and saw the birth of the Mormon and Seventh Day Adventist churches. The Third Great Awakening began around 1850 and continued into the early 1900s. See Robert William Fogel, *The Fourth Great Awakening & the Future of Egalitarianism* (Chicago: University of Chicago, 2000).

called for the prohibition of alcohol and the regulation of sexual behavior; both were widely influential.

At the same time, more liberal manifestations of the Third Great Awakening arose in the form of new religious movements like Christian Science, Divine Science, and New Thought. Although nominally Christian, they introduced new beliefs that emphasized the immanence of spirit and the ability of the mind to heal the body. Other spiritual groups springing from this fertile period included those with Utopian visions, like the Brotherhood of New Life established by Thomas Lake Harris in Fountain Grove, California and the Oneida Community founded by John Humphrey Noyes in upstate New York, both of which incorporated nontraditional marriage and sexual practices.

Spiritualism was another pervasive influence throughout the last half of the 19th century. The primary feature of Spiritualism was communication with the spirits of the dead, which usually took place during a séance in the form of table turning, table rapping, automatic writing, or speaking through a medium. The Ouija board, or *planchette,* was also a favorite Spiritualist instrument. Introduced in 1848, Spiritualism rapidly gained in popularity after the Civil War, when a grieving nation was eager to establish contact with its huge number of dead husbands, fathers, and sons. It was by no means a fringe movement; séances were held even in the White House and attended by Abraham Lincoln. Spiritualism also assumed a political dimension because most mediums were women, affording them unprecedented standing as spiritual leaders within their communities. Thus it naturally became aligned with causes associated with women's rights.

Related to, but distinct from, Spiritualism was a rise in organized occultism. The most successful metaphysical organization of the period was the Theosophical Society, founded in New York in 1875 by the spiritualistic medium Helena Petrovna Blavatsky, along with Henry S. Olcott and William Q. Judge. Other occult groups, like the Triplicate Order founded in 1874 by Paschal Beverly Randolph and the Hermetic Brotherhood of Luxor founded in 1884 by Peter Davidson, Thomas Burgoyne, and Max Theon, also had esoteric sexual teachings.

Coincident with this explosion of spiritual activity was an increasing amount of discourse on sexual activity. The new science of sexology had just been established in Europe, and the groundbreaking works of sexologists

Richard von Krafft-Ebing and Havelock Ellis were best-sellers in the United States. The medical profession began to regard "the sex question" as part of its domain, competing with the clergy who had hitherto held a monopoly on sexual matters, considered to fall within their moral purview. Meanwhile, Hargrave Jennings and others had demonstrated that the origins of modern religion could be traced to ancient phallic and sex worship, influencing the doctrines of the occultists and titillating the public.

All of these trends were reflected in the political activism of the day. The Freethought movement emerged to counter sectarianism and the repression of the social purity crusades by supporting free speech, especially in matters of religion and morality. The Free Love movement went a step beyond this and advocated the reform of patriarchal marriage and divorce laws. Social hygiene proponents sought to accomplish the same goals espoused by social purity reformers—to reduce prostitution, venereal disease, and unwanted pregnancy—but from a medical, rather than moralistic, perspective. Women fought for dress reform, to shed the corsets of the Victorian era in favor of simpler and more comfortable undergarments. Many of these movements were interrelated, and factions within them sometimes were split over a single issue.

At the nexus of all of these trends—spiritual, sexual, and political—was a remarkable woman named Ida C. Craddock. She was a Spiritualist and a Freethinker, a proponent of New Thought and Divine Science, an occultist and an activist. She advocated free speech but not free love, social purity but not moral asceticism, social hygiene but not artificial birth control. In some ways, she appeared to be a paradox: rational and scientific, yet spiritual and religious.[3] She was progressive on many issues, especially those relating to sexual and social reform, and yet uncompromisingly conservative on others— for example, maintaining that marriage was the only permissible context for sexual activity. But she was neither confused nor ambivalent; she had very definite and well-justified beliefs, and a strong sense of personal morality. Her activities eventually brought her squarely into conflict with the law, but she held fast, motivated by her conviction that her efforts served a higher purpose and a greater good. To sacrifice her life for these principles was entirely consistent with her

3 This apparent paradox is resolved by the principle of "Scientific Illuminism" described by Aleister Crowley as "the Method of Science, the Aim of Religion." See Egil Asprem, "Magic 'Naturalized'? Negotiating Science and Occult Experience in Crowley's Scientific Illuminism," *Aries*, vol. 8, no. 2, 2008.

idealism. Although her suicide was tragic in its necessity, it was ultimately triumphant in achieving its purpose.

Ida's father, Joseph T. Craddock, was born in Maryland in 1817. Although raised a Quaker, at some point he appears to have repudiated the faith of his family and become non-religious. He was an inventor, holding two U.S. patents for improvements to the process of refrigeration. At the age of twenty-two, he married Mary J. Crow, also twenty-two, and they had four children: Rebecca, Edwin, William, and Joseph Jr. Mary died tragically in 1852 at the age of thirty-five. Perhaps it was this cruel twist of fate that led Joseph to abandon his belief in a personal, benevolent God.

Two years later, Joseph married twenty-one-year-old Elizabeth "Lizzie" Selvage. Her origins are somewhat vague; census records list her as having been born in either New Jersey or Maryland, and indicate that her parents had emigrated from France. Joseph and Lizzie were married on April 27, 1854 at the First Methodist Episcopal Church in Baltimore, but soon thereafter, they moved to Philadelphia. Their first child, Nana, died in infancy. Ida was born on August 1, 1857.

Ida never knew her father. Joseph Craddock died of tuberculosis when she was just four months old. On his deathbed, he extracted a promise from Lizzie that she would not give Ida a religious upbringing. It was a promise that she would not keep, however. Although Lizzie was a spiritualist and dabbled in séances and the Ouija board, after Joseph died she became a devout evangelical Christian and even served as treasurer of the WCTU in Philadelphia. She raised Ida with puritanical discipline, giving her intensive religious training at home and later sending her to a Quaker school. She also had an irritable temper, and subjected Ida to physical punishment well into her twenties. Ida later recalled that her mother "instructed me carefully that I must never allow a man to kiss me or put his arm around me, or even hold my hand."[4] Lizzie, on the other hand, married again twice after Ida's father died: once to a man named Brown, and then to a man named Decker, whose name she kept for the remainder of her life.

By her mother's account, Ida was a precocious child, already reading from the Bible when she was two and a half years old, and able to write by the time she was five. In spite of being a single parent, Lizzie was able

4 Quoted by Theodore Schroeder, "The Religious Erotism of Ida C." (SCRC, 1930).

to provide a comfortable standard of living for their household, which in 1860 consisted of Lizzie, age twenty-seven, Ida, age three, Ida's twenty-year-old half-sister Rebecca (from Joseph's previous marriage), an Irish maid, and a middle-aged female lodger. They also had a vacation cottage in New Jersey and a horse named Daisy. Overall, Ida reported fond memories of her childhood, but her mother's strictness would remain a potent force throughout her life.

Soon after Joseph's death, Lizzie founded a patent medicine business, Craddock & Co. Her sole product was a liquid preparation of *Cannabis indica* (Indian hemp), an early example of what we today call medical marijuana. It was advertised as a cure for consumption (as tuberculosis was then called), the same disease that had killed Ida's father. It was also marketed to treat "bronchitis, night sweats, irritation of the nerves, difficult expectoration, nausea at the stomach, and will break up a fresh cold in 24 hours" according to one advertisement from a newspaper of the time.[5] This business provided Lizzie with a steady source of income until about 1897.

CRADDOCK & CO.,
PROPRIETORS OF
DR. H. JAMES'
CANNABIS INDICA,
For the Cure of Consumption,
No. 1032 Race St., Philadelphia.

Figure 1. Advertisement for Craddock & Co., from the Ida Craddock papers, courtesy of SCRC.

Upon reaching adulthood, Ida embarked upon her lifelong vocation as a writer and teacher. In 1878, at the age of twenty, she wrote a review of Goethe's *Faust* that was published in the *Saturday Evening Post*. She also taught shorthand at Girard College in Philadelphia, and authored a textbook on the subject called *Primary Phonography*. Published in 1882, the book received favorable reviews in the *Post* and the *Atlantic Monthly*. But even this seemingly innocuous occupation harbored seeds that would grow in significance later in her life.

5 Today the original Craddock & Co. medicine bottles are collector's items, commanding prices of $200 or more.

First was the fact that the standard method of shorthand Ida taught was originally developed by Sir Isaac Pitman (1813–1897), who happened to be a member of the New Church founded by the Swedish mystic Emmanuel Swedenborg (1688–1772). It seems a bit more than coincidence that several prominent advocates of sexual reform were also practitioners of stenography, including Stephen Pearl Andrews[6] and Henry Parkhurst.[7] Another synchronicity arose from a controversy in 1888 over the fact that Girard College provided religious instruction to its students, in violation of the conditions set forth in the will of its founder, Stephen Girard.[8] The primary instigator of this protest was Richard B. Westbrook,[9] who was later to become Ida's employer and a significant influence on her life.

By the time she was twenty-five years old, Ida had already begun to challenge the status quo. In 1882, she became the first woman to apply for admission to the University of Pennsylvania. Although she passed the entrance examination and was recommended for admission by the faculty, the board of trustees quickly passed a resolution expressly prohibiting the admission of women, and Ida's application was denied. This setback would later limit her opportunities to pursue a career as a schoolteacher. Not having a college degree made it harder for her to find work, but also probably contributed to the channeling of her energies toward less conventional aspirations.

In 1887, at the age of twenty-nine, Ida left home for the first time and moved to California, mainly to escape the overbearing attention of her mother. She lived in the San Francisco Bay area for about two years, during which time she worked as a bank clerk. She also taught typing and stenography classes at the Women's Educational and Industrial Union, which was dedicated to improving opportunities for a rapidly growing class of working women. In her spare time, she read the works of Laurence Oliphant[10] and started attending a Unitarian church.

---

6 Stephen Pearl Andrews (1812–1886) was an American attorney, abolitionist, and founder of the Free Love League. He invented the word "scientology" in 1871, long before it was taken up by L. Ron Hubbard.

7 Henry Martyn Parkhurst (1825–1908) was a professor of astronomy whose writings on male sexual continence would later influence Ida's ideas about sexual mysticism.

8 Stephen Girard (1750–1831) was an American banker and philanthropist, and the wealthiest man in the country at the time of his death. In his will, he endowed Girard College as a boarding school for poor white orphan boys in grades 1–12.

9 Richard Brodhead Westbrook (1820–1899), an attorney and ex-clergyman, was the author of *Girard's Will and Girard College Theology* (1888).

10 Laurence Oliphant (1829–1888) was a British author, traveler, and mystic. He was a follower of Thomas Lake Harris (1823–1906), American spiritualist and founder of the Utopian Brotherhood of the New Life, which taught unorthodox sexual doctrines.

Unitarianism was a breath of fresh air for Ida after her rigid evangelical upbringing. The adult class that she attended at the church each week broadened her horizons and challenged her intellect. She wrote: "I have never yet been in any class or club that went quite fast enough for me . . . and I have always longed to be thrown with a set of people where I should have to work to keep up with the others, rather than have to restrain my steps to hold back with them. Now, at last, I am thrown with such a set of people."[11] They studied such works as Herbert Spencer's *Principles of Psychology* and had lively and spirited discussions. As a result, she continued, "not only is my horizon of scientific knowledge widening; not only is my mode of thinking becoming more consecutive and logical; but my sense of the nearness of God, of the truth of the assertion that *in* him we live and move and have our being, grows daily more vivid."[12]

In 1889, she took a month-long vacation to Alaska, which refreshed and invigorated her. Her encounters with the native art and culture prompted her to write an article on phallic symbolism in Alaskan mythology, although the magazine to which she submitted it had to edit it heavily for publication. This work marked the beginning of her enduring interest in sexual customs and their religious implications. Now all she had to do was find an outlet for its expression.

An opportunity would soon present itself.

11 Letter from Ida Craddock to Katie Wood, December 8, 1887, SCRC.
12 Letter from Ida Craddock to Katie Wood, December 8, 1887, SCRC.

Chapter 1

Belly Dancing in Chicago

Chicago was abuzz with excitement in 1893. Three years earlier, the city had narrowly beaten New York to be chosen as the site of the World's Columbian Exposition, popularly known as the World's Fair. After twenty-six months of feverishly paced construction, at a cost of over $18 million (an astronomical sum at that time, equivalent to about $17 *billion* today), the fair finally opened to the public on May 1, 1893. In sheer size and grandeur, it was without precedent, and it would not be surpassed for years to come. Covering over 600 acres of mostly reclaimed land on the shore of Lake Michigan south of the city, it encompassed 200 purpose-built structures—pavilions for the exhibits and concessions—set among meticulously landscaped gardens, artificial lakes, canals, and islands. In the short six months of its operation, the fair drew in more than 27 million visitors, equal to about half the U.S. population at the time. It was a monumental achievement.

Among the many attractions of the fair, the promenade extending west from its entrance, called the Midway Plaisance, was undoubtedly the most colorful and exciting. This area was leased to private concession operators for carnival rides, sideshows, food stands, and other amusements. "The Midway," as it came to be known, was home to the first Ferris wheel, built on a colossal scale—at over 260 feet high, it had thirty-six Pullman-sized carriages that could carry sixty people each. Other popular venues included Buffalo Bill Cody's Wild West Show and the nation's first commercial movie theater.

In keeping with the international character of the fair, many of the Midway attractions were modeled after exotic locales. There were Chinese, Javanese, Aztec, and Turkish villages; a Moorish palace, an Indian bazaar, and a Persian theater; and scale models of the Eiffel Tower and St. Peter's Basilica. Occupying a prominent spot in the shadow of the Ferris wheel (near the intersection of what is 59th Street and University Avenue today), the "Street in Cairo" entertained visitors with a chaotic mix of astrologers, conjurers, snake charmers, and trained monkeys. But its most famous—and most controversial—attraction was a show called the "Danse du Ventre" (French, literally "dance of the abdomen.") This was America's introduction to the art of Middle Eastern dance, destined to become known simply as "belly dancing."

Figure 2. A performer of the Danse du Ventre, from Halsey C. Ives, *The Dream City: a Portfolio of Photographic Views of the World's Columbian Exposition* (St. Louis: N. D. Thomson Co., 1893).

By today's standards, the show was downright tame. No bare midriff or flash of thigh could be seen; the dancers wore ankle-length skirts with muslin trousers underneath, and ample chemises that fully covered their torsos, arms, and shoulders. But it wasn't *what* they displayed, it was *how* they displayed it that caused such a sensation in 1890s America. The provocative undulations of the performers' waists and hips, and the deliberate sensuousness of their movements, fascinated even as it scandalized the public. The Danse du Ventre quickly became one of the fair's most popular draws.

The performance also drew the attention of Anthony Comstock (1844–1914), self-appointed guardian of American public decency. In 1873, Comstock founded the New York Society for the Suppression of Vice (NYSSV), a private moral enforcement squad that was spun off from the YMCA and funded by a cadre of wealthy conservative businessmen, including J. Pierpont Morgan and Samuel Colgate. After intense lobbying by Comstock, Congress passed a law aimed at the suppression of "obscene literature and articles of immoral use," which became known as the Comstock Law after its chief proponent and enforcer. This law made it illegal to send any "obscene, lewd, or lascivious" materials through the U.S. mail, including contraceptive devices and any information concerning sex, birth control, or abortion.[13] Many states followed suit by passing their own versions of the Comstock Law.

Although he was not a government employee, through his influence in Congress Comstock was able to obtain an appointment as a volunteer postal inspector that allowed him to conduct investigations, order arrests, and seize and destroy materials he found objectionable. Since the postal service fell under federal jurisdiction, this gave Comstock broad powers to intercept, examine, and proscribe virtually anything sent through the mail, even personal correspondence. Along with a gang of private "detectives" in his employ, he often used undercover sting operations and other subterfuges to gather his evidence and secure legal convictions against those who dared to offend his sensibilities. Comstock boasted that he was responsible for 4,000 arrests and fifteen suicides over the course of his career. Among his earliest targets was the famous women's suffragist and free-love advocate, Victoria Woodhull.[14]

13 This law is still on the books and enforced today. See "Adult Entertainment Producer Sentenced to 46 Months in Prison on Obscenity Charges," Department of Justice Press Release, October 3, 2008. The provisions pertaining to contraception were determined unconstitutional in 1936, although some state laws continued to outlaw sending contraceptives and birth control information through the mail as late as 1972.

14 Victoria Claflin Woodhull (1838–1927) was arrested by Comstock in 1872 for printing an article that revealed a sex scandal involving the prominent Congregationalist pastor Henry Ward Beecher.

Figure 3. Anthony Comstock (1844–1915), frontispiece from *Anthony Comstock, Fighter* (1913).

After viewing the Danse du Ventre for himself, Comstock deemed it "distinctly and disgustingly obscene" and attempted to have it shut down. He appealed to the Board of Lady Managers, an advisory group constituted to represent women's interests at the fair. Although the Board was not unanimously opposed to the performance (one member insisted that it was "very fascinating"), they nevertheless lodged a formal complaint with the fair's director-general, George R. Davis. Davis immediately authorized an investigation. No doubt mindful of the show's popularity, however, and the fact that the fair was still running in the red, he ultimately took no action against it. Meanwhile, Comstock took his campaign to the public, threatening to have the fair's commissioners indicted for "keeping a disorderly house," a charge usually reserved for those who managed houses of prostitution.

The press had a field day with Comstock's absurd prudery. The August 5, 1893 edition of the *New York World* quoted him fuming: "It's got to stop. The whole World's Fair must be razed to the ground or these [belly dancing] shows must stop. It is an assault upon the pure dignity of womanhood." The paper went on to describe how Comstock, "a pretty stout man," attempted to imitate the dance and nearly fell on his sofa instead. In an editorial on August 11th, the *World* sarcastically noted that the "tears and virtuous indignation" of the Lady Managers arose only after Comstock's arrival, when the fair was already half over. And on the 13th, the *World* dedicated almost an entire page to letters it had received in response to the controversy. Seven of these were from clergymen, most of whom supported Comstock's efforts, even though they had not seen the performance themselves. The remaining two letters were from women, and the longest letter of all, spanning almost two full columns, was from Ida Craddock. Comstock had provided just the opening she needed to introduce her ideas to the broader public.

Ida defended the Danse du Ventre as "a religious memorial of a worship which existed thousands of years ago all over the world, and which taught self-control and purity of life as they have never been taught since." She went on to describe the movements and attire of the dancers in detail, noting that even such elements as the number of tassels hanging from the dancers' costumes had symbolic meaning. Those who understood that meaning, she contended, would not misinterpret the belly dance as immoral. She concluded with a direct challenge to Comstock:

> To suppress this dance, as Anthony Comstock and others propose to do, strikes a blow at social purity and at the diffusion of scientific truth. It is our American men and women, and not the Oriental women, who are responsible for the atmosphere of indecent suggestions surrounding the very mention of the Danse du Ventre in the Midway Plaisance at the World's Fair. . . . Let the real significance of this dance as a religious memorial of purity and self-control be broadcast, so that Anthony Comstock and his helpers may be enlightened on the subject and may refrain from their attacks on the Danse du Ventre in the Cairo Theatre of the Midway Plaisance—attacks which, if successful, will certainly blacken the cause of social purity for many a long year to come.[15]

Ida's challenge would not go unanswered. Anthony Comstock was apparently *not* enlightened on the subject. Although his attempts to suppress the dance itself had been fruitless, he now had a new target. When an expanded version of Ida's letter was published in the medical journal *Chicago Clinic*, Comstock used his powers as a volunteer postal inspector to declare the issue obscene, making it a crime to send it through the U.S. mail.

Ida responded by typing up copies of the essay and offering them for

15 *New York World*, August 13, 1893, p. 17.

sale herself, at fifty cents each. The notoriety generated by her public defiance of Comstock led to her making contact with like-minded supporters, among whom she found ready customers for her work. In November 1893, she was invited to give a lecture to the Ladies' Liberal League in New York, one of several organizations in the burgeoning Freethought movement that opposed religious meddling in affairs of state. The lecture was entitled "Survivals of Sex Worship in Christianity and Paganism: What Christianity Has Done for the Marital Relation." She gave the same lecture again a few months later at the Manhattan Liberal Club, which also drew press coverage; the *World*'s headline read "A Very Shocking Time" and said that the lecture was unprintable, albeit very well attended.[16] A new phase of Ida's life had begun, one dedicated to public activism.

The essay presented here is reproduced from one of Ida's self-published copies. It was expanded significantly beyond the edited letter that appeared in the *World*, and quoted other letters in support of the dance that appeared in the same issue of the paper. In this version, Ida elaborates on the symbolism of the six tassels on the dancer's costume as representing the five days of a woman's menstrual cycle, plus a sixth day for the resumption of sexual intercourse. She also discusses at some length the practice of "male continence" (ejaculatory control) as taught by John Humphrey Noyes, founder of the Oneida Community in upstate New York. In the methods of the Danse du Ventre, Ida found what she believed to be the female counterpart of male continence, a method by which women could effect their own sexual self-control. These principles became the bedrock upon which all her future works (and personal practice) were based. Her essay, "The Danse du Ventre," is especially significant as her first articulation of these principles in printed form. It is also Ida's first published admission of her marriage to a spirit husband, a bombshell that she casually drops in the very last paragraph.

16 *New York World*, February 10, 1894, p. 2.

The Danse du Ventre (Dance of the Abdomen) as performed in the Cairo Street Theatre, Midway Plaisance, Chicago: Its Value as an Educator in Marital Duties[17] (1893)

The Danse du Ventre in the Cairo Street Theatre of the Midway Plaisance, at the World's Fair, Chicago, has been so little understood by the crowds that have flocked to see it, that it is usually spoken of as demoralizing. On the contrary, it is a strictly moral dance in its significance. It is a religious memorial of a worship that existed thousands of years ago, all over the world, and which taught self-control and purity of life as they have never been taught since. We have travelled fast and far since those old uplifting days of Phallic or Sex Worship. That worship, the vehicle of moral and social teaching to all humanity, at length became corrupt, through causes which it is unnecessary to mention here, and was gradually displaced by Sun Worship; this, in turn, yielding to Christianity in some portions of the world. We have gained much by this religious evolution; but we have also lost something; and that something is (1) the clean-minded consideration of the human form divine, and (2) the recognition of sex as the chief educator of the human race in things material and things spiritual. We have still something to learn from heathen nations in these matters; and I, for one, rejoice that this Danse du Ventre should have been one of the appointed means of grace.

But—but—but—why do people all say it is so demoralizing, and so disgusting, and . . .

All people do not call it these things, my friend. Archbishop Corrigan,[18] in reply, apparently, to a question asked of him by the *New York World*, gave his opinion on the Danse du Ventre in the edition of Sunday, August 13th, as follows: "I presume that the dances in the Midway Plaisance which Mr. Comstock objected to were national dances, and, as such, gave one an idea of the manners and customs of the peoples. No doubt the poor creatures meant no harm by it and thought no wrong of it. They would hardly come so far to exhibit a performance they were ashamed of. It is all in the way one looks at it.

17 Part of this essay originally appeared in the *New York World*, Sunday, August 13, 1893. (ICC note)

18 Michael Augustine Corrigan (1839–1900), the well-respected but at times controversial Roman Catholic Archbishop of New York.

I should have gone to see it and would not have been scandalized, I believe. Perhaps Mr. Comstock was too sensitive in the matter, he and the good old ladies who were so shocked. They might have seen worse dances of a Saturday night in New York, dances where real evil is meant. It will not do to criticize semi-savages on the same basis as our high-toned American ladies and gentlemen."

In the same issue of the *World*, Miss Loie Fuller,[19] the serpentine dancer, spoke in high terms of the artistic grace of this dance, which she had seen performed, not in Chicago, but in Paris (where, if anywhere, one might look for refined immorality). She thought that to those who wish it suppressed, the Venus of Milo would probably seem an equally fit subject for suppression. She adds: "I am well aware that dancing may be immoral and graceful and artistic at the same time; but the dancer whom I saw, who was said to be a very good and experienced one, impressed me only with her art. She really expressed thoughts and ideas in her graceful pantomime . . . those zealots who are looking for suggestiveness would doubtless find it, but then people of that sort would doubtless find something suggestive in the dainty raising of skirts in the stately minuet."

I talked this summer with a commercial traveler who had been told by a friend: "Now, you can look at that dance which you are going to see, in one of two ways. You can view it as a vulgar show, or you can view it as a presentation of their religion." This gentleman, while watching the dance, overheard another gentleman explaining to his wife that the dance was a religious memorial of ethical teaching.

The above were but a few of the numerous instances within my knowledge where the Danse du Ventre has been looked on as the reverse of impure.

The Danse du Ventre (Dance of the Abdomen) is not a dance at all, as we understand the term. It consists mainly of swaying, undulating movements of the hips and contortions of the abdomen; and at first sight, one is lost in wonderment as to what it all means. But it is not long before most spectators realize that it sets forth the movements of a passionate woman, elaborated, conventionalized into a series of rhythmic actions, and performed with

19 Loie Fuller, née Marie Louise Fuller (1862–1928) was a modern-dance performer and choreographer famed in America for her "Serpentine Dance." She later moved to France where she performed at the Folies Bergère in Paris and also developed new stage lighting techniques. She arranged European tours for early modern dancers, including Isadora Duncan.

deliberation, in harmony with musical beats of time. The dance was usually performed by one woman at a time, and consisted almost entirely in a slight swaying of the body from the pelvis as a fulcrum, with powerful contortions of the abdomen and undulations of the hips. That these contortions might be clearly visible to the spectators, the skirt band dipped in front to about the navel. The entire trunk and the arms were clothed in a netted silk undervest—no doubt in deference to the prejudices of an American audience—and the girl was adorned with numerous bangles and neck chains looped over her bosom, and waist chains looped over her abdomen. Ugly black stockings, high heeled slippers and wide white muslin drawers reaching to the knee and visible under the short peasant skirt only at such rare times as the dancer whirled about quickly, completed the costume. The lower limbs were distinctly uninteresting and unattractive, both in costume and attitude, thus differing from our ballet-dancers, whose limbs, as we know, are always clothed so as to enhance the charm of graceful posturing.

A universal adornment of those who danced (though sometime absent from the skirts of those who remained sitting cross-legged on the divan at the rear of the stage) was a number of tassels, hung each on a streamer that usually extended from the waist to the bottom of the skirt. In one or two instances, the side tassels lacked a streamer, and were suspended directly from the waist; but these tassels, whether with or without streamers, were always on the dancer's skirt, and played their part in accentuating her pelvic contortions and quiverings. These tassels (except in certain cases referred to farther on) were invariably six in number. Now, to a student of Phallic antiquities, these six tassels are conclusive evidence of a memorial which, in all heathen lands, recognizes a prohibition laid upon the man not to approach the woman during her *tapu*[20] time of five days monthly, and the rejoicing consequent upon the removal of that prohibition upon the sixth day, when Nature ensures that the woman shall be most affectionate. This memorial, which, in one form or another, is universal in heathen countries, and which also exists among the Jews, emphasizes a teaching sadly needed in Christian countries to save amiable wives from the incessant demands of those husbands who respect no physical condition and no night in the month—as every physician knows.

20 Polynesian word meaning both "sacred" and "forbidden," from which the English word "taboo" is derived. Craddock uses it to refer to the period of a woman's menstrual bleeding.

In exceptional instances, the six tassels were lacking, only four or five tassels of irregular length being worn, as if they were growing out, but had not yet finished growing—that is to say the sixth tassel and the sixth day of rejoicing had not been reached. But in all these cases, the dancer had the waistband of her skirt made of a coiled snake. The serpent is a well-known Phallic symbol of the male organ; and where the tassels were not yet six in number, the snake was shown coiled around the dancer, and not free to erect its head until the sixth day comes, which is the day of rejoicing and union at the close of the woman's monthly *tapu* of five days.

A charming picture in *Frank Leslie's Illustrated Weekly* shows a dancing girl with four short tassels in addition to the usual six tasseled streamers, or ten in all.[21] It is possible (supposing the artist has represented the number correctly) that this symbolizes the ten lunar months of gestation, during which modern and ancient sexology alike forbid sexual excitement to the mother. Here, too, the coiled snake occurs as the waistband of the skirt, showing that the phallic serpent is no more free to erect its head during gestation than during the five days of monthly *tapu*.

The dancer held in each hand a castanet with a bell-like clapper, which she kept actively in motion—a symbol recognizable by any Phallic student as typifying the agitation of the female. These castanets seem to serve as a guide to the musicians to regulate the measures of the discordant wailings which their instruments produced, and which the Orientals call music. Usually she walked slowly about on the stage as she contorted, pausing at intervals to perform some especially complicated movement. At such times she often spoke to the musicians, to give them some direction about changing the measure, or to one of the other women on the divan, or to some of her own people in the audience.

One woman tried hard to captivate some of the male spectators, by smiling boldly at one after the other; but the rest of the women danced modestly, and with an eye to the business of the stage only. This one would-be cajoler has been emphatically condemned by every man with whom I have talked as being the only blemish on an otherwise pleasing entertainment. It is justice to

21 *Frank Leslie's Illustrated Weekly* was a popular literary and news magazine founded in 1852 by illustrator and engraver Frank Leslie (1821–1880). The drawing referred to here was chosen by the editors of the *World* to illustrate Ida's letter, and is similar to the photograph reproduced on p. 2.

the management of Cairo Street to say here that she was, later on, sent back to Egypt, with one or two other girls who had been found unsatisfactory.

As the ardor of the dancer increased, the agitation of her castanet clappers would likewise increase; sometimes, in her vehemence, she would throw her castanets away entirely for several moments; at other times she would crouch nearly to the floor, or even sit on the floor for a moment, all the time keeping up her powerful movements of the hips and abdomen, and then, rising once more to her feet, resume her dance. Several times during the progress of the dance, she would stand perfectly still for a moment, and then be seized (as was indicated by the tremblings of her tasseled streamers) with a gentle agitation which increased in violence until it seemed as though she would become too much exhausted to continue. But just as one may sometimes, in fording a stream, fear he will be swept away, and yet, by a struggle, keep his footing and pass through safely to the other shore, to resume his journey, so this dancer was never quite swept away by the final quiverings of her passion, but passed through without losing her emotional balance, *and continued her dance.* And in this final quivering of passion, which never wholly submerged her self-control, and through which she passed mistress of herself, to resume her Danse du Ventre as before, is presented what was the great object of Phallic teaching in the ancient days when Sex Worship was the uplifting religion of the whole world—the acquirement of absolute self-control in both men and women. The wise men of those days well knew what our wise men either have forgotten or shrink from teaching publicly—that the divine power who rules the world requires from us all, not asceticism, but the self-controlled and pleasurable use of *every* passion in His service. This Danse du Ventre must have been, in its origin, a striking lesson to women, not only in their powers, but in their duty of self-control on that sixth and most passionate day of all the twenty-eight, when *tapu* time is ended.

It was easy to tell who among the spectators were unduly agitated by the sight of the Danse du Ventre, since these usually ejaculated "disgusting," and precipitately fled. But to those whose sexual self-control, or whose intelligent purity, or both, enabled them to appreciate and enjoy the Danse du Ventre, it could not help being a most valuable object lesson, since it was, so to speak, the apotheosis of feminine passion. And it was no doubt originally intended as an object lesson to women in what corresponds to the especial kind of male continence advocated alike by the ancient Sex Worship and by the most advanced sexology of today—i.e., the full control of the orgasm at supreme moments, so that it may be enjoyed leisurely, and in absolute purity and self-control. Thus women, as well as men, were trained in that marital self-control which prolonged the satisfaction of husband and wife for an hour or more, prevented the waste of nervous tissue resulting from the orgasm, conserved their physical and mental energies, and united them more closely in bonds of affection and mutual respect than is possible by any other method.

In some cases, a woman danced with a huge bottle of water on her head, and with two *crossed* sabers, which she at intervals pointed against her breast or her abdomen. The *cross* was a well-known symbol, in nearly all lands, for thousands of years before Christianity, of the union of man with woman, when Sex Worship was the uplifting worship of the whole world. She repeatedly struck the bottle of water with one of the sabers. This bottle, which thus remained erect upon her head, despite the blows it received, and in spite of her multitudinous contortions of body, is symbolical of the organ which never spills its creative water of life, no matter how great the friction—that is, where the man has acquired the ability to practice the controlled orgasm and the sustained thrill.

It is, of course, possible that the religious meaning of this dance, and of the memorial of the six tassels on the dancer's skirt, may have long since been forgotten by the Oriental women who dance, and by the Oriental men before whom they perform—although the modest bearing of most of the Cairo Theatre troupe, and the studied intellectual presentation of the dance by their most finished dancers, would indicate that a reverence, however vague, still attaches to it in their minds. (In this, they are in striking contrast to their imitators in other theaters on the Midway Plaisance, who present it as a meaningless muscular contortion, and who, for the most part, wriggle and shake themselves through it as superficially as a child jingles off Shakespeare.) But in the days when the spectators knew what the six, or the ten, or the less than six tassels meant, and why the Danse du Ventre was prolonged (symbolically) through orgasm after orgasm, *without loss of energy*, for an hour at a time, we cannot doubt that it taught the man and the woman who witnessed or performed it, both their capacities for conferring, and their duties toward one another in the relation of husband and wife, as no mere preaching, by the wisest of priests, could have taught them.

Such a dance as the Danse du Ventre, therefore, was and is distinctly uplifting to those who witness it with a full knowledge of its meaning, for the following reasons:

First, it inculcates purity of thought toward the sexual relation, since the movements of the woman in this dance are performed modestly, and with no evident attempt at lewdness, but merely as a natural and legitimate act which has been deemed worthy of a clear and simple presentation, without comment, in a public dance, where all may see its details.

2nd. It teaches that prolonged pleasure goes hand-in-hand with sexual self-control.

3rd. It teaches directly, by the six tassels on the dancer's skirt (or by the fewer number of tassels in connection with the waistband of the coiled serpent) the duty of respecting the woman's *tapu* period of five days monthly, since these tassels, placed so conspicuously, are a memorial of rejoicing on the sixth day, when the prohibition is removed, and the man is once more free to approach the woman. This prohibition is memorialized in all heathen beliefs, the world over, and also by the Jews. Christianity is the only religion within the writer's knowledge which fails to memorialize in its symbolism some teaching, direct or indirect, to its young people, about the prohibited five-days period and other sexual obligations, thus leaving the prospective fathers of the race to pick up what knowledge they can, haphazard, mostly from prostitutes or depraved men of the world; and leaving the prospective mothers of the race to be trained on the wedding night by these male graduates from the school of impurity. And here, also, we can learn something from this dance of heathen women; since, as I have already said, nearly every physician knows of a brute or unthinking husband, for the lack of this training of respecting five nights out of every twenty-eight as free from his approach. A physician lately told me that he knows of a flourishing house of prostitution in Philadelphia, whose proprietor is accustomed to regularly notify certain male patrons in New York of the monthly illness of any of the women, as these New York men will come over from that city on purpose at such times.

4th. The picture given in Frank Leslie's Illustrated Weekly would indicate, as I have already shown, that the ten lunar months (forty weeks) of gestation are also memorialized by this dance, as being a time when sexual excitement is forbidden to the mother—a most wise prohibition, which cannot be too clearly presented as the duty of every woman great with child.

5th. The Danse du Ventre trains the muscles of the woman in the endurance desirable in the wife whose husband has acquired the ability to practice the controlled orgasm and the sustained thrill, and therefore increases her capacity, not only for receiving, but also for conferring pleasure.

6th. The Danse du Ventre teaches that the controlled and directed orgasm may be passed through without loss of nervous energy; and it thus conveys a hygienic lesson, which people in general would be better physically for knowing.

7th. Most important of all, the Danse du Ventre, if practiced by husband and wife in accordance with its true interpretation, would do away with the horrors of accidental or forced maternity, and without, on the other hand, violating the natural law by putting asunder those whom God hath joined together as husband and wife. That is to say, while it insures that children cannot be born accidentally, it requires no unnatural self-denial or sinful modes of prevention, but permits the freest possible intercourse in the marital relation, prolonging the physical and spiritual bliss of both parties. I say spiritual bliss advisedly, since it would appear that the controlled orgasm and the sustained thrill reach their perfection between husband and wife only when an atmosphere of mental purity and aspiration to the highest obtains during the entire progress of the orgasm.

As to whether the Danse du Ventre practiced between husband and wife injures the health, I would refer the reader to the report made in the *New York Medical Gazette* by Dr. Theodore R. Noyes concerning statistics of nervous diseases in the Oneida Community.[22] The Oneida Community, as is well known, was managed from 1848 until 1879 under some peculiar social

22 The Oneida Community was a Utopian religious group founded in 1848 by John Humphrey Noyes (1811–1886) in Oneida, New York. It grew to about 300 members before its decline and eventual dissolution in 1881. Theodore R. Noyes was John Humphrey Noyes' son.

laws, one of which included the universal practice of male continence,[23] except when the Community had distinctly authorized the creation of a child by a picked man and woman of the society. Their social custom further included one of what *Appleton's Encyclopedia* terms "community of women"—regulated, to some extent, by ordinance. This latter custom was finally frowned down by clergymen and others in the districts adjoining the Oneida Community, and abolished. As to the practice of male continence, however, it is said that "all the best members hold it in high honor and are faithful to it" today. And for at least thirty years previous to the giving up of their system of "community of women," male continence (which, as John Humphrey Noyes taught it, is physiologically the same thing as the Danse du Ventre) was the almost universal practice, the main exceptions being youths who had not yet acquired self-control, and who were therefore forbidden to mate with any woman who had not passed the child-bearing age, as the community desired that all its children should be the result, not of accident, but of intention. Professor Goldwin Smith said of the children born of these unions: "They are a fine, healthy-looking, merry set";[24] and this opinion is borne out by other writers.

Concerning the health of the Community at large, John Humphrey Noyes writes:

> The *New York Medical Gazette* of October, 1870, in a review of our article on Scientific Propagation published in the *Modern Thinker* of that year, took occasion to criticize our practice of Male Continence as likely to prove injurious . . . and expressed a wish to see the statistics of nervous diseases in the Community. Whereupon a professional examination was instituted and a report made by Theodore R. Noyes, M.D., in which it was shown, by careful comparison of our statistics with those of the U.S. census and other public documents, that the rate of nervous diseases in the Community is considerably below the average in ordinary society. This report was published by the *Medical Gazette*, and was pronounced by the editor "a model of careful observation, bearing intrinsic evidence of entire honesty and impartiality."

23 Male continence, as advocated by Noyes and practiced by members of the Oneida Community, involved prolonged sexual intercourse without ejaculation by the male partner. It was regarded as both a spiritual discipline and a practical measure for eugenic birth control.

24 Goldwin Smith, "The Oneida Community and American Socialism," *Canadian Monthly*, Nov. 1874, republished in Smith, *Essays on Questions of the Day Political and Social* (New York: Macmillan; Toronto: Copp, Clark, 1893), appendix.

> It was, however, admitted in that report that there had been one or two cases of nervous disorder in the Community, which could be traced with probability to a misuse of Male Continence in the way suggested by the *Gazette*; and I will here take occasion to add that I have no doubt the greatest danger attending the practice of Male Continence is, the temptation to make a separate hobby of it, and neglect the religious conditions out of which it originally issued and to which it belongs. Male Continence in its essence is self-control, and that is a virtue of universal importance. To cultivate self-control in respect to the seminal crisis, but neglect it in other sexual indulgences, is evidently Male Continence in a spurious and dangerous form. It is certain that this spurious self-control may be cultivated for the purpose of gaining freedom for sexual and riotous pleasure. We may be thankful that such a counterfeit cannot escape the checks prepared for universal vice. Nothing less than heart-abandonment to the grace of God, which teaches and gives *temperance in all things*, can ever release us from the old tutelage of suffering. Our theory in its oldest form defined the sexual organs as conveyances, not only of the seed, but of the "social magnetism." Now it is certain that the social magnetism is a vital element, as real as the seed, and as really limited in its supply; and that the loss of it in excessive quantities entails diseases as atrocious as those which follow seminal waste, and to this liability women are as much exposed as men.[25]

The pamphlet from which I quote the above details the philosophy and method of male continence. It is written from such a high and pure standpoint that I wish every man in the country could read and ponder over its teachings.

The plain teachings of that pamphlet to men, however, need to be supplemented by equally plain teachings to women. It is with this end in view that I have written this little pamphlet, as an entering wedge for detailed scientific instruction from those sexologists who are more widely conversant with the matter than I.

It is usually assumed that propagation is nature's only reason for man and woman entering into marital relations; whatever physical pleasure accrues therefrom being looked on as merely a bait to propagation, and as at least a

25 John Humphrey Noyes' *Male Continence*, pp. 22, 23. Published in Oneida, N.Y., 1877. (ICC note)

sensual, if not positively impure indulgence. But Noyes clearly shows in the pamphlet above referred to, that there are two distinct functions concerned in those relations—the social and the propagative—and that the sexual union of husband and wife is for the purpose, not alone of perpetuating the species, but of "giving a medium of magnetic and spiritual interchange." It is this possibility of the twain becoming one flesh by being welded through their sexual relations into a spiritual union, which lifts husband and wife above the merely physical relations which obtain among animals. In such a spiritual and magnetic union, strengthened in each meeting in accordance with the principles of the Danse du Ventre and of Male Continence, children will not be produced until the parents are ready for them, and can beget them under the best conditions. In savage or sparsely settled countries, or in countries frequently depopulated by war, it is perhaps well to urge wholesale propagation, but in countries and civilizations like ours, the need is not for quantity, but quality. Every woman knows, when she stops to think about it, that to create a child by accident, and carry it for nine months in the womb of an unwilling mother—a mother who perhaps hates it for coming—is a sin, not only against the moral law, but also against the community into which that unwelcome comer, cursed before its birth with undesirable traits, is to be introduced. But, on the other hand, it is unreasonable to expect married people who are true lovers to abstain from intercourse. And if intercourse be considered sinful between them, save for purposes of child-bearing, unduly large families will result, as is so often the case with ministers and other pious and well-meaning people. The device most frequently relied upon to prevent conception—abstaining from intercourse until two weeks after the menses—is a sin against nature (and therefore, to truly devout men and women a sin against God) since the day after the menses is the proper time of all times for intercourse, it being the period when the woman is most affectionate and most passionate. The husband who allows this natural wedding-night to go by, and who approaches his wife two weeks later, need not wonder if she feels disgust, instead of tender passion, at being compelled to receive him only when she has least inclination to be approached. The practice of the Danse du Ventre, however, disposes of these objections.

The method of training in this, as in most things, consists in attempting it by slow degrees; going to the verge of orgasm, and resolutely stopping there, time after time, until one is able to suppress it altogether at will. Then, and not until then, may one attempt to enter that state of ecstasy with any expectation of controlling it. On one point I cannot be too emphatic. Unless the attempts at suppressing and finally controlling the orgasm be made throughout in a mood of aspiration to the highest, there will not be complete satisfaction, nor will the ecstasy result in the twain becoming one in flesh and one in spirit. If you believe in Jesus, aspire to be in unison with his will from the moment the ecstasy sets in; if you believe only in God the Father, aspire in joy and thankfulness to him; if you are an Atheist, aspire to be in harmony with the Law of the Universe. If, however, you look on such advice as religious cant, then think and talk with your partner of poetry, sculpture, good books, plans for helping other people, etc.; in short, strive then, of all times in your life, to enter into harmonious relations with the ideal, the generous and the pure outside and beyond the act, if you would consummate it in its perfection.

The ancients were right when they recognized the union of man with woman as a religious, but not necessarily a propagative act. Cupid, the God of Love, was a child—passion-inspiring but non-creative. His antitype is found in the famous *Mannekin Pis* statue of Brussels (whose phallus serves as the conduit and gargoyle of a drinking fountain); in the Christ-Child on his folklore side; in the boy-saint, Nicholas,[26] etc.—all of them bestowers of abundance, but non-creative as a little child. In Matthew 19, after a long and earnest talk on marriage duties, Jesus finishes by commending those who make themselves eunuchs for the kingdom of heaven's sake, adding, significantly, "He that is able to receive it, let him receive it."[27] St. Origen and several other early Christians interpreted this text to mean literally castration; and they accordingly mutilated themselves, apparently not noticing that among those to whom Jesus referred as making themselves eunuchs "for the kingdom of heaven's sake" he did not include those who were made "eunuchs for men." But the Danse du Ventre renders it possible for men to carry out the recommendation of Jesus without unnatural mutilation.

---

26 Eleventh century Roman Catholic and Orthodox saint Nicholas Peregrinus. See Patricia Healy Wasyliw, *Martyrdom, Murder and Magic: Child Saints and their Cults in Medieval Europe* (New York: Peter Lang Publishing, 2008), pp. 95–96.

27 Matthew 19:12.

A great deal of sentiment is talked about "sexual purity." But it rarely seems to occur to anyone that purity means absence from material as well as moral uncleanness, and that the sexual act, as usually performed, is anything but cleanly. This objection does not apply when husband and wife perform the Danse du Ventre. The wasteful scattering of seed where no sowing is intended, and the consequent wanton drain on the male energies, is something against which every wife who ever hopes to be a mother should protest on behalf of the children whom she expects one day to bear to her husband.

So far from suppressing the Danse du Ventre, we should have it performed far and wide throughout our country, accompanied by an explanation of its symbolism of purity and self-control, as a prenuptial educator of our young people in the marital duties which they are about to assume. This dance is a bit of the old pure and uplifting Sex Worship preserved by God's grace through the barbaric and corrupt customs intervening between prehistoric times and now. Let us rejoice that He who doeth all things well has preserved for this nineteenth century—when the facts of heredity and the claims of a future generation are brought to our notice—this memorial of the Danse du Ventre, which, rightly understood and practiced between man and wife, will purify the marital relation, and render it impossible for any child to come into this world through an accident of sensuality. Should it be objected that sensualists would then choose the Danse du Ventre always for its physical pleasure and to escape having children, I answer, so much the better! The intelligent, the devout, the well-ordered classes will not fail to propagate when they are free to use the time and environment (inasmuch as children are dear to all but the sensualist), and the human race will then be the gainer, since those only who realize their duty to God and humanity will seek to perpetuate the species, and intending parents will then select the most favorable conditions under which to propagate. Moreover, those who seek only sensual enjoyment, instead of the affectional and spiritual bliss of wedded love, in the Danse du Ventre, will not find the game worth the candle, since the Danse du Ventre between man and woman can be practiced successfully only in an atmosphere of mental purity and spiritual uplifting.

There are, then, three reasons for practicing the Danse du Ventre between man and wife:

First. No child can be born by accident.

Second. The physical enjoyment is more prolonged and intense than in the ordinary way.

Third. In order that the Danse du Ventre may be enjoyed in its perfection, it must be practiced throughout in an atmosphere of clean thoughts and aspiration to the highest, thus purifying the fountains of life at their very source, and educating those who practice this method to become worthy creators of the children who may be born from their loins.

To all those, then, who value marital purity, wedded happiness and the bearing of children into the world under the most suitable conditions, I commend the study of the Danse du Ventre, in its pure aspect of an educator and uplifter to that ideal sexual life which is the only one that is in accordance with natural and divine law.

I would say that I speak from the standpoint of a wife. My husband, however, is in the world beyond the grave, and had been for many years previous to our union, which took place in October, 1892. In accordance with angelic laws, he can come clearly to me when I keep the way of right living and clear thinking. Since right living cannot coexist with a sexual intercourse which is uncontrolled—as I have endeavored to show throughout this pamphlet—we are both of us compelled to carry out those principles of ideal marital relations which are taught by the symbolism of the Danse du Ventre. How far the reader may value my testimony as being the result of my personal experience, he will decide of course according to his bias for or against the possibility of communicating with our deceased friends beyond the grave. However, whether my psychical experience be a fact or a hallucination, I can truthfully say that I have gained from it a knowledge of sexual relations which many years of reading and discussions with other people never brought me. But I do not rely exclusively on my own experience with my spiritual husband for authority. The statements in this pamphlet regarding the Danse du Ventre are amply borne out by the testimony, both of books, and of men and women whose earnest seeking for the better way is undoubted.

Chapter 2

Spiritual Union

At the end of "The Danse du Ventre," Ida anticipated a potential objection to her work: how could she write knowledgably about sex if she were unmarried? In 19th-century America, this would either mean that she had no sexual experience, which would diminish her credibility, or that she had had *illicit* (premarital) sexual relations, which would damage her reputation and undermine her moral standing to speak as an authority on such matters. She answered this concern by informing her readership that she was indeed married, to a husband "in the world beyond the grave" with whom she had regular sexual intercourse.

Ida's first biographer, New York lawyer and free-speech advocate Theodore Schroeder (1864–1953), believed that she had, by this time, gained sexual experience in the material world as well, although Ida left no direct admission of this in any of her surviving diaries or letters. Reading between the lines, Schroeder asserts that Ida had "illicit relations" with two different men before 1892. The first was Euclid Frick, the son of a family friend, who was entrusted to her care during her move to California in the spring of 1887. He and Ida lived together in a small house on 22nd Street in Oakland. Ida was working as a bank clerk while the younger man attended medical school. In a letter to her life-long friend, Katie Wood, dated December 8, 1887, Ida reported that she had no other friends or social life outside of her relationship with Euclid, and yet she "never was so happy in my life as I am now." She also admitted that she felt secure not having to sleep there alone, although whether this meant "in the same bed" or "in the same house" is a matter of conjecture. Eventually, Euclid graduated and married another woman, and Ida returned to Philadelphia. Later in her life, Ida would write that she and Euclid were good friends "in a brotherly and sisterly way," but contended that "there was never the slightest exchange of caresses between us"—a bit *too* insistently in Schroeder's estimation.[28]

The second source of Ida's earthly sexual experience was identified by Schroeder only as an "ex-clergyman and heretical mystic" for whom Ida worked as a secretary after she returned from California in 1889. The name of this alleged lover has never before been divulged in print, but from the evidence, it is certain that Schroeder was referring to Richard Brodhead Westbrook (1820–1899). Westbrook had been a Presbyterian minister, but became a lawyer and prominent Freethinker who challenged such Christian dogmas as the infallibility of the Bible and the historicity of Christ. In the preface to the second edition of his book *The Eliminator,* he wrote:

> There is indubitable evidence that this *Christ character* . . . was mainly *mythical, drawn from the astrological riddles of the older Pagan mythologies*. In fact, almost everything in Christianity seems to have been an *afterthought*. It is the least original of any of the ten great religions of the world, and the great mistake has been in making almost everything *literal* which the wise men of ancient times regarded as *allegorical*.[29]

Heretical indeed! In 1888, Westbrook was elected President of the American Secular Union (ASU), a leading Freethought organization founded in 1876 as the National Liberal League. The following year, at the ASU's thirteenth annual congress in Philadelphia, Westbrook was re-elected President, and Ida was elected Secretary. It is during this period, according to Schroeder, that Ida began a sexual relationship with her second lover.

Unlike her previous companion, Westbrook was much older and more experienced. He was also an avid student of Eastern mysticism and had apparently mastered the practice of prolonging intercourse without ejacu-

28 Theodore Schroeder, "The Religious Erotism of Ida C." (SCRC, 1930), pp. 8–9.

29 Richard Westbrook, *The Eliminator: Skeleton Keys to Sacerdotal Secrets* (Philadelphia: J. B. Lippincott,1894), p. iv. Italics in original.

Figure 4. Richard B. Westbrook (1820–1899), president of the American Secular Union, 1889–1891. Frontispiece from *The Eliminator: Skeleton Keys to Sacerdotal Secrets* (1894).

lation. Schroeder speculated that, in contrast to her previous experience, his technique "must have seemed wonderfully entrancing" and induced in her "extraordinary ecstasies."[30] Soon afterward, Ida enthusiastically endorsed the method of male continence in "The Danse du Ventre."

Westbrook and Ida resigned from the ASU in October of 1891, ironically because they disagreed with a faction of "free-lovers" within the organization who wanted the group to defend those who were being prosecuted for sending "obscene literature" through the mails. With the termination of their working relationship came the cessation of their intimacy as well.

Ida's spirit husband arrived a year later. His name was Soph, and he was the spirit of a young man whom Ida had known when she was a teenager. He had been a business associate of her mother's and a frequent visitor to her household. During these visits he would always find some excuse to chat and joke with young Ida, and often gave her little presents. He died, however, before she reached adulthood. Soon thereafter, Ida took up her mother's early interest in Spiritualism and began to experiment with Ouija boards and automatic writing. Eventually, as her mediumship

30 Theodore Schroeder, "Puritanism through Erotomania to Nymphomania" (SCRC, 1930).

abilities developed, she was able to make contact with Soph once again. After a brief astral courtship, they were wedded in the spirit world.

At first, she was tentative about revealing her new relationship. In a letter to a Freethought associate, she wrote:

> The little paragraph pinned on the last page [of "The Danse du Ventre"] forms no part of the essay. I merely send it out with the essay to such of my friends and acquaintances as many be interested in knowing upon what authority I, an unmarried woman, presume to express an opinion on the duties of the marital relation.[31]

She knew full well that such a claim would likely be greeted with skepticism, but she was unprepared for the response it provoked in those closest to her. In early 1894, after she prepared a lecture entitled "Celestial Bridegrooms" for the Ladies' Liberal League, Westbrook secretly attempted to have the talk cancelled. Failing that, he instead addressed the assembled audience, disavowing her conclusions as "unworthy of consideration," an act that left Ida "exceedingly hurt."[32] Even worse was being betrayed by her own mother, who attempted to have her committed to an insane asylum. She learned of the plot at the last minute and fled to the Westbrook residence for sanctuary. Although Richard was fed up with her "silly delusions in regard to the Spirit Husband"[33] and sought to distance himself from Ida, his wife, Henrietta,[34] was sympathetic and took her in.

After a brief stay with the Westbrooks, Ida escaped to New York under the protection of a prominent Freethinker, E. B. Foote, Jr.[35] But she soon learned that her mother was hot on her trail, and had hired two men to abduct her and take her to an asylum against her will. With remarkable cunning, she arranged a series of false trails to throw her mother off the scent, sending her luggage to Jersey City and making arrangements to

31 Letter from Ida Craddock to E. B. Foote, Jr., November 22, 1893, SCRC. The "paragraph pinned on the last page" became integrated into the main text in later versions of the essay, after Ida had more widely announced her spirit husband.

32 Letter from Ida Craddock to James B. Elliot, July 14, 1894, SCRC. Westbrook's attempt to have Ida's lecture suppressed was thwarted by the famous anarchist and early feminist author Voltairine de Cleyre (1866–1912), one of the founders of the Ladies' Liberal League and mother of a son by Elliott born out of wedlock.

33 Letter from R. B. Westbrook to E. B. Foote, Jr., February 14, 1894, SCRC.

34 Henrietta Payne Westbrook (1834–1909), a physician, author, and activist in the woman's suffrage movement. Henrietta would steadfastly continue to support Ida until the very end.

35 Edward Bond Foote (1854–1912), a physician and staunch opponent of the Comstock Act.

have her precious typewriter sent to Canada. She then redirected them under assumed names back to New York, from whence she could collect them in time to leave the country. Meanwhile, she met with a sympathetic colleague, the British journalist and spiritualist W. T. Stead,[36] who was in New York on business. After hearing of her plight, Stead agreed to employ Ida as his research assistant, and arranged for her passage to England with him on the next steamer. They set sail just ahead of the private investigators sent by Ida's mother to track her down. The ocean voyage was uneventful, but not until she had safely set foot on British soil did Ida finally breathe a sigh of relief.

In London, Ida assumed the alias "Mrs. Irene S. Roberts," and lived quietly by herself in a boarding house near Hyde Park. She spent much of her time conducting research at the British Museum, with the support and encouragement of Stead. She also helped out at the offices of the *Borderland* and made use of their extensive library as well. It was during this period of refuge and study that Ida wrote *Heavenly Bridegrooms*, beginning the manuscript on May 11, 1894.

Heavenly Bridegrooms was Ida's attempt to justify her relationship with her spirit husband by demonstrating that her claim was by no means unique or historically unprecedented. She cited numerous Biblical and classical references to the phenomenon of intercourse between humans and angelic beings, not the least of which was the Virgin Mary's impregnation with Jesus. The influence of her research in the British Museum is evident in the many scholarly authorities from which she liberally quotes. She also drew upon a variety of spiritualist and occult sources, providing a little bit of something for everyone among her intended audience of "Occultists, Freethinkers and Christians." The result was an impressive and exhaustive proof that her experience was well-represented in the recorded history and literature of mankind across many cultures and time periods.

It would be easy to dismiss *Heavenly Bridegrooms* as an elaborate cover-up for the likelihood that Ida had already experienced sex in the conventional manner, and to suspect her spirit husband of being nothing more than a convenient fiction to explain her illicitly-gained sexual knowledge. Ida herself acknowledged the possibility that some of her readers would come to such a conclusion. To do so, however, would be erroneous. Ida

36 William Thomas Stead (1849–1912) was editor of the *Pall Mall Gazette* and the *Review of Reviews*, as well as the spiritualist journal *Borderland*. He died on the *Titanic*.

kept detailed diaries of her spiritual experiences from the spring of 1894 until the end of her life. These diaries document her conversations and other interactions with several distinct personalities whom she identifies as discarnate beings, including her husband Soph. Her descriptions are clearly detailed, logically consistent, and evenly matter-of-fact in tone. In the same entries, she also often recorded her dealings with the people around her and events in her daily life. She is able to distinguish clearly between these "real world" and "spirit world" occurrences, which happen with her fully conscious participation—as distinct from her dreams, which she also records. Her writing does not appear to be dissociative or fantastic, nor does it seem to degenerate in quality or temperament over hundreds of pages spanning a period of eight years. In short, these personalities and her experiences with them were clearly an integral part of her subjective reality, whether or not they can be considered objectively true. Her diaries provide the best evidence that, even if she was in some way "delusional" in the conventional sense, she was neither lying nor clinically insane.[37]

Heavenly Bridegrooms is also significant in that it allows us to trace the evolution of Ida's principles of sexual mysticism. About midway through the text, she asserts that one of the benefits of sexual intercourse, whether with an earthly partner or a heavenly one, is that it is "the surest and safest method of seeking union with the Divine Heart of the Universe and becoming one with all God's world." But to accomplish this, she explains, requires a program of strict training in self-control, divided into three degrees. Later, she describes these degrees, and promises that they will be elaborated upon further in a forthcoming treatise entitled "Psychic Wedlock." We will take up the details of "Psychic Wedlock" in the next chapter, but in *Heavenly Bridegrooms,* we can discern many clues to the origin and development of its key points.

The eight months during which Ida worked on the manuscript were intensely productive in a number of ways. Not only was she conduct-

37 Most 19th-century doctors would likely have disagreed, judging her insane according to their assessment of the factual merits of her claims. Modern psychology, however, generally evaluates mental disorders according to the degree to which they cause distress or otherwise interfere with an individual's ability to function productively in society. By these standards, it would be difficult to condemn Ida's behavior as pathological. Her symptoms do not neatly fit any of the diagnostic criteria for conditions such as schizophrenia or personality disorders. It is important to note that, although Ida eventually did submit to psychiatric observation for a period of three months at the Pennsylvania Hospital for the Insane, she was never legally judged insane, and the hospital had no grounds upon which to commit her involuntarily. (Letter from Owen Copp to Theodore Schroeder, September 20, 1913, SCRC.)

ing historical research at the museum and writing the text, she was also expanding her horizons on other fronts. It was during this stay in London that she first made contact with the Theosophical Society, and expressed serious interest in receiving formal training in occultism. She also met other individuals from a variety of backgrounds, each of whom provided pieces of the overall puzzle as it took shape. But she did not confine herself solely to abstract intellectual pursuits. She began earnest and diligent work on practical psychic development as well, undertaking experiments in automatic writing, meditation, levitation, crystal gazing, and divination with a Ouija board. On October 6, she wrote in her diary:

> I have learned more from the *Borderland* library the past month and from Miss X.[38] and the various books of the S.P.R. and other occult works while in London, than I could have learned in five years at home. I have dipped into Theosophy, Mysticism, Faith Cure, Christian Science, Hypnotism, Crystal Gazing, Telepathy, et al., and have learned to recognize *the Power of Thought* which is their great underlying principle. It has been a wonderful training. Had I chosen, I could not have chosen one spot in the world where I could have been so helped in my studies.

During the whole time, she kept in constant contact with several spirit guides, conferring with and learning from them—and, at least in the case of her husband, Soph, having sex with them. She kept a detailed record of all of these experiences in her spiritual diary, which she evidently submitted to Stead for his review; occasionally she would address him directly in an entry, to clarify a point or supply additional explanation.

The most extraordinary feature of Ida's life with the spirits, of course, was her sexual contact with them. Rather than attempt to describe her experiences, I shall provide a few quotes from her diary, verbatim:

> Monday, May 21st, 1894.
>
> Last night, on retiring, my dear husband was with me as he has not been for some time—I mean, in a different way—and we united sexually. I cannot describe how happy I was to possess and be possessed by him. I felt as though I could not

38 Ada Goodrich-Freer (1857–1931), an English author, psychical researcher, and co-editor of *Borderland* with Stead. She wrote under the pseudonym "Miss X."

give myself sufficiently to him. The union was satisfactory in every way, physically and mentally. Iason, the German physician,[39] assisted me, as he sometimes does, by helping me to rotate and perform other abdominal movements, such as the girls in the Danse du Ventre in the Cairo Theatre performed. Whenever he "assists" at one of our unions, it seems to me as though it were more of a success. When the orgasm approached, Soph begged me to not give way just yet. Twice this occurred; and, as I felt that he would enjoy as prolonged a union just before the culminating point quite as much as I, and, indeed, more than I, because of his increased sensibility, as compared with mine, he being in a world of greater development, and because I wanted last night to give him all the pleasure I could—and then, too, I think, because I vaguely felt how pleasant it would be, and what a fine thing it would be to be able to exercise this power, I did control myself just as Soph wished; and the bliss was very, very, very great. I cannot express the joy it is to be able to control one's self just as one is going over the verge, and to realize in the same moment that this prolonged union just as the spasm is about to begin is a delight to one's partner. When the third time came, the agony was too exquisite, it seemed to me, to be wasted, and my husband and I went through it with more prolongation of the spasm than I can ever recollect my having before. This may sound as if it were merely physical pleasure to which I refer; but it is not so; it was mental, affectional, on a high plane. I loved him and he loved me, and we twain were one flesh, and also, it seemed to me, one heart, in a certain sense. It was so good, so good, to have my dear husband with me in this union after last week's frightful psychical experiences!

Saturday, June 2nd, 1894.

Last night my husband and I united, I lying on my face. After awhile, he began to manifest at the clitoris, telling me not to fear, but to allow the excitement to develop there; that it was under law; and that, as soon as the orgasm began, he would present at the vagina. I was rather fearful, but I

39 Iason was one of Ida's spirit guides.

asked God not to let it come if it were wrong.[40] Iases[41] and Soph both insisted it was all right, and that it was to secure variety of manifestation. So I rather gingerly allowed myself to be worked up at that locality. Presently, I discovered my husband was praying to God, so I knew the orgasm must be near, and redoubled my willingness to become ardent there. Sure enough, the orgasm did come with a rush, and my husband straightaway slipped down to the entrance, as he had promised he would, and we had several reciprocal movements there. I was praying to God all the while, but, as they have since told me, I was *"chétif, craintive,"*[42] and not in thorough control of my faculties, being so scared and dubious as to whether it was really under moral law to unite thus. It was a decided disappointment to me, and I felt as though it were a masturbation, such as is treated of in that French book on "Onanisme."[43] However, I continued my movements, partly in hopes that I should have the sort of orgasm I was accustomed to; for the one I had just passed through had left me weak, as from mere masturbation, to some extent, and I thought that for my physical welfare, it might be well to have an interchange of strength with my husband in what seemed to me the more normal and right way. I would say that at no time during our union, save when he was at the clitoris, was his organ objectively as manifest as it is sometimes. Well, we continued our union, and then I began to feel an affectional yearning toward him, which I declared was a great deal nicer than that horrid orgasm at the clitoris; so I continued to perform my abdominal movements upon him, from affection, rather than passion. After awhile, I was aware that he was penetrating all the way in, and I knew intuitively, but only the least bit objectively, that his organ was filling the interior of the vagina. I longed more than ever to be able to feel him at the uterus, as he assured me his organ was now

40 Ida is apprehensive due to her belief, widely prevalent at the time, that an orgasm arising from stimulation of the clitoris was masturbatory and therefore immoral and unhealthy.

41 Iases is a spirit guide with whom Ida does not have sex, but with whom she is most commonly in contact, a "guardian angel" or "genius" who often advises and assists her.

42 "stunted, anxious"

43 *L'Onanisme: dissertation sur les maladies produites par la masturbation* by Samuel Auguste David Tissot (Lausanne: François Grasset, 1764) was the most well-known anti-masturbation polemic of the time.

resting upon it; and I tried to act passionately toward him, to possess him, so as to feel it. As I have said, I have never yet been able, from sensation, to locate my uterus, as I am not aware of ever having had any sensation there. But last night, I felt intuitively his contact, but, I fear, not objectively, unless in an infinitesimal degree. But it was a very great pleasure mentally to realize that he had thus penetrated to the extreme limit; and, though there was little physical pleasure on my part from that contact at the uterus, if, indeed, any physical pleasure, there was a great deal of pleasure in my mind and also, I may say, psychically; I cannot express it otherwise than by this term.

Thursday, October 11th, 1894.

Last night, Soph and I united, mainly at the clitoris, where his organ was for a great part of the time strongly perceptible in its texture, as it is in his clearest manifestations. At the entrance it was mostly vague; but, had I succeeded in passing through one of the final ordeals in the self-control and aspiration at which I was aiming, I doubt not that it would have been very satisfactory. As it was, however, I had a partial orgasm at the moment, in spite of myself. At first, Soph thought I could not continue; but I did manage to, to his delight. Nevertheless, when the final orgasm came, his organ did not clearly manifest. But, on the other hand, over and over again I was able to check myself on the verge of an orgasm. At each one of these successful attempts at suppression I felt myself growing stronger and stronger. I cannot express in words the delight it is to thus control one's self on the very verge of the precipice. It is indeed a carrying out of my favorite comparison of one's animal nature to a fast horse, and the Ego to its driver who holds the horse well under the guidance of bit and rein, while the creature is dashing furiously along. Toward the last, I became quite passionate. The joy, the joy, the joy of self-control at such a moment! The joy of wanting to share one's delight with the Pantheos of the Universe! And the joy of feeling—vague as is my perception at present—that my partner is one with me in these things!

Another important aspect of *Heavenly Bridegrooms* is that Ida considered it a work of semi-automatic writing—that is, a collaboration with one of her spirit guides, Iases, working through her. In her diary, she wrote that *Heavenly Bridegrooms* "is much, much more due to his [Iases'] directing intellect than I should have ever dreamed possible for me as a psychic." The full entry is reproduced at the end of the text.

Heavenly Bridegrooms is Ida's best-known work, thanks to the efforts of Theodore Schroeder. Schroeder had never met Ida, but became interested in her case about a decade after her death due to its significance in the history of the Free Speech movement. He began making inquiries and collecting documents, and was eventually able to retrieve the bulk of Ida's letters and manuscripts from the estate of W. T. Stead in England. Her story, and in particular *Heavenly Bridegrooms*, perfectly illustrated Schroeder's theories on what he called "the erotogenesis of religion"—that is, the sexual origin of religious phenomena. He submitted *Heavenly Bridegrooms,* along with a short introduction, to the psychological journal *The Alienist and Neurologist* in 1915. The journal published it over six issues between November 1915 and August 1917. It was then reissued as a book in 1918, with the full title *Heavenly Bridegrooms: An Unintentional Contribution to the Erotogenetic Interpretation of Religion,* by "Ida C." The version presented here is based upon the proofs of the 1918 edition as hand-corrected by Schroeder, who added this explanatory note:

> In the course of my studies on the erotogenesis of religion I became interested in the life work and mental characteristics of one Ida C., a woman who committed suicide in her forty-fifth year. I first heard of her after her death, but it seemed to me that a psychologic study of her would yield rich materials as a contribution to the psychology of religion. Consequently, I bestirred myself to secure information, both biographical and autobiographical. Among the materials gathered was her lifelong correspondence with friends, a number of published essays written by her, some scraps of manuscripts, and two completed but unpublished book manuscripts. This material will later constitute the subject of my analysis. Ida C. was for a number of years a college teacher and for a long time associated with various kinds of free-thinking heretics. She was never married. In due time she became the victim of erotic hallucinations to which she gave a "spiritual" interpretation. Later, when her conduct brought her to the verge of incarceration in a jail or in an asylum,

she endeavored frankly to meet the issue of her own insanity. The resultant investigation to her mind seemed a complete vindication, not only of her sanity, but also, of the objective reality and spirituality of her erotic experiences. This vindication she reduced to writing. The manuscript is now in my possession. It seems to me under the circumstances of this case and the future studies which I am going to make, partly from other papers of the same author, that this is too valuable a document to be mutilated by editing. Furthermore, others should be given equal opportunity with myself in the interpretation of this material. The manuscript had been revised by its author and in a number of places it was quite impossible to decipher the pen interlineations, or replace words destroyed by the tearing of the manuscript through frequent handling before it came into my possession. At such places a word may be occasionally omitted or a connection left defective,[44] otherwise the following document is in the exact words of its author. This essay, I believe, was written before her thirty-fifth year, that is ten years before her suicide, and twenty-two years before the present publication. Her subsequent development will be brought out in my own study of her. Just before she wrote this she was [for] a short time a voluntary inmate of an asylum and pronounced incurably insane. She left the country to escape legal commitment.

44 These have been marked in the text by the present editor.

Heavenly Bridegrooms (1894)

The Sons of God saw the daughters of men
that they were fair; and they took them wives
of all that they chose. (Genesis 6:2)

Preface

It has been my high privilege to have some practical experience as the earthly wife of an angel from the unseen world. In the interests of psychical research I have tried to explore this pathway of communication with the spiritual universe, and, so far as lay in my power, to make a sort of rough guide-book of the route. For not all wives of heavenly bridegrooms travel the same path at first. There are roads running into this one from every religion and folklore under the sun, since the pathway of marital relations on the Borderland[45] was once, and still is, as I hope to show, one of the main thoroughfares connecting our world with the world beyond the grave. This thoroughfare, along part of which I hope to conduct the reader in imagination, is marked with signposts, many crumbling under the religious storms of centuries, others preserved as sacred trellises upon which to train a rank growth of flourishing superstition, and still others fresh with modern paint and gilding. Part of this thoroughfare runs straight through the Christian Church, or, to speak more accurately, the foundations of the Church are laid upon this very principle. For Jesus himself is said to be the child of a union between an earthly woman and a heavenly bridegroom who (however godlike, and whatever the details of the relation) certainly seems to have manifested to Mary on the occult plane. If it be objected that Mary's Borderland spouse was not an angel, but God himself, and therefore Borderland laws could be laid aside in His case, I reply that modern philosophy holds apparent miracles to be no violation of natural laws, but to have happened in accordance with some law as yet unknown to us, for God never breaks His laws, and if He became a Borderland spouse to Mary, it must have been in accordance with Borderland laws. And we, as made in His likeness, are bound by the same natural laws as God. Moreover, as Mary and

45 A spiritualist term referring to the threshold between the material world and the afterlife, within which the spirits of the dead may interact with the living.

me are sharers in a common humanity, she and me are bound alike, sharers in the glorious possibilities of Borderland.

The abraded survivals of an ancient religious teaching of marital purity and self-control is of so lofty a type that it has been obscured by the fogs in the lowlands of modern sensuality. Enlightened by my experiences as the wife of my unseen angel visitant, I wrote a defense (from a folklore standpoint) of the Danse du Ventre, which was published in the *New York World.* This I afterwards added to, and issued in a typewritten essay for private circulation. As the essay showed that I wrote from experience, as I was still "Miss" Craddock, and as my social standing had hitherto been above suspicion, I deemed it only prudent to state to my readers that I had acquired my knowledge from a spirit husband. This I did on a little slip of paper pinned to the last page of the essay. The persecutions which—in consequence of this straightforward effort to tell the truth simply and clearly—I suffered at the hands of those who deny the possibility of angelic communication, need not be dwelt on here. Suffice it to say that, while my non-occultist readers who did not know me personally, pooh-poohed the idea of a spirit husband, and declared that I must surely speak from an illicit experience, my non-occultist friends, who knew my habits of life from day to day, could find no explanation for the essay but that I must have gone crazy; and two physicians made efforts to have me incarcerated as insane. One of the latter remarked, "Had that essay been written by a man, by a physician or by any other scientist (and the paragraph about the spirit husband omitted) it would have been alright; but coming from an unmarried woman, neither a physician or a scientist, and with that claim of a spirit husband, there is no explanation possible but (1) illicit experience, which is denied by all who know her, or (2) insanity." That is to say, because I had, by means of knowledge gained through channels of which he was ignorant, given utterance to what would have passed unquestioned if coming from a scientist, therefore, I must be insane. To put it more tersely, a diamond of truth is to be considered genuine only when discovered by A or B; if the same diamond be discovered by X, Y, or Z, it is to be considered paste. My worst offense, however, in his eyes, seemed to be that, as a woman, I was out of my province in openly preaching marital reform, however high the ideals advocated; and, as my sense of duty did not conform with his conventional prejudices, he felt justified in seeking to incarcerate me until I should recant my heresy.

The factors in this case were:

1st. An unmarried woman of known reputation and integrity.

2nd. An essay written by that woman, dealing with the marital relation along lines not known to one married couple in a thousand.

3rd. A claim by the essayist, that she wrote from an experience gained as the wedded partner of a ghost.

To ignore any one of these factors in arriving at a theory to explain the other two, is to invalidate that theory.

Now, there is one creed to which all genuine Freethinkers[46] are faithful. It is to seek the truth, wherever it leads, and whatever the traditional belief upon the subject under investigation. This being so, I feel that I may confidently appeal to Freethinkers to consider carefully the evidence herewith submitted as to marital relations on the Borderland.

Last, but not least, I appeal to Spiritualists, Theosophists and Occultists generally. Psychics and sex, Laurence Oliphant has shown, are so interwoven that you cannot take up one wholly separate from the other. Only an occultist—and [a] somewhat experienced occultist, at that—knows anything of the perils which await the developing psychic on the Borderland. The Middle Ages are strewn with wrecked lives—mainly those of illiterate women, who, beginning by dabbling with magic in an empirical fashion, ended by confessing themselves as witches, devil-haunted in body as well as in mind, and pledged to sins against nature. Within the sheltered precincts of the most conservative of all Christian churches—the Roman Catholic—"*Congressus cum daemonis*."[47] And among the non-churchly practicers of modern occultism we too often find a tendency, on the one hand, not only to justifiable freedom, but also to unjustifiable looseness of life; or on the other hand, to a rigid asceticism and unnatural suppression of the sex instinct as impure. All these

46 Adherents of the Freethought movement, popular in the United States and Britain in the last half of the 19th century. Freethinkers generally stood for secularism and freedom of expression, especially for subjects that were likely to be suppressed by religious authorities.

47 Latin, "intercourse with demons." Incomplete sentence, as in original.

things point to the necessity for some teaching as to the fundamental principles of sex morality on the Borderland—all the more, as spirit bridegrooms and spirit brides are much more frequent than is generally supposed. Between the witch who held diabolic assignations as a devil's mistress, and the psychic who has been trained to self-control and reverent wedlock with an angel, it must surely be admitted, there is a wide stretch of road.[48] Nevertheless, both are on the same road, and the downward grade is very slippery. In so far as I have been able to explore this road, therefore I think it my duty to map out its perils and its safeguards, as help to my fellow occultists. For, no matter on what obscure by-path a psychic starts, he or she can never be sure of not coming upon this road unexpectedly, since it is, as I have said, one of the main thoroughfares of occultism.

To all three classes, then—to Occultists, Freethinkers and Christians—I respectfully offer this treatise for consideration in the hope that each may find in it something of interest, and, mayhap, of profit.

Heavenly Bridegroom

The celestial being, who, whether as God or angel, becomes the Heavenly Bridegroom of an earthly woman, is better known to the literature of the Christian Church than most people who are not theologians are aware. But he is not peculiar to Christianity. He has been known and recognized throughout the world in all ages. The woman to whom he comes is, as a rule, distinguished for her purity of life. Usually she is a virgin; but where already married and a mother, she must be recognized as chaste, or, at least, there must be no stigma of impurity upon her reputation. I am not at the present writing aware of a single exception to this.

Let us, however, first consider the Heavenly Bridegrooms of Christianity, from the popular orthodox standpoint.

There are two Heavenly Bridegrooms—the Holy Spirit and Christ. The first of these, the Holy Spirit, is, according to the New Testament, the Being through whose agency she whom the Catholic Church delights to honor as the Blessed Virgin became incarnate with Jesus. The second of these, Christ,

48 For an analysis of the former, see R. E. L. Masters, *Eros and Evil: The Sexual Psychopathology of Witchcraft* (New York: Julian Press, 1962).

is the Being honored alike by Catholics and by Protestants as the Bridegroom of the Church; by Catholics also as the mystic Spouse of the ecstatic and purified nun, as in the case of Saint Teresa; and by Protestants as the Bridegroom of the Soul, in that popular hymn beginning:

> Jesus, Lover of my soul,
> Let me to Thy bosom fly!

I once attended a young women's revival meeting at Ocean Grove, held under the auspices of an evangelist who was noted for his success in converting young girls. When the enthusiasm flagged, and his hearers were slow in responding to his appeals to "come to Christ," he started the above hymn, and the ardor of his fair congregation was at once kindled, girl after girl rising to publicly give herself to Christ. That which earnest pleading for their soul's salvation had failed to accomplish, was brought about by this simple suggestion of the "Lover of the Soul." In thus stimulating the untrained emotions of the maiden to aspire to the Divine through the symbolism of earthly affection, this revivalist not only showed keen insight into human nature, but he was also instinctively true to the teachings of the innermost truth of all religion, as I hope to show further on.

In the Bible an entire book—the Song of Solomon—is given up to expressing the raptures of the Heavenly Bridegroom and his Bride. At least, this is the interpretation which the Christian Church universally puts upon Canticles—the reciprocal Joys of Christ, the Bridegroom, and His Bride, the Church. Various phases of the sensuous relations of husband and wife are there set forth, in figurative but unmistakable terms of passion—passion which the Christian world has, unfortunately, long since forgotten how to utilize as the most important means of growth toward the Divine.

But there are other Heavenly Bridegrooms besides Christ and the Holy Spirit referred to in the Bible. In the sixth chapter of Genesis may be found a curious text, which reads:

> The sons of God saw the daughters of men, that they were fair; and they took them wives of all that they chose.

The Septuagint originally rendered the words "Sons of God" by αγγελοι του Θεου (angels of God) and this rendering is found in Philo, de Gigantibus, Eusebius, Augustine and Ambrose. This view of Genesis 6:1-4 was held by most of the early fathers.[49]

In fact, in the Book of Enoch, these sons of God are spoken of all through as angels who wedded earthly women; and it is further stated that these angelic husbands broke the law, living in depravity with their earthly wives, and laying the foundation of evils which required the Deluge to sweep away. Critical scholarship usually holds these angels to be fallen, but St. Augustine protests against this very saying: "I firmly believe that God's angels could never fall so at that time."

Nevertheless we find in the Book of Enoch, 15:4, the following:

> Whilst you were still spiritual, holy, in the enjoyment of eternal life, you have defiled yourselves with women, have begotten (children) with the blood of flesh, and have lusted after the blood of men, and produced flesh and blood, as those produce them who are mortal and short-lived.[50]

Here we see that the angels, whatever their [. . .] after depravity, were "still holy" when they united themselves as heavenly bridegrooms with earthly women.

However, from the above, and from other texts in Enoch, it would appear that the angels are blamed for having broken the laws of right living so far as to turn the relations existing between them and their earthly wives into the grossest sensuality. They, rather than the women, seem to be credited with the responsibility for evil-doing. But it is noticeable that Genesis is silent as to the character of these angelic bridegrooms, while it lays stress on the fact that the imaginations of men's hearts were evil continually, as though this last were the real cause of the wickedness which required the purification of the Deluge.

Now, let us remember that the Book of Enoch, although referred to in Jude, is not canonical. It belongs to the Hebrew Apocalyptic literature, and was for some time lost, save for a few fragments preserved in references made

49 See R. H. Charles, *The Book of Enoch, Translated from Professor Dillmann's Ethiopic Text* (Oxford: Clarendon Press,1893). (ICC note)

50 Charles, *The Book of Enoch,* p. 83. (ICC note)

by ecclesiastical writers. However valuable to scholars, it is un-canonical and thus cannot be accepted by Christians as the Word of God. Genesis, on the contrary, *is* accepted by Christians today as the Word of God; and therefore, the total omission of this sacred book to bring any charge against these angelic "sons of God," while the depravity of *man* is dwelt upon at this period of the world's history, is not a matter to be passed over lightly by a Christian.

According to the Christian Scripture, then, it was not the wickedness of the angels who wedded earthly women, but the evil imaginations of the human heart that brought about the punishment of the Deluge. And in this, Genesis is in strict accord with modern Theosophy—the only philosophy, so far as I know, which professes to know the Alpha and Omega of occultism. Theosophy lays stress on the punishment which awaits the black sorcerer—the earthly being who uses magical powers for selfish or impure purposes. But Theosophy is not alone in this teaching. All occultism, by whatever name it is called, however imperfect in deductions, learns at least to beware of the occultist who breaks the moral law, or who, whether willfully or carelessly, through prejudice or through crafty desire to advance his own selfish interests, closes his eyes to the truth. In other words, clear thinking and correct living are the only passport to trustworthiness in an occultist.

I have said that *all* occultism learns this lesson at last.

It is true that there are many psychical phenomena which at first sight do not seem to require any special exercise of morality on the part of the percipient. Such are the carefully attested phenomena of thought transference and wraith-seeing (especially of the astral form or "double" of people at the point of death or undergoing a sudden shock) which the Society for Psychical Research[51] have collated from a multitude of sources, in the case of the double to the number of some three thousand. The percipients in these instances are probably the average sort of folks, no better and no worse than their fellows. Yet they see or they hear by means of senses which are still unrecognized by most people, and which are, therefore, termed occult; and what they perceive is afterwards proved to be an actual occurrence, often of something taking place miles away. But it is to be observed that the reliable cases collated by

51 The Society for Psychical Research was founded in London in 1882 for the purpose of scientifically examining and validating claims of psychic and paranormal phenomena. It was generally sympathetic to spiritualism.

the Psychical Research Society are furnished by people who seem to be clear-headed enough, at least, to form definite mental conceptions. The majority of these cases are perceptions of occurrences in this earthly life. Where the thing claimed as seen or heard by the percipients no longer belongs to this world, but to the world beyond the grave, as in the case of visions or voices of those now deceased, the phenomena, collated by the Society of Psychical Research, seem not only to be capricious but they also seldom furnish a veridical (i.e., truth-telling) communication.

In the case of Spiritualist mediums, professional or amateur, where the phenomena assume some show of regularity, and are claimed by the medium to come entirely from the world beyond the grave, or through its aid, one always has to be on one's guard against the subtle interpolation among otherwise truthful matter of fantastic or misleading statements made apparently by the communicating spirits themselves. Occultists in all ages have invariably assumed such statements to be the work of "lying spirits." But it is noticeable that the medium of correct life and clearness of intellectual conception is less troubled by such lying spirits than is the medium of halting intellect or morals. This of itself should indicate to the thoughtful student of occult phenomena that the medium, and not the spirits, may be to blame when lying communications are made.

It is generally assumed that the false or fantastic remarks so subtly interpolated into communications which are otherwise truthful and uplifting are due to evil spirits getting temporary control of the medium. But this theory presupposes a state of society in the spirit-world far worse regulated than with us. It is often claimed, for instance, that throngs of spirits crowd about a powerful medium as a crowd of people on earth sometimes flock about a telegraph operator in times of excitement, each man selfishly striving to get his message sent off first. But, even in our imperfect civic life, is such an occurrence usual? By no means. Is it likely that in a new life with its added experience, such gross violations of law and order should be allowed to continue right along? *By no means.* Even if Heaven be not as Christians believe, the abode of God and the angels; even supposing that it is merely, as most Spiritualists claim, an improved edition of this world; it is but logical to infer that law and order will obtain there as here, and even more so, because the tendency of human society is always in the direction of systematizing its work for mutual convenience of its members. The idea of a good spirit may at any moment be temporarily displaced by an evil one, and that the laws of that clearer thought-world beyond the grave are powerless to cope with this annoyance is absurd, and contrary to common sense. The fault of imperfect communication is just as likely to be ours as others. Let us see to it that the lines of telegraphic communication are laid in correctness of moral living, and clearness of intellectual conception (on our side of the abyss of death), before we rashly assume the fault to be theirs. In other words, if they are in a world where new laws of matter obtain, as they must be, if they live at all after the death of the body—to communicate intelligently with us may not be so easy for them as we imagine. They may find themselves confronted at every turn by such difficulties. Therein will be found also a statement requiring an occult principle which seems not only to forbid spirits from communicating accurately with an immoral medium, but which seems to positively enjoin upon them the utterance of all the foolish, depraved and even criminal ideas that the medium is willing to receive, and places us mentally at a standpoint where all else is out of focus. Thus the slightest prejudices on any given subject under discussion between our celestial visitors and ourselves will render us liable to distorted conceptions of their ideas. Such is the law of our own thought-world here on the earthly plane; and we must remember that they have left our plane and entered into a far wider thought-world than ours. Hence the need for rigidly clear thinking on the part of every would-be occultist. And, since, as has been well said: "All badness is madness," we must not forget to also reckon a well-ordered moral life as among the attributes of the really clear-headed man or woman. This correct living and clear thinking go hand in hand as vouchers for accuracy of mediumship between this world and the world beyond the grave. The philosophy which deals with the subjective consciousness, as an important factor in fantastic and misleading psychic phenomena from spirits, will be found set forth at length. Sufficient to say here that in all such cases, however varied the manifestations, whether of an abnormal subconsciousness or of outside intelligences, failure to think clearly as to live in accordance with the moral requirements of self-control, duty, aspiration to the highest, unselfishness and genuine purity, will be found responsible for the disappointing psychic manifestations on the Borderland.[52]

When, therefore, the Book of Enoch blames the angelic sons of God, rather than their earthly wives, for the depravity of relations said to exist between them as spirits and mediums, we may well ask if this be not a matter on which the writer of the Book of Enoch has carelessly accepted current legends. May it not be that he, too, believed all depraved psychical manifestations to be due to "evil spirits" and that he was totally unaware of the occult law which brings these things to pass with a medium who, ignorantly but persistently, fails in clear thinking or correct living on the Borderland?

Once more let us note that the Book of Genesis, which is canonical, lays stress on the fact that at this epoch the imaginations of men's hearts were evil continually.

When the Christian Church appeared on the stage of history, it found several varying traditions current about those sons of God who, so many centuries before, had taken unto themselves wives from among the daughters of men.

One after the other, the early Church Fathers wrestled with these traditions, and strove to fit them into the Christian theological system. Beginning with Paul, we find that he asserts in the first chapter of I Corinthians, that a woman ought to be veiled, as a token of her inferiority and dependence upon man, and he adds: "For this cause ought the woman to have a sign of authority on her head because of the angels?"[53] Irenaeus, in his work *Against Heresies*, quoting this text, makes it read, "A woman ought to have a *veil* upon her head because of the angels."[54] From Tertullian we learn what this means. He says in his work *Against Marcion*:

> The apostle was quite aware that spiritual wickedness (Ephesians 6:12) had been at work in heavenly places when angels were entrapped into sin by the daughters of men.[55]

52 See Aleister Crowley, "Notes on the Nature of the 'Astral Plane'" in *Magick in Theory and Practice* (London: privately printed, 1930), pp. 245–264.

53 I Corinthians 11:10 (Revised Edition).

54 Alexander Roberts and W. H. Rambaut, *The Writings of Irenaeus*, *ANCL*, vol. 5 (Edinburgh: T. and T. Clark, 1868), p. 33.

55 Peter Holmes, *The Five Books of Quintus Sept. Flor. Tertullianus against Marcion*, *ANCL*, vol. 7 (Edinburgh: T. and T. Clark, 1868), p. 468.

In sundry places Tertullian waxes wroth over this supposed "entrapping" of angels by earthly women. In a treatise *On the Veiling of Virgins*—written for the purpose of compelling all unmarried women to be veiled as were the married, one reason being that they were "Brides of Christ"—he speaks his mind thus:

> So perilous a face, then, ought to be shaded, which has cast stumbling-stones even so far as heaven; that when standing in the presence of God, at whose bar it stands accused of the driving of the angels from their (native) confines, it may blush before the other angels as well; and may repress that former evil liberty of its head—(a liberty) now to be exhibited not even before human eyes.[56]

The author of the *Testaments of the Twelve Patriarchs* is, if anything, more severe. He remarks:

> Hurtful are women, my children; because, since they have no power or strength over the man, they act subtilly through outward guise how they may draw him to themselves; and whom they cannot overcome by strength, him they overcome by craft.... By means of their adornment, they deceive first their minds, and instill the poison by the glance of their eye, and then they take them captive by their doings, for a woman cannot overcome a man by force. . . . my children . . . command your wives and your daughters that they adorn not their heads and their faces; because every woman who acteth deceitfully in these things hath been reserved to everlasting punishment. For thus they allured the Watchers before the flood.[57]

He adds that these angelic Watchers manifested as apparitions to the women at the times of their union with their earthly husbands; "and the women, having in their minds desire towards their apparitions, gave birth to giants, for the Watchers appeared to them as reaching even unto heaven."[58]

Here we see an attempt to account for the resulting progeny of "giants" by such simple and natural means as Jacob made use of when he desired to

56 *On Veiling of Virgins*, 7. (ICC note) [S. Thelwall and R. E. Wallis, *The Writings of Quintus Sept. Flor. Tertullianus*, vol 3, *ANCL*, vol. 18 (Edinburgh: T. and T. Clark, 1870), p. 166.]

57 *Testament of Reuben*, 5. (ICC note) [Robert Sinker, *The Testaments of the Twelve Patriarchs*, *ANCL*, vol. 22 (Edinburgh: T. & T. Clark, 1871), p. 16.]

58 Sinker, *Testaments*, p. 16.

produce "ringstraked, speckled and spotted" goats (Genesis 30:35). No mention is made of marital relations being established directly between earthly women and angels. Elsewhere the same writer speaks of these same Watchers as having "changed the order of their nature, whom also the Lord cursed at the flood, and for their sakes made desolate the earth."[59]

This follows a reference to Sodom, the writer seeming to trace a similarity between the two causes of the two punishments. Justin Martyr, however, makes the offence of the sinning angels to consist rather in ambition for power over mankind. He says:

> God . . . committed the care of men and of all things under heaven to angels whom He appointed over them. But the angels transgressed this appointment, and were captivated by love of women, and begat children who are those that are called demons; and besides, they afterwards subdued the human race to themselves, partly by magical writings, and partly by fears and the punishments they occasioned, and partly by teaching them to offer sacrifices, and incense, and libations, of which things they stood in need after they were enslaved by lustful passions; and among men they sowed murders, wars, adulteries, intemperate deeds, and all wickedness.[60]

These things, according to Justin, the poets (unaware that they were due to sinning angels) ignorantly ascribed to God (Jupiter), and to those who were called his brothers, Neptune and Pluto, and to the Olympian deities in general.

Lactantius lays the blame principally upon Satan. Speaking of the repeated efforts of the serpent ("who from his deeds received the name of devil, that is, accuser or informer") to corrupt mankind, he adds:

> But when God saw this, He sent His angels to instruct the race of men, and to protect them from all evil. He gave these a command to abstain from earthly things, lest, being polluted by any taint, they should be deprived of the honor of angels. But that wily accuser, while

59 *Testament of Naphthali*, 3. (ICC note) [Sinker, *Testaments*, p. 56.]

60 *Second Apology of Justin*, 5. (ICC note) [Marcus Dods, George Reith and B. P. Pratten, *The Writings of Justin Martyr and Athenagoras*, *ANCL*, vol. 2 (Edinburgh: T. and T. Clark, 1867), pp. 75–76.]

> they tarried among men, allured these also to pleasures, so that they might defile themselves with women. Then, being condemned by the sentence of God, and cast forth on account of their sins, they lost both the name and substance of angels. Thus, having become ministers of the devil, that they might have a solace of their ruin, they betook themselves to the ruining of men, for whose protection they had come.[61]
>
> Thus from angels the devil makes them to become his satellites and attendants. But they who were born from these, because they were neither angels nor men, but bearing a kind of mixed (middle) nature, were not admitted into hell, as their fathers were not into heaven. Thus there came to be two kinds of demons; one of heaven, the other of the earth.[62]

In one place Justin Martyr speaks of "evil demons" who "in times of old, assuming various forms, went in unto the daughters of men."[63] Elsewhere he also speaks of these demons manifested as apparitions and misled boys as well as women. He said that they "showed such fearful sights to men, that those who did not use their reason in judging of the actions that were done were struck with terror . . . and not knowing that these were demons, they called them gods."[64] Justin evidently looks upon the angelic bridegroom as demoniacal from the start. Clement of Alexandria says that the angels "renounced the beauty of God for a beauty which fades, and so fell from heaven to earth."[65]

Athenagoras asserts that the angels "fell into impure love of virgins."[66] But Tertullian calls attention to the fact that sacred Scripture terms these angels *husbands*; and he argues at length very ably to show that we are bound to infer from Scripture that the earthly wives of these angelic husbands were virgins, pure and undefiled, at the time of their marriage. From which it is evident that these marriages were acceptable to virtuous women, and therefore, we may infer, not an infringement of the civil law of the time, or the sex

61 *Epitome of the Divine Institutes*, 27. (ICC note) [William Fletcher, *The Works of Lactantius*, vol. 2, *ANCL*, vol. 22 (Edinburgh: T. and T. Clark, 1871), pp. 109–110.]

62 *The Divine Institutes*, II, 15. (ICC note) [William Fletcher, *The Works of Lactantius*, vol. 1, *ANCL*, vol. 21 (Edinburgh: T. and T. Clark, 1871), p. 127.]

63 Temple Chevallier, *First Apology of Justin Martyr* (New York: Henry M. Onderdonk & Co., 1846), p. 129.

64 Dods, *Justin Martyr and Athenagoras*, p. 10.

65 William Wilson, *The Writings of Clement of Alexandria*, vol. 1, *ANCL*, vol. 4 (Edinburgh: T. and T. Clark, 1867), p. 283.

66 Dods, *Justin Martyr and Athenagoras*, p. 406.

which is proverbially conservative would never have contributed so largely to these unions from among its best members. Nor could they have been unions which transgressed the laws of nature, or the resulting offspring would not have been so well developed physically (as giants) nor mentally (as "mighty men which were of old, men of renown").

Clement of Alexandria, in his Miscellanies (*Stromata*), appears to blame the sinning angels in addition because they "told to the women the secrets which had come to their knowledge; while the rest of the angels concealed them, or rather, kept them against the coming of the Lord."[67] These "secrets," we learn from several of the Christian Fathers, were the arts of metallurgy, dyeing, the properties of herbs, astronomy and astrology, etc. Reasoning from this assumption that certain sciences and industrial arts were imparted to mankind from sinful angels, we need not wonder that Tertullian pertinently asks:

> But, if the self-same angels who disclosed both the material substance of this kind and their charms—of gold, I mean, and lustrous stones—and taught men how to work them, and by and by instructed them, among their other (instructions) in (the virtue of) eye-lid powder and the dyeing of fleeces, have been condemned by God, as Enoch tells us, how shall we please God while we joy in the things of those (angels) who, on these accounts, have provoked the anger and vengeance of God?[68]

This thought seems to have been to him a matter of serious moment, for he enlarges upon it, as follows, when speaking of the dress and ornamentation of women:

> For they, withal, who instituted them are assigned, under condemnation, to the penalty of death—those angels, to wit, who rushed from heaven on the daughters of men; so that this ignominy also attaches to woman. For when to an age much more ignorant than ours they had disclosed certain well-concealed material substances, and several not well-revealed scientific arts—if it is true that they had laid bare the operations of metallurgy, and had divulged the natural properties

67 Wilson, *Clement of Alexandria*, p. 226.

68 *On Female Dress*, II, 10. (ICC note) [S. Thelwall and R. E. Wallis, *The Writings of Quintus Sept. Flor. Tertullianus*, vol. 1, *ANCL*, vol. 11 (Edinburgh: T. and T. Clark, 1869), pp. 327–328.]

> of herbs, and had promulgated the powers of enchantments, and had traced out every curious art, even to the interpretation of the stars—they conferred properly and as it were peculiarly upon women that instrumental mean of womanly ostentation, the radiances of jewels wherewith necklaces are variegated, and the circlets of gold wherewith the arms are compressed, and the medicaments of orchil with which wools are colored, and that black powder itself wherewith the eyelids and eyelashes are made prominent. What is the quality of these things may be declared meantime, even at this point, from the quality and condition of their teachers; in that sinners could never have either shown or supplied anything conducive to integrity, unlawful lovers anything conducive to chastity, renegade spirits anything to the fear of God. If these things are to be called teachings, ill masters must of necessity have taught ill; if as wages of lust, there is nothing base of which the wages are honorable. But why was it of so much importance to show these things as well as to confer them? Was it that women, without material causes of splendor, and without ingenious contrivances of grace, could not please men, who, while still unadorned and uncouth, and—so to say—crude and rude, had moved the minds of angels? Or was it that the {angelic} lovers would appear sordid and—through gratuitous use—contumelious, if they had conferred no compensating gift on the women who had been enticed into connubial connection with them? But these questions admit of no calculation. Women who possessed angels as husbands could desire nothing more; they had, forsooth, made a grand match! Assuredly they who, of course, did sometimes think whence they had fallen, and, after the heated impulses of their lusts, looked up toward heaven, thus requited that very excellence of women, natural beauty, as having proved a cause of evil, in order that their good fortune might profit them nothing; but that, being turned from simplicity and sincerity, they, together with the angels themselves, might become offensive to God. Sure they were that all ostentation, and ambition, and love of pleasing by carnal means, was displeasing to God.[69]

Cyprian, when blaming virgins for wearing jewels, necklaces and wool stuffs colored with costly dyes likewise remarks:

---

69 *On Female Dress*, chap. II. (ICC note) [Thelwall and Wallis, *Quintus Sept. Flor. Tertullianus*, pp. 305–307.]

> All which things sinning and apostate angels put forth by their arts, when, lowered to the contagions of earth, they forsook their heavenly vigor.[70]

When we remember that early Christianity sets its face like a flint against all delights of the senses and that this extreme reaction of the spiritual against the sensuous has largely shaped our social customs of today, we begin to see how important and far-reaching were these opinions of the Church Fathers that feminine adornment had been taught by angels who had sinned in wedding earthly women, and that it was therefore a sinful thing in that it has emanated from a depraved source. Some of the theories built upon this assumption are quite curious. Here are a few:

> That which He Himself has not produced is not pleasing to God, unless He was *unable* to order sheep to be born with purple and sky-blue fleeces! If He was *able*, then plainly He was *unwilling*: what God willed not, of course ought not to be fashioned.[71]
>
> For it was God, no doubt, who showed the way to dye wools with the juices of herbs and the humours of conchs! It had escaped Him, when He was bidding the universe come into being, to issue a command for the production of purple and scarlet sheep![72]
>
> Why should she walk out adorned? Why with dressed hair, as if she either had or sought for a husband? Rather let her dread to please if she is a virgin. . . . It is not right that a virgin should have her hair braided for the appearance of her beauty.[73]
>
> You are bound to please your husbands only. But you will please them in proportion as you take no care to please others. Be ye without carefulness, blessed sisters; no wife is ugly to her own husband. She pleased him enough when she was selected by him as his wife; whether commended by form or by character. Let none of you think that, if she abstain from the care of her person {*compositione sui*}, she will incur the hatred and aversion of husbands. Every husband is the exactor of chastity; but beauty a believing husband does not require, because we

70 *On the Dress of Virgins*, 14. (ICC note) [Robert Ernest Wallis, *The Writings of Cyprian, Bishop of Carthage*, vol. 1, *ANCL*, vol. 8 (Edinburg: T. & T. Clark, 1868), p. 344.]

71 Tertullian, *On Female Dress*, I, 8. (ICC note) [Thelwall and Wallis, *Quintus Sept. Flor. Tertullianus*, p. 312.]

72 Tertullian, *On Female Dress*, II, 10. (ICC note) [Thelwall and Wallis, *Quintus Sept. Flor. Tertullianus*, p. 327.]

73 Cyprian, *On the Dress of Virgins*, 5. (ICC note) [Wallis, *Writings of Cyprian*, pp. 337–338.]

> are not captivated by the same graces which the Gentiles think to be graces.[74]
>
> Do ye, O good matrons, flee from the adornment of vanity; such attire is fitting for women who haunt the brothels. . . . To a wife approved of her husband, let it suffice that she is so, not by her dress, but by her good disposition.[75]

Let us remember that these and similar teachings by the early Christian Fathers have laid the foundation of our present marriage customs. The theory [is] that a woman sins in adorning herself to please a husband (whether present or prospective), and this theory is still indescribably popular among devout Christians.

Commodianus ascribes the teaching of "arts, and the dyeing of wool, and everything which is done," not to the angels but to the giant progeny. And he adds:

> To them, when they died, men erected images. But the Almighty, because they were of an evil seed, did not approve that, when dead, they should be brought back from death. Whence wandering they now subvert many bodies, and it is such as these especially that ye this day worship and pray to as gods.[76]

The author of the *Clementine Homilies* records a tradition concerning these gigantic "wanderers" on the borders of Ghostland[77] which seems to him that they were not unable to beget children. After speaking of the Deluge he says:

> Since, therefore, the souls of the deceased giants were greater than human souls, inasmuch as they also excelled their bodies, they, as being a new race, were called also by a new name. And to those who survived in the world a law was prescribed of God through an angel, how they should live. For being bastards in race, of the fire of angels and the

74 Tertullian, *On Female Dress*, II, 4. (ICC note) [Thelwal and Wallisl, *Quintus Sept. Flor. Tertullianus*, pp. 319–320.]

75 *The Instructions of Commodianus in Favor of Christian Discipline Against the Gods of the Heathens*, 59. (ICC note) [Thelwall and Wallis, *Quintus Sept. Flor. Tertullianus*, p. 464.]

76 *The Instructions of Commodianus in Favor of Christian Discipline Against the Gods of the Heathens*. (ICC note) [Thelwall and Wallis, *Quintus Sept. Flor. Tertullianus*, p. 435.]

77 An alternative term for Borderland.

> blood of woman, and therefore liable to desire a certain race of their own, they were anticipated by a certain righteous law.[78]

Inasmuch as the Deluge had already destroyed everyone on the earth except Noah and his family, we see that the author cannot mean by those who survived in the world any giants still in the flesh. Moreover, the decree which followed and which prescribed that they are to have power over only those human beings who break the moral law and practice magic would indicate these "giants" had then entered upon what Theosophists would call astral, and from the paragraph quoted above, it is evidently taken for granted that these astral giants would propagate their kind. This is an important point—the testimony of a Christian Father of a tradition that human beings (not created angels) who had once inhabited bodies, could beget children on the plane of the astral unless prevented by the direct prohibition of Heaven. If it be objected that the author refers to giants still in earthly form when he speaks to "those who survived in the world," I am sure that the statement follows a remark about the Deluge and that in that case the surviving giants must have been Noah and his family. This view, however, is absurd, when we consider that the decree forbade the giants to assume power over any but the human race. If Noah and his family were the surviving giants, where would be the sense in promulgating such a decree to them? This same author gives an account of the doings of the angelic fathers of these giants which reminds one strongly of the spirit séances of the late Rev. Stainton Moses,[79] when under conditions which precluded all fraud or illusion, tiny pearls and other precious stones suddenly materialized before the sitters. Here is the tradition recorded by the Christian Fathers:

> For of the spirits who inhabit the heaven, the angels who dwell in the lowest region, being grieved at the ingratitude of men to God, asked that they might come into the life of men, that, really becoming men, by more intercourse they might convict those who had acted ungratefully towards Him, and might subject every one to adequate

78 *Clementine Homilies*, VIII, 18. (ICC note) [Thomas Smith, Peter Peterson and James Donaldson, *The Clementine Homilies*, *ANCL*, vol. 17 (Edinburgh: T. and T. Clark, 1870), p. 145.]

79 William Stainton Moses (1839–1892) was an English clergyman and spiritualist, editor and author, and one of the founders of the Society for Psychical Research.

> punishment. When, therefore, their petition was granted, they metamorphosed themselves into every nature; for, being of a more godlike substance, they are able easily to assume any form. So they became precious stones, and goodly pearl, and the most beauteous purple, and choice gold, and all matter that is held in most esteem. And they fell into the hands of some, and into the bosoms of others, and suffered themselves to be stolen by them. They also changed themselves into beasts and reptiles, and fishes and birds, and into whatsoever they pleased. These things also the poets among yourselves, by reason of fearlessness, sing, as they befell, attributing to one the many and diverse doings of all.[80]

(Then, "having assumed these forms, they convicted as covetous those who stole them, and changed themselves into the nature of men, in order that, living holily, and showing the possibility of so living, they might subject the ungrateful to punishment."[81] However, "having become in all respects men, they also became subject to masculine infirmities and fell."[82])

Does it not seem as though we had here a survival of Animism—a state of mind frequent among savages, children and animals in which an inanimate object which moves without visible cause or manifests in any peculiar way is thought to be alive. A horse is often terrified by a piece of paper blown in front of him, evidently he takes it for a live creature. Savages speak of the sun and moon as living individuals because of their apparently voluntary journeys through the sky; among the Kukis of Southern Asia, if a man was killed by a fall from a tree, his relatives would take their revenge by cutting the tree down, scattering it in chips. A modern King of Cochin, China, when one of his ships sailed badly, used to put it in the pillory as he would any other criminal.[83] In classical times, the stories of Xerxes flogging the Hellespont and Cyrus draining the Gyndes occur as cases in point, but one of the regular Athenian legal proceedings is a yet more striking relic. A court of justice was held at the Prytaneum, to try any inanimate object, such as an

80 *Clementine Homilies*, VIII, 12. (ICC note) [Smith, et.al., *Clementine Homilies*, p. 142.]

81 Smith, et.al., *Clementine Homilies*, p. 143.

82 Smith, et.al., *Clementine Homilies*, but misquoted. The original reads "having become in all respects men, they also partook of human lust, and being brought under its subjection they fell into cohabitation with women."

83 Adolf Bastian, *Die Völker des östlichen Asien*, vol. 1 (1866), p. 51. (ICC note)

axle, a piece of wood or stone, which had caused the death of anyone without proved human agency, and this wood or stone, if condemned, was with solemn form cast beyond the border. The spirit of this remarkable procedure reappears in the old English law (repealed in the present reign), whereby, not only a beast that kills a man, but a cart-wheel that runs over him, as a tree that falls on him, kills him, is dead and is given to God, forfeited and sold for the poor. The pathetic custom of "telling the bees" when the master or mistress of a house dies, is not unknown in our own country. In Berlin, Germany, the idea is more fully worked out; and not only is the sad message given to every bee-hive in the garden and every beast in the stall, but every sack of corn must be touched and everything in the house shaken, that they may know the master is gone. And we all know that even an intelligent nineteenth century man is not above administering an angry kick to a chair against which he has bruised himself.

Now the author of the *Clementine Homilies* seems to have similarly lighted on an instance of Animism in connection with gold, pearls, precious stones, etc. In prehistoric times this tradition, rational and intelligible, may suppose that these precious articles had moved or otherwise behaved as though endowed with life in the ancient times to which the tradition relates. Could it be that they suddenly appeared to those prehistoric gazers, coming from no one knew where, and moved about by unseen hands, as tables are lifted, bells rung, banjos played or flowers materialized at a modern spiritual séance, evidently reported to have come by occult means, supposed to be heavenly. The people who witnessed the phenomena were probably not accustomed to clear-headed and intelligent investigation of such phenomena, see at once it was an Animistic explanation such as is given in the *Clementine Homilies.* As to the frightened horse, and to the ignorant savage, inanimate things seem to be alive, so may the precious objects which materialized at those prehistoric séances have seemed to the beholders to be living creatures, inasmuch as they sped through the air without visible support. If alive, they surely (so would argue the witnesses) must be angelic beings since they were said to come from heaven and the attendant phenomena of the séance no doubt would increase the awe with which these "angels" were received and treasured. An "angel" is simply a vehicle for a message in the original signification. Let us glance in passing at the accounts of materializing through the psychic power. In this sense a pearl materialized through the psychic power of so reliable a modern medium as the Rev. Stainton Moses, plainly by occult means, might be called an "angel"—i.e., the means by which the message from the unseen reached the sitters. In after times when the word angel had come to be specialized as a personal envoy from Heaven, the old tradition about the pearls and precious stones which had evidently come as "angels" (vehicles for a heaven-sent message) whenever told would probably be adapted to the specialized meaning and it would be said as above, that personal beings transformed into these inanimate things. First, as to the manifestations through the Rev. Stainton Moses lately declared, in his journal occurs the following entry:

> *Tuesday, September 9th, 1873.* Same conditions. Plentiful scent as before. Sixteen little pearls were put on the table, six having been previously given during the day. Mrs. Speer and I were writing at the same table, and a pearl was put on my letter as I was writing. After that I saw a spirit standing by Mrs. Speer, and was told that it was Mentor, who had put a pearl on Mrs. Speer's desk. After that four others came. They seemed to drop on the table, just as I have seen them with Mrs. A—h. We have in all twenty-one now. They are small seed pearls, each perforated.

A week later, there is this entry:

> When we broke up we found a little heap of pearls was put before each. One hundred and thirty-nine little pearls have been brought to us, one hundred and ten in the last two days.

(This, it appears from another witness, occurred in daylight.)

Dr. Speer[84] (referred to by Miss X. in *Borderland*[85] as "a highly intelligent and by no means credulous witness") gives a striking instance of the materialization of a precious object:

> *December 31st, 1872.* A very successful séance. A blue enamel cross was brought, no one knew whence, placed before my wife, who was told to wear it.

84 Stanhope Templeman Speer (1823–1889), a physician and associate of Stainton Moses.
85 Here referring to the quarterly Spiritualist journal *Borderland*, edited by W. T. Stead.

Mrs. Speer testifies as follows:

> *Ventnor, November 29th, 1893.* I wish to state that the most convincing evidences of spirit-power always took place when hands were held.
>
> Other manifestations occurred, often in light, such as raps, raising of table, scent, musical sounds, and showers of pearls. . . . Two cameos were carved in light while we were dining.

Before leaving this part of the subject, it may be well to quote the following by Miss X. in *Borderland* (Miss X., I would add, is by no means a Spiritualist, but is distinctly opposed to the Spiritistic hypothesis):

> Mr. Stainton Moses has for many years been one of the most important witnesses for Spiritualism. The fact that, like Professor Crookes[86] and Alfred Russel Wallace,[87] he was a gentleman, a scholar, and a man of recognized position and character, was, to say the least, a good letter of introduction. . . . It may be said, once and for all, that it is unnecessary to insist on the absolute sincerity of Mr. Stainton Moses. It is a point which has never been so much as raised. His life has been of a kind not to be called in question—obscure without mystery, dignified without pedantry, lived in the sight of just that class of the public which demands the strictest respectability of conduct, the most unequivocal correspondence between life and profession. As a clergyman he was beloved by his parishioners, as a schoolmaster he was respected by his boys, as a personal friend he commanded the confidence and esteem of all his intimates.[88]

May it not be that the phenomena recorded by the author of the Clementine Homilies are essentially the same in kind as those referred to above in the case of the Rev. Stainton Moses?

St. Augustine, considering the possibility of occult sex relations between earthly women and beings from the unseen world, remarks:

---

86 Sir William Crookes (1832–1919), an important British chemist and physicist who studied Spiritualist phenomena and concluded that they were genuine. He was also a member of the Hermetic Order of the Golden Dawn.

87 Alfred Russel Wallace (1823–1913), a British anthropologist, biologist, and explorer who also studied Spiritualism and accepted it as valid.

88 W. T. Stead, ed. Borderland, vol. 1 (1894), p. 307.

> The Scriptures plainly aver that the angels have appeared both in visible and palpable figures. And seeing it is so general a report, and so many aver it either from their own experience or from others, that are of indubitable honesty and credit, that the sylvans and fauns, commonly called incubi, have often injured women, desiring and acting carnally with them, and that certain devils from whom the Gauls call dusii, do continually practice this . . . and tempt others to it, which is affirmed by such persons, and with such confidence that it were impudence to deny it, I dare not venture to determine anything here as to whether the devils being embodied in air (for this air being violently moved is felt) can suffer this lust, or move it so as the women, with whom they commix, may feel it; yet do I firmly believe that God's angels could never fall so at that time.[89]

Notice the perplexity of St. Augustine as a logician. He cannot deny that occult sex relations exist on the Borderland, the testimony to this is too widespread and of too reliable a character. But (we can imagine him saying), how reconcile these phenomena with the belief that the inhabitants of the world beyond the grave are immaterial, vapory, mist-like beings?

How can such a hazy, ethereal creature as a ghost produce objective sensations of touch upon an earthly being? And if possible—as he ingeniously supposes, by such means as air becomes perceptible to us when violently put in motion—how reconcile such phenomena with the belief that sex is impure, and that it does not exist in the world beyond the grave? How could God's angels ever fall so? It were impossible.

But St. Augustine evidently starts from two hypotheses —the unsubstantiability of ghosts and the impurity (as will be seen by a perusal of the quotation in full) and, therefore, non-existence of sex, neither of which two hypotheses has ever been definitely proven. As a logician therefore, he is at fault, and I have already shown the danger of starting from mistaken premises when dealing with occult phenomena. The two hypotheses, however, were not peculiar to St. Augustine. They were, and are, the common property of the majority of mankind. But it does not follow that they are correct: and the psychic who rashly assumes their truth to start with (through prejudice or

89 St. Augustine's *City of God*, XV, 23. (ICC note) [John Healey, trans., *The City of God (De Civitate Dei)*, vol. 2 (London: Griffith, Farran, Okeden and Welsh, 1892), p. 90.]

because other people think so) may expect to be deluded, and to come upon all sorts of fantastic, and possibly diabolical manifestations. Such is the occult law. Start with a false premise or with a premise which you have not investigated with scrupulous care, and you are certain to get phenomena of either a misleading or a depraved character.

But all the Christian Fathers did not accept the possibility of bridegrooms from the unseen world. There were then, as now, Materialist minds which disbelieved in ghosts. Alexander, Bishop of Lycopolis, endeavored to explain away angelic bridegrooms as myths, thus:

> When the Jewish history relates that angels came down to hold intercourse with the daughters of men . . . this saying signifies that the nutritive powers of the soul descended from heaven to earth.[90]

Hence the "injuring" of women by incubi to which St. Augustine refers, an injuring either wholly subjective and illusory, or, if objectively real, was brought about in part by the woman's ignorance of the occult requirements for correct living and clear-headedness on the Borderland, in part by her failure to thus live and think on the earthly plane.

It would be interesting to know his authority for this. Rationalistic theories cannot rest, as do folklore traditions, upon a mere say-so; they must be supported either by testimony or by argument. Otherwise, we are obliged to dismiss them as the whimsical fancies of a solitary individual.

Origen says he will "persuade those who are capable of understanding the meaning of the prophet, that even before us there was one who referred this narrative to the doctrine regarding souls, which became possessed with a desire for the corporeal life of[91] men," and thus in metaphorical language he termed them "daughters of men." But Origen does not give his authority, nor advance any argument in support of this explanation.

Julius Africanus suggests another Rationalistic explanation, but is candid enough to give it as his own notion. He says:

---

90 *On the Tenets of the Manicheans*, XXV. (ICC note) [W. R. Clark, J. B. H. Hawkins, B. L. Pratten and S. D. Salmond, *The Writings of Methodius, Alexander of Lycopolis, Peter of Alexandria, and Several Fragments*, ANCL, vol. 14 (Edinburgh: T. and T. Clark, 1869), pp. 264–265.]

91 Frederick Crombie, *The Writings of Origen*, vol. 2, ANCL, vol. 23 (Edinburgh: T. and T. Clark, 1872), p. 325.

> When men multiplied on the earth, the angels of heaven came together with the daughters of men. In some copies I found "the sons of God." What is meant by the Spirit, in my opinion, is that the descendants of Seth are called the sons of God on account of the righteous men and patriarchs who have sprung from him, even down to the Saviour Himself; but that the descendants of Cain are named the seed of men, as having nothing divine in them, on account of the wickedness of their race and the inequality of their nature, being a mixed people, and having stirred the indignation of God.[92]

This ingenious theory has been eagerly grasped at by succeeding Christian writers who disbelieve in the substantiality of ghosts. So able a commentator in modern times, however, as Delitzsch[93] *On Genesis* decides against this view, and quotes various authorities which I give elsewhere. He also quotes Keil as demonstrating that two of the Hebrew words in the text in Genesis show that "the contraction of actual and lasting marriages" is meant.

Julius Africanus, indeed, seems to have had doubts as to whether the current tradition about angelic bridegrooms might not be true after all, for he adds directly upon the heels of the above theory:

> But if it is thought that these refer to angels, we must take them to be those who deal with magic and jugglery, who taught the women the motions of the stars and the knowledge of things celestial, by whose power they conceived the giants as their children, by whom wickedness came to its height on the earth, until God decreed that the whole race of the living should perish in their impiety by the Deluge.[94]

Nevertheless, Rationalists and Materialists are in the minority among the Fathers of the Church as regards this subject. The majority accepted the accounts in Genesis and Enoch at their face value.

To briefly sum up the majority's views of the early church on this matter:

1. Angels of a superior order did come into the earthly life—whether (a)

---

92 Cleveland Coxe, *Fathers of the Third Century, The Ante-Nicene Fathers, Translations of the Writings of the Fathers Down to A.D. 325*, vol. 6 (Edinburgh: T. and T. Clark, 1890), p. 131.

93 Franz Delitzsch (1813–1890), a theologian and co-author of a series of commentaries on the Old Testament with Johann Friedrich Karl Keil (1807–1888).

94 Coxe, *Fathers of the Third Century*, p. 131.

because God sent them, or (b) because they were moved with indignation at the ingratitude of men toward God and came voluntarily in order to reconcile God and man, or (c) because they were enticed by women on the earth, the traditions do not agree.

2. Having come into this earthly life, they became either the lovers or the husbands of women, whether beguiled thereto in part by the Devil, or wholly by the women, or partially or wholly by their own desires, the traditions again do not agree. One tradition, as we have seen, hints at the sin of Sodom; and an interference on the astral plane with the rights of earthly husbands; others hint at illicit amours; but Tertullian demonstrates unanswerably from sacred Scripture that the angels were the wedded husbands of the daughters of men, and that these daughters were virginal at the time of wedding their angelic lovers.

This was not, however, all their sin. One tradition, as we have seen, makes a vague allusion to the sin of Sodom in connection with the intercourse of angels with women.

3. That an angelic woman should seek an honorable marriage, especially an earthly woman, it would appear, was reckoned a sin. When asked why, we find that the Church Fathers, one and all, treated marriage as a mere expedient. Tertullian said that the reason why "marrying" is good, is that "burning" is worse. Minncius Felix remarks that "with some even the modest intercourse of the sexes causes a blush."[95] Methodius has an entire book devoted to an argument offered by ten virgins against wedlock and on behalf of perpetual virginity. Origen says: "God has allowed us to marry, because all are not fit for the higher, that is, the perfectly pure life."[96] Cyprian says that, "Chastity maintains the first rank in virgins, the second in those who are continent, the third in the case of wedlock."[97] He also says:

> What else is virginity than the glorious preparation for the future life? Virginity is of neither sex. Virginity is the continuance of infancy. Virginity is the triumph over pleasures. Virginity has no children; but what is more, it has contempt for offspring; it has not fruitfulness, but neither has it bereavement; blessed that it is free from the pain of bring-

95 *Octavius*, XXXI. (ICC note) [Wallis, *The Writings of Cyprian*, p. 503.]
96 Crombie, *The Writings of Origen*
97 Wallis, *The Writings of Cyprian*, pp. 255–256.

> ing forth, more blessed still that it is free from the calamity of the death of children. What else is virginity than the freedom of liberty? It has no husband for a master. Virginity is freed from all affections; it is not given up to marriage, nor to the world, nor to children.[98]

Justin Martyr exults that "many, both men and women, of the age of sixty and seventy years, who have been disciples of Christ from their youth, continue in immaculate virginity."[99]

In a spurious fragment credited to "Hippolytus, the Syrian Expositor of the Forum," the writer refers to an ancient Hebrew MS., which tells of Noah being commanded by God to stake off each male animal in the ark from the corresponding female. The other and principal object of marriage which runs through all nature from protoplasmic cells up to man—of mutual exchange of strength and mutual happiness, seems to have been totally ignored by the early Christian Fathers. Lactantius held that it is impossible the two sexes could have been instructed except for the sake of generation. Justin Martyr says frankly:

> Either marry at first, for no other object than to rear children, or else abstaining from marriage, continue to live in a state of continence.[100]

He notes with approval a Christian youth who begged Felix, the governor of Alexandria, for permission to be made a eunuch by a physician, in order to attest his continence to the world. (Felix, however, had the good sense to refuse.) To such an extent was this unnatural loathing for wedlock carried, that Constantine found it judicious to remove the old-time penalties against celibacy, because of the many Christians who continued celibates from motives of religion.

Since marriage on natural grounds was thus depreciated by the early Church as impure when occurring between earthly men and women, we need not wonder that she viewed with horror the very thought of wedlock with an angel inasmuch as angels were supposed to be above earthly weaknesses. Having thus started from a false premise, i.e., that marital passion cannot be

98 *Of the Discipline of Chastity*, 7. (ICC note) [Wallis, *The Writings of Cyprian*, pp. 257–258.]
99 Dods et al., *Justin Martyr and Athenagoras*, p. 18.
100 *Apology*, I, 37. (ICC note) [Chevallier, *Translation of the Epistles*, p. 154.]

pure in God's sight, there was no other deduction to be made regarding these love-matches between angels and women but that they were sinful.

4. But, according to the Christian Fathers, the angels committed other sins, in addition to seeking a woman in honorable marriage. They actually endeavored to beautify the world into which they had come, and to make men wiser and happier by teaching them various arts and sciences. One might have thought this a cause for gratitude; but the Church Fathers, having started from a false premise, were logically bound to deduce the theory which Tertullian did—that as these spirit husbands were fallen angels, what they taught could not possibly be conducive either to integrity, chastity, or the fear of God. Therefore, dress and adornment and the industrial arts of dyeing and metallurgy were sinful, and consequently, displeasing to the Almighty. Very different is the view taken by a more modern writer, Sir Thomas Browne, the author of the *Religio Medici* who, advocating the doctrine of this celestial guardianship over marriage on earth, observes: "I do think that many mysteries ascribed to our own inventions, have been the courteous revelation of spirits; for those noble essences in heaven bear a friendly regard unto their fellow natures on earth."[101]

5. Ambition plays a prominent part in the traditions, it will be noticed. It is said that these angels were ambitious for earthly power and exacted libations and sacrifices; and also that they were the beings whom the heathen ignorantly supposed to be gods.

But if the reader will recall what I have said about the misleadings in spirit manifestations when the psychic starts from a false premise, he will understand how possible it is that we have to deal here with subjective illusions, and not objective realities; and that the lower estimate in which these angelic visitors came to be held was due entirely to the failure of psychics to keep the laws of correct moral living or common sense and his weaknesses and vanities and superstitions will be played upon *ad libitum*. As for the giant offspring said to have resulted from these unions—offspring which in the male line became evil-doers, and finally demons on the astral plane—if the reader will consider that necessity to which I have referred for correct living and clear thinking on both sides of the abyss of death, if the bridge of

101 Bourchier Wrey Savile, *Apparitions: A Narrative of Facts* (London: Longmans and Co., 1874), pp. 3–4. (ICC note)

communication is to hold, he will see that if these "giants" continued to influence the world from the astral plane they could not be evil demons, but must be beneficent helpers of mankind. But there is, I think, grave doubt as to whether such offspring ever resulted from these unions between angels and earthly women, as the reader will see when I come to speak of the occult laws governing such unions. Nevertheless, there is something to be said on both sides, and we should do well to reserve our judgment until all the evidence is before us.

We have seen that Commodianus says that these giants are the gods to whom the heathen ignorantly prayed. Justin Martyr, mindful of certain similarities between the stories told of those same heathen gods and the Scriptural account of Jesus, advances the theory that the demons had some imperfect perception of the coming Messiah, gleaned from the Old Testament prophecies, and that they tried to forestall Christianity by ascribing Christ's possible attributes in advance to the gods.

> The demons, then, hearing these prophetic words {Genesis 49:10–11,} asserted that Bacchus was born the son of Jupiter; they ascribed to him also the invention of the vine, and in the celebration of his mysteries led an ass in procession, and taught that Bacchus was torn in pieces and taken up into heaven.[102]

Justin also draws a comparison between some of these gods and Christ, to show that Christianity claims no more for its god than aid the heathen for those whom they called "Sons of Jove." He says:

> When we affirm that the Word, which is the first-begotten of God, was born without carnal knowledge, even Jesus Christ our Master, and that he was crucified, and died, and rose again and ascended into heaven, we advance no new thing different from what is maintained respecting those whom ye call the sons of Jupiter. For ye well know how many sons your approved writers attribute to Jupiter: Mercury, the word of interpretation and the teacher of all men; Esculapius, who was a physician, and yet struck with lightning and taken up into heaven; Bacchus, who was torn in pieces; Hercules, who burned himself upon the pile to escape

102 Justin Martyr's *Apology*, I. 71. (ICC note) [Chevallier, *Translation of the Epistles*, p. 177.]

> his torments; Castor and Pollux, the sons of Leda; Perseus the son of Danae; and Bellerophon, born of human race, and carried away upon the horse Pegasus. . . . Neither is it necessary that I should relate to you, who already know well, of what kind were the actions of each of those who were called the sons of Jupiter; I need only say, that the writings in which they are recorded, tend only to corrupt and pervert the minds of those who learn them; for all take a pride in being the imitators of the gods. . . . But if we say that he {Jesus} was begotten of God, in a manner far different from ordinary generation, being the Word of God, as we have before said, let this be considered a correspondence with your own tenets, when ye call Mercury the word who bears messages from God. And if any one objects to us that He was crucified; this too is a point of correspondence with those whom ye call the sons of Jupiter, and yet allow to have suffered. . . . Again, if we affirm that he was born of a virgin; let this be considered a point in which he agrees with what you (fabulously) ascribe to Perseus. And whereas we say that he made those whole, who were lame, palsied, and blind from their birth, and raised the dead; in this too we ascribe to him actions similar to those which are said to have been performed by Esculapius.[103]

We thus see that the heathen gods and heroes whose father was Jupiter, the Christian Messiah whose father was the holy spirit and the traditional "giants" whose fathers were angels, were, in the eyes of at least one Church Father, but different aspects of the same underlying principle—the possibility of marital union between dwellers in the unseen world and dwellers upon the earth, for the purpose of begetting children. Today, however, we look upon the story of virgin born Perseus as fabulous.[104] But the ancient heathen opponents of Justin seem to have accorded a scant respect to the story of the virgin-born Jesus as we do to the story of virgin-born Perseus. Now to laugh to scorn the birth of Perseus from the occult union of God with one virgin, and then to accept without question the birth of Jesus from the occult union of God with another virgin, is somewhat inconsistent. On strictly logical grounds, if one story be false, so may the other be false; if one be true, so may

103 Justin Martyr's *Apology* I, 28, 29, 30. (ICC note) [Chevallier, *Translation of the Epistles*, pp. 146–148.]

104 His mother, Danae, was said to have been imprisoned, while yet a virgin, in a high tower, that she might have no children. Jupiter, however, visited her manifestly as a shower of gold, and Perseus was the result of the union. (ICC note)

the other be true. But Perseus is only one of many virgin-born heroes or gods. We find these children of a visible earthly mother and an invisible, celestial mysterious father, the world over, in all ages.

There was Buddha, the child of Māyā and a celestial being god who, in the form of a white elephant, entered her side, or according to De Gingnes,[105] his mother conceived by a ray of light without defilement.

The Hindu Krishna was born of a chaste matron, who, though a wife and a mother, is always spoken of as the Virgin Devaki. Krishna, by the way, has many attributes in common with Kama, the East Indian god of love, corresponding to the Latin Cupid. He is represented as black—a symbolism to which I will return later on.

The Egyptian God Ra was born from the side of his mother, "but was not engendered."

The Mayas of Yucatan had a virgin-born god, named Zama.

Among the Algonquin Indians we find the tradition of a great teacher, by name Michabou, who was born of a celestial Manitou and an earthly mother.

> Upon the altars of the Chinese temples were placed behind a screen, an image of *Shin-moo*, or the "Holy Mother," sitting with a child in her arms, in an alcove, with rays of glory around her head, and tapers constantly burning before her.[106]

In ancient Mexico,

> The Virgin Chimalman, also called Sochiquetzal or Suchiquecal, was the mother of Quecalcoatle.[107] In one representation he is shown hanging by the neck holding a cross in his hands. His complexion is quite black. Sochiquetzal means the *lifting up of roses*.[108] Eve is called

105 See Godfrey Higgins, *Anacalypsis, an Attempt to Draw Aside the Veil of the Static Isis; or, an Inquiry into the Origin of Languages, Nations, and Religions* (London: Longman, Rees, Brown, Green, and Longman, 1836), vol. 1, p. 157. (ICC note)

106 Rev. Joseph B. Gross, *The Heathen Religion in its Popular and Symbolical Development* (Boston: John P. Jewett and Company, 1856), p. 60, quoted in T. W. Doane, *Bible Myths and their Parallels in Other Religions* (New York: Commonwealth, 1882), p. 327. (ICC note)

107 Evidently the same as Quetzelcoatl, who was crucified as a Saviour for the Mexicans, as Jesus was for the Christian world. (ICC note)

108 This is really our Sukey, and the Greek ψυχε, Psyche, which means the soul, and which was appropriately applied to the bride of the spirit-lover, Cupid. (ICC note)

> Ysnextli, and it is said she sinned by plucking roses. But in another place these roses are called *Fruta del Arbor.*[109]
>
> The Mexican Eve is called Suchiquecal. A messenger from heaven announced to her that she should bear a son, who should bruise the serpent's head. He presents her with a rose. This was the commencement of an Age, which was called the Age of Roses.[110]

Is this the age when angels became the husbands of pure-minded women—an age fitly symboled by the rose, the flower of perfect love? Note, also, the resemblance between this tradition and the Christian tradition, concerning the angel's offering Mary a lily-branch at the Annunciation. Evidently, these are two different aspects of the same symbolism.

Higgins, continuing, says: "All this history the Monkish writer is perfectly certain is the invention of the Devil,"[111] and Justin Martyr strove to account for the analogy between the story of Christ and the story of Bacchus by supposing that demons had imitated the Christian Scriptures in advance, so totally unaware was he that both stories had the same esoteric meaning to the initiate. "Torquemada's Indian history was mutilated at Madrid before it was published. Suchiquecal is called the Queen of Heaven. She conceived a son, without connection with man, who is the God of Air. . . . The Mohammedans have a tradition that Christ was conceived by the smelling of a rose."[112]

In the Finnish epic of the *Kalevala* there is a heroine by the name of Mariatta (from Marja, "berry") who becomes pregnant through unwittingly eating a berry—the berry here playing a similar part to the rose referred to above in the Mohammedan tradition. She goes from one to another person, vainly seeking a place in which to bring forth her child. At last she is referred by one household to the stable of "the flaming horse of Hisi"; and she then appeals to the horse of Hisi in the following words:

> Breathe, O sympathizing fire-horse,
> Breathe on me, the virgin-mother!
> Let thy heated breath give moisture,

109 Árbol? (ICC note)
110 Higgins, *Anacalypsis,* vol. 2, p. 32.
111 Higgins, *Anacalypsis,* vol. 2, p. 33.
112 Higgins, *Anacalypsis,* vol. 2, p. 32. (ICC note)

Let thy pleasant warmth surround me,
Like the vapor of the morning;
Let this pure and helpless maiden
Find a refuge in thy manger!

Observe that, although the mother of an illegitimate child, she, like all the mothers of such children when their father is divine or mysterious, is "pure," the "virgin-mother," etc.

These virgin-mothers are not copies of the Christian Mary. Most, if not all of them, were known long before the days of Christianity.

The mother of the Siamese "Somona Cadom" was impregnated by sunbeams, another form of Danae's golden shower. She was called Maha Maria or Maya Maria, i.e., "the Great Mary." And this brings out some curious coincidences in name among virgin-mothers. Thus:

Marietta of the *Kalevala* has already been referred to above.

The mother of Hermes or Mercury was Myrrha or Maia.

Maya, the mother of Buddha, is identical in name with the Hindu goddess Maya, who is represented as walking upon the waters, with her peplum teeming with animals, to show her fecundity. *Maya* is also a well-known Hindu term for "illusion."

The month of May (so nearly like the name of Maia) was sacred to some of the virgin-goddesses of ancient times, as it is now to Mary, the Mother of Jesus. The Christian Virgin Mary was also called Myrrha; and she is still called Santa Maria in Southern Europe and in Mexico. The title bestowed on her of "Star of the Sea"—a title given to the Egyptian Virgin-mother, Isis, perhaps two thousand years earlier—shows how close a resemblance tradition and folklore have traced between both of these virgin-mothers and the ancient genitrix of the waters. Also, the Latin *mare* and the French *mer* for "the sea," and the French *mère* for "mother" bear a striking resemblance to the name Mary in sound. And Venus was, born from the foam of sea, presiding divinity of love between the sexes. She is credited with having been "indulgent Venus"[113] to a mortal man, Anchises, to whom she bore the hero of Virgil's *Aeneid*—a Borderland espousal, this; though here it is the wife and not the husband who comes from the invisible world.

113 *Venus obsequens* in Latin.

The Apocryphal Gospels speak of the Virgin Mary's being brought up as an orphan, in the temple, and they refer to her as an obedient and pure-minded maiden, accustomed to holding daily converse with angels. That she should have been called by the same root-name as these ancient virgin-mothers, is, therefore, the less remarkable, if we consider the possibility of her having been trained in the temple by the priests as an initiate in the sacred mysteries, and of her having passed the various ordeals so successfully as to entitle her to be called by the name sacred to the type of womanhood accounted worthy to sustain marital relations on the Borderland.

In some cases it would appear that ambitious princes or other designing politicians of ancient days did not scruple to avail themselves of the current belief in the possibility of divine paternity, when it would serve their purpose. It was an open secret among the Greeks that Alexander the Great had not hesitated to do this, on the occasion of his march into Egypt and Syria, when the oracle at the temple of Jupiter Ammon (doubtless for a bribe) declared Alexander to be the son of Jupiter, saying that this god, in the form of a serpent, had manifested to Alexander's mother.

The serpent is, in ancient sex worship, a well-known symbol of the phallus, and therefore, of the creative fatherhood. It appears in several stories of divinely begotten children.

Scipio Africanus was another politician who availed himself of the popular belief in these matters, it would seem. "There is no doubt," remarks Higgins in his *Anacalypsis*, "that he aimed at the sovereignty of Rome, but the people were too sharp-sighted for him."[114] A. Gelline says, "The wife of Publius Scipio was barren for so many years as to create a despair of issue, until one night, when her husband was absent, she discovered a large serpent in his place, and was informed by soothsayers that she would bear a child. In a few days she perceived signs of conception, and after ten months gave birth to the conqueror of Carthage."[115]

The Emperor Augustus was said to have been the result of a mysterious connection of his mother with a serpent in the temple of Apollo.

Ovid in his *Fasti* records a story that Servius Tullius was a mysterious

114 Higgins, *Anacalypsis*, vol. 1, pp. 212–213.

115 Ten lunar months, 28 days presumably, meant here. (ICC note) [Higgins, *Anacalypsis*, vol.2, p. 287.]

shape, claiming to be a vulcan, which appeared to the mother, Ocrisia, among the ashes of the altar, when she was assisting her mistress (Ocrisia was a captive) in the sacred rite of pouring a libation of wine upon the altar.

Pythagoras, who lived more than five hundred years before Christ, was said to be the offspring of Apollo. He was born on a journey, his father (or rather, his mother's earthly husband) having traveled up to Sidon on business. Pythais, the mother, had been beloved by a ghostly personage who claimed to be the god Apollo. Afterwards this same apparition showed itself to the husband, informing him of the parentage of the coming child, and bidding him to have no connection with his wife until after its birth.

A similar event is said to have transpired in the case of Plato, Apollo his father also. His mother was Perictione, a virgin, who was betrothed to one Ariston at the time. In this case, also, Apollo appeared to inform the earthly lover of the child's paternity. Higgins, relating this tradition, adds:

> On this ground, the really very learned Origen defends the immaculate conception[116] assigning, also, in confirmation of the fact, the example of Vultures (*Vautours*) who propagate without the male.[117]

The Vulture was an accompaniment of Hathas [Hathor], the Egyptian Venus; and it would therefore seem as though Origen had unwittingly stumbled on a bit of folklore. Graves, in his *Sixteen Crucified Saviors*, remarks (I know not on what authority, but give his remark rather for its suggestiveness than as a vouched-for historical fact):

> Many are the cases noted in history of young maidens claiming a paternity for their male offspring by a God. In Greece it became so common that the reigning King issued an edict, decreeing the death of all young virgins who should offer such an insult to deity as to lay to him the charge of begetting their children.[118]

---

116 Higgins evidently refers, not to the Roman Catholic Doctrine of Mary's stainlessness by that term signified, but to the conception of Jesus. (ICC note)

117 (!!) (ICC note) [Higgins, *Anacalypsis*, vol. 2, p. 194.]

118 Kersey Graves, *The World's Sixteen Crucified Saviors, or, Christianity before Christ* (Boston: Colby and Rich, 1876), p. 49.

The vestal virgin Rhea Sylvin, who bore Romulus and Remus to the god Mars, is well-known. It is a curious co-incidence that the name Rhea, which was one of the names of the Mother of all the gods, is applied by one writer to the Virgin Mary who likewise became the "Mother of God."

The Mongolian conqueror, Genghis Khan, and his two twin brothers were said to be the result of an occult union of the earthly mother with a mysterious intelligence.

> His mother having been left a widow, lived a retired life; but some time after the death of her husband . . . she was suspected to be pregnant. The deceased husband's relations forced her to appear before the chief judge of the tribe, for this crime. She boldly defended herself, by declaring that no man had known her; but that one day, lying negligently on her bed, a light appeared in her darkroom, the brightness of which blinded her, and that it penetrated three times into her body, and that if she brought not three sons into the world, she would submit to the most cruel torments. The three sons were born, and the princess was esteemed a saint. The Moguls [Mongols] believe Genghis Khan to be the product of this miracle, that God might punish mankind for the injustice they had committed.[119]

Of the conqueror, Tamerlane, who claimed direct descent from Genghis Khan on the mother side, it is related that he was the result of a connection of his mother with the God of day.

Dean Milman says, in his *History of Christianity*:

> Fo-hi [Fu-His] of China—according to tradition—was born of a virgin, and the first Jesuit missionaries who went to China were appalled at finding, in the mythology of that country, a counterpart of the story of the Virgin of Judea.[120]

But, had those same Jesuit missionaries apprehended the idea which lies back of both stories—the substantiality of the unseen world beyond the grave and the possibility of marital relations on the borderland of that world and this,

119 [Higgins, *Anacalypsis*, vol. 2, p. 353.] (ICC note)

120 [Henry Hart Milman, *History of Latin Christianity; including that of the Popes to the Pontificate of Nicolas V* (London: John Murray, 1854), vol. 1, p. 97, quoted in Doane, *Bible Myths and their Parallels in Other Religions*, p. 119.] (ICC note)

they would not have been thus "appalled." The mother of Confucius, says one tradition, when walking in a solitary place, was impregnated by the vivifying influence of the heavens.

The Chinese philosopher, Lao-tzu, born 604 B.C., the founder of the Religion of the Supreme Reason, was said to have been born of a virgin of a black complexion—a forerunner this, by hundreds of years, of the Black Madonnas in the Italian Churches.

Do those black Madonnas typify, mystically, the darkness of the unknown world beyond the grave whence the Heavenly Spouse emerges?

The Earls of Cleve were said to descend from a union between the heiress of Cleve and a being from the upper air, "who came to Cleve in a miraculous ship, drawn by a swan, and after begetting divers children, 'went away at Noon-day, in the sight of a World of People, in his Airy Ship.' "[121]

The famous Robert le Diable, according to one tradition, was the child of an incubus.

The enchanter Merlin, "son of an incubus and of a holy woman, became the center and the master of all nature," says Peyrat.[122] [. . .]

> Still greater was the number of those adventurers during the Middle Ages who asserted themselves or others to be the bastards of devils and human beings. But if they led a blameless life, evincing a firm belief in the dogmas of the Church, the danger of such a pedigree was not greater than the honor. The son of a fallen angel did not need to bend his head before a man of noble birth.[123]

"But," it will be objected, "these stories are myths of ancient, or at most, mediaeval times. You don't find virgin-born children nowadays."

Stay:

In the establishment of Schweinfurth, that individual in Rockford, Illinois, who today claims to be the Christ, a woman a few years since bore a child, and steadfastly declared her belief that it was immaculately conceived.

121 Original source of quote unknown. See Sylvanus Urban, ed., *Gentleman's Magazine and Historical Chronicle* (1735), vol. 5, p. 313.

122 Original source of quote unknown. "Peyrat" is Alphonse Peyrat (1812–1890), author of *Histoire et religion* ("History and Religion," 1858) and *Histoire élémentaire et critique de Jésus* ("Basic History and Criticism of Jesus," 1864).

123 Viktor Rydberg, *The Magic of the Middle Ages* (New York: Henry Holt and Company, 1879), p. 204. (ICC note)

Trial, it is said, before a jury of the women of Schweinfurth's establishment, did not succeed in shaking the faith of these women in the possibility of such a thing.[124]

In the *Truth Seeker* of New York occurs this paragraph: "Mrs. Helen Fields, of Wichita, Kansas, has given birth to a child whose father she avers is the Holy Ghost."[125] Moncure D. Conway, in his *Demonology and Devil-Lore*, says:

> When in Chicago in 1875, I read in one of the morning papers a very particular account of how a white dove flew into the chamber window of a young unmarried woman in a neighboring village, she having brought forth a child, and solemnly declaring that she had never lost her virginity.[126]

It is, of course, easy to dismiss all these stories, ancient, medieval and modern, with contempt, as so many falsehoods, or, at best, self-delusions. I have already said that, despite the immense number of traditions and miraculous births, I doubt if such ever occur upon the borderland of the two worlds, owing to certain occult principles to which I shall briefly refer further on. Nevertheless, this mass of folklore belief is too overwhelming in quantity and too widely diffused to be dismissed lightly. Back of it all there must be some objective realities and some fire for all this smoke. And we must not forget that there is one miraculous birth which is accepted throughout Christendom—the birth of Jesus from a Divine Father and an earthly Virgin-Mother. Nevertheless, by the cultured heathen opponents of Justin, the story of the divine paternity of Jesus seems to have been regarded with a scorn similar to that with which we regard the above tales today, and that Church Father showed his wisdom when he placed heathen and Christian stories upon the same logical basis. Am I not right in saying that to impugn the possibility

---

George Jacob Schweinfurth (b. 1853) was the founder of the Church Triumphant of Rockford, Illinois, in which the sole condition of membership was recognizing Schweinfurth as the "Christ of the Second Coming." He was arrested in 1895 for living openly with three unmarried women. (San Francisco Call, April 28, 1895, p. 2.)

125 *The Truth Seeker* was a Freethought periodical published from 1873 to 1929. This was probably a skeptical report. *The Truth Seeker* would later become a major supporter of Ida Craddock in her conflict with the authorities.

126 Moncure Daniel Conway, *Demonlogy and Devil-Lore* (New York: Henry Holt and Company, 1881), vol. 2, p. 231. (ICC note)

of marital relations between earthly women and heavenly bridegrooms is to strike at the very foundations of Christianity?

In folklore customs and fairy tales, fantastic though these may be, we find numerous indications of the world-wide belief in bridegrooms and brides from the unseen world of spiritual beings, or, as they were termed in the middle ages, incubi and succubae.[127]

We may set out with that description among the islanders of the Antilles, where they are the ghosts of the dead, vanishing when clutched; in New Zealand, where ancestral deities "form attachments with females, and pay them repeated visits"; while in the Samoan Islands, such intercourse of mischievous inferior gods caused "many supernatural conceptions"; and in Lapland, where details of this last extreme class have also been placed on record. From these lower grades of culture the idea may be followed onward. Formal rites are specified in the Hindu *tantra* which enable a man to obtain a companion—nymph—by worshipping her and repeating her name by night in a cemetery.[128]

Among the Metamba negroes, a woman is bound hand and foot by the priest, who flings her into the water several times over with the intention of drowning her husband, a ghost, who may be supposed to be clinging to his unfeeling spouse.[129]

In China, it is not considered respectable for widows to remarry, for the express reason that their husbands are expected to return to them from the world beyond the grave and resume marital relations with them upon the Borderland.

In the case of widows it would appear to be but a resumption of a relation previously established between the two upon earth. And there are indications that the same stress is not laid upon passing preliminary ordeals as is the case with the virgin, who "has never known man." May it not be because of the

127 Latin, *incubo*, "to lie upon"; *succubo*, "to lie under." (ICC note)

128 Edward Tylor, *Primitive Culture: Researches into the Development of Mythology, Philosophy, Religion, Language, Art, and Custom* (London: John Murray, 1891), vol. 2, pp. 189–190. See also William Ward, *A View of the History, Literature, and Religion of the Hindoos: Including a Minute Description of their Manners and Customs, and Translations from their Principal Works* (Serampore: Mission Press, 1815), vol. 2, p. 151, and Christoforo Borri, "An Account of Cochin China," in John Pinkerton, *A General Collection of the Best and Most Interesting Voyages and Travels in All Parts of the World* (London: Longman, Hurst, Rees, Orme, and Brown, 1811), vol. 9, p. 823. (ICC note)

129 T. F. Thiselton-Dyer, *The Ghost World* (London: Ward and Downey, 1893), p. 182. (ICC note)

virgin's greater ignorance, physiologically speaking, so that she has to enter upon a more extended course of training than does the widow, who already has experience?

The myths and fairy tales which speak of maidens with mysterious lovers from the realm of the unseen are certain to contain, so far as I have observed, reference to some rule or pledge which the woman must strictly observe. If she fails to do this, her lover vanishes, and she can find him again only after passing long and toilsome ordeals. Such was the case with Psyche, who broke the command of her heavenly lover, Cupid, not to look upon him while he slept. He had come to her night after night in the darkness, unseen, as is the wont with so many of these heavenly bridegrooms; and she naturally desired to see his face. But, in her eagerness to know him more intimately, she let fall a drop of hot oil from the lamp upon him, which awoke him, and he vanished. This myth is an evident euphemism for a broken law of marital self-control. In other words, she wanted to enter upon the second step in the occult training which she was receiving from her husband, before she had fully mastered the first step. What those steps were—first, second and third (for there is a third)—through which the earthly wife of a heavenly bridegroom must pass, will appear further on in this book.

In one of the oldest of the Vedas—those books which contain the legends of the Aryans before they split up into fragmentary races—we find a similar story about Urvasi and Pururavas.

These two stories are usually explained as myths which show how the dawn vanishes as soon as it looks upon the sun. In solar myths, the dawn is often typified as a maiden, the sun-god being her lover who pursues her vanishing form through the heavens—an idea picturesquely brought out in the myth of Cinderella. If these two stories really are a bit of sun and dawn folklore then, Urvasi and Psyche must each be the dawn-maiden, and Pururavas and Cupid must be the sun-god on whose glorious form, unveiled by any clouds, the dawn-maiden dare not look, for, as she looks, the two lovers become separated—i.e., the dawn vanishes before the rising sun. But it is a little curious that in one story, the maiden disappears, while in the other it is the lover himself who flees. Obviously there is some other myth than a purely solar one involved in these two stories—stories so strikingly similar and yet so strikingly at variance in the one feature in which they should agree, if true sun and dawn myths.

May not their likeness be due to their being memorials of the belief in Borderland marriages and in the self-control which is obligatory upon the earthly partner in such marriages? May not their unlikeness as to the sex of the partner who disappears when that self-control is violated, be due to there being heavenly brides, as well as heavenly bridegrooms?

To these same myths, I take it, belong all those fairy stories of which Beauty and the Beast is the type. Here a maiden—noted, as a rule, for her amiability and gentleness—is served each day by invisible hands, and at night receives her lover in the form of a handsome prince. By the ordinary light of day he is a monster, appalling to behold, or, in some of the stories, he is invisible; but night and the marriage couch cause him to materialize in his true shape. Finally, her family and friends—themselves quite outsiders as to these experiences—work upon her feelings and make her believe that this union is evil (in occult parlance, it would be termed diabolical) and she breaks off her connection with him. In the end, true love triumphs, and the lovers are reunited—under happier auspices, that is, in the fairy story; in actual life, it too often happens that Beauty and the Beast are permanently separated by meddling outsiders who ignorantly assume that everything which they cannot understand comes from the Devil. The poor earthly psychic has so constantly dinned into her ears the fact that her mediumship has revealed glimpses of monstrosities and deceptions, that she comes at last to fear lest her invisible visitor be in truth the evil demon which at times, by the sober light of day, he seems to be. All unaware of the law by which her own failures and peccadilloes bring about subjective hallucinations which mislead, she ascribes to her angelic bridegroom a tendency to evil which he does not possess, and finally comes to shrink from him as demoniacal. And the laws of Borderland forbid his undeceiving her so long as she hold fast to her prejudice as if it were gospel truth. Thus Beauty too often turns away from her princely lover forever, so far as this earth-life is concerned, as Beauty, in the fairy story, did from the husband whom ignorant outsiders had led her to look upon as Beast.

Pyramus and Thisbe, the lovers who, separated by a huge wall, were fain to satisfy themselves with kisses exchanged through a hole therein, are a euphemistic expression for those marital unions one of the parties to which is invisible and his earthly love impalpable to the physical senses. In this story a bloodthirsty lion puts an end to the lovemaking. This is probably the solar lion, the meaning being that the ancient faith is superseded by the later and (in some respects) purer Sun Worship which seems to have been a reform movement of the science and materialism of the time against the Borderland sensuality which obtained in the declining age of Sex Worship.

Isis and Osiris are also types of the husband and wife who unite upon the Borderland. Egyptian sacred traditions were wont to relate that Osiris was killed by the Typhon, who then cut up his victim's body into fourteen pieces, enclosed it in an ark, and set it adrift upon the River Nile. Isis, the Virgin-Mother, sought far and wide for these remnants of her husband's body. One legend states that she found all, except the phallus; another, that she found nothing except the phallus, and from that solitary fragment, she reconstructed her husband, entire. Here we evidently have two sides of the same esoteric idea—that the loss of sex power constitutes the true death of the soul (not, of course, the spirit) and that in the finding of one's marital partner on the Borderland the ghost may be gradually materialized into substantiality by beginning at the same starting-point as did Isis.

Heavenly *bridegrooms*, it will be noticed, predominate over heavenly *brides* in Borderland traditions. The reason, I take it, is that women, because of their social environment, usually lead a more self-controlled and temperate life than men do, and thus are in most (though not all) respects more worthy of marital union with an angel. Custom allows men more freedom—a privilege which the masculine sex is not slow to avail itself of, especially in the direction of wine, women and tobacco. These three dissipations not only exhaust the nerve force of men, but blunt both their physical and their moral sensibilities; so that the man for whom, in all possibility, his angel mate may be waiting upon the Borderland, may find himself handicapped at the outset, should he ever essay an adventure into Borderland romance while still on the earth. In this connection we may remark that in India, where the attempt to obtain a spirit wife is said to be of common occurrence (and it would appear often rewarded with success), we find a nation singularly gentle and peaceable in disposition, unaccustomed to drunkenness until taught it by outside peoples (there is a proverbial saying among the Hindus "as drunk as a Christian"), and endowed by nature with a tendency to aspire to union with God. Last, but not least, it is a nation whose religions, for the most part, recognize the truth that sex is holy; and in this it is in strong contrast with our Western "civilization," where the most sacred function of humanity is looked upon as vile. We Occidentals have a whole life's teaching to unlearn before we can approach the subject of marital relations on the Borderland from a natural and pure-minded standpoint.

The chief tradition regarding spirit brides relates to Lilith or Lilis or Lilot and is mostly Rabbinical. As in the case of the angelic bridegrooms, she is supposed to be demoniacal. Lilith is said to have been Adam's first wife; one tradition says that by her he begat only demons; another says that she rebelled when Adam assumed authority over her and fled from him to the evil angel Samael, to whom she bore a demon progeny. Another legend has it that, being jealous of Eve, she slipped back into Eden behind the *particeps criminis*[130] in the temptation.

Another says that Adam kept himself apart from Eve for a hundred years in order not to fill hell with their offspring; but that in a weak moment a female devil, called Lilith, seduced him and became his wife, and from their union arose devils, ghosts and evil night dreams; and Eve in like manner became the wife of a demon.[131] Of a similar tenor is the tradition about the Zoroastrian Yeina, who fell from a state of innocence by means of a great serpent, the Azis-Dahaka:

> For a long period Yeina and his subjects were in the power of this evil serpent, Azis-Dahaka, the demons. . . . Yeina himself in order to oblige his masters, had to abandon his own wife, who was also his sister, and to take a female devil for his wife, and to consent to the union of his former wife with a demon. From these unions were produced apes, bears, and black men. During this evil period women much preferred young devils to young men for husbands, and men married young seductive "Paris," or "female devils."[132]

---

130 Latin, "partner in crime."

131 *The Serpent in Paradise*. London. (ICC note) [Anon. [Robert Willis,] *The Serpent in Mythology: A Contribution to Comparative Mythology. The Serpent in Paradise, and the Fable of the Fall of Man from a State of Perfection, which Never Existed*, (London: Thomas Scott, 1876).]

132 *The Serpent in Paradise: The Serpent in Mythology*. (ICC note) [Willis, *Serpent in Mythology*, p. 20.]

The psychic who can sustain marital relation on the Borderland must above all be sensitive at the extremities of the nerves of touch. Neither blind people nor deaf people are hindered by their respective infirmities from marrying in this earth-life, and on the Borderland a psychic may be clairvoyant and clairaudient to only a limited extent, and yet be a partaker in connubial joys. For the Borderland husband must materialize more or less fully to enable her to understand the relation clearly upon the physical side: Whereas for most men this is unnecessary, and the spirit bride may remain in all *save a few essentials*, invisible, inaudible, intangible—a veritable "woman of air." Hence her ghostliness and her philological connection with the idea of pale blue or pale purple—the color of air and the mist.

Lilith is said to come to young mens' bedsides at night to seduce them, under the aspect of a beautiful and finely dressed woman with golden hair. And, afterwards, she strangled them, and they are known to be Lilith's victims because one of her golden hairs is found tightly wound around the victim's heart. In the Zoroastrian legends, she is much connected with night and night-dreams; and men are cautioned not to sleep alone for fear of the evils of Lilith. She also lies in wait for children to kill them if they are not protected by "Amulets."

> Herodotus says that the Arabians called the moon "Alilat," the Assyrian word for night is *Lilat*, and Talbot supposes that the Arabians really called the moon "*Sarrat ha Lilat*," the queen of night.
>
> Mr. Talbot also says "Alilat" may also mean the star Venus.
>
> The Greeks considered Lilith evidently to be the moon, as with them she is Ilithyia, the sister of Apollo, one of the birth goddesses. Night in Hebrew is *layelah*.
>
> That the moon should be selected to represent the feminine principle is readily accounted for by her waxing and waning propensities, to say nothing of her controlling or coinciding with the feminine periods.[133]

Summing up these varying traditions we find the following incidents prominent:

1. A woman who is not of the earth but evidently from an unknown world enters upon relations with Adam or with the men of later generations.

133 *The Serpent in Paradise*, etc. (ICC note) [Willis, *Serpent in Mythology*, p. 21.]

2. The relation is in most cases that of husband and wife and not a mere liaison.

3. {In those cases where the relation is illicit, the earthly partner comes to an unfortunate end.}

4. This woman from the unseen world is credited with being a seducer and a devil.

5. She bears no children save demons and is reputed to destroy children.

6. She causes men to dream evil dreams at night.

Lilith is evidently the complement of the tradition about angelic bridegrooms. That the typical spirit bride should have so much more unsavory a reputation than has the typical spirit bridegroom of nowadays. The masculine nature is proverbial for its lack of self-control where women are concerned, and in this it has usually contrasted unfavorably with the self-control of women in similar cases. On the other hand, the men of our Western civilization are mostly superior to our women (of the virtuous classes) in the ardent, dramatic and artistic expression of love for the opposite sex—a desirable qualification in the romance and uncertainties and trying ordeals of Borderland wedlock.

If, therefore, the propositions which I have laid down as to the necessity for self-control in occult investigations be correct, we need not be surprised that the spirit bride is ere long denounced as demoniacal and seducing. But it is the ignorance or the willful wrongdoing of her earthly lover that is to blame, and not the spirit-bride—unless in some rare instance, where the celestial visitor is exceptionally careless. In that case, her superiors in the invisible world interfere and remove her. The connection with her earthly partner is snapped, never to be resumed, until he passes over to her world at death. But such failures on the part of the heavenly visitor are rare; and if the resulting phenomena are diabolical, it is the earthly medium's own fault.

That she should bear no children except demons points to the proposition which I have already advanced: that children cannot be begotten from Borderland marriage unions. If the earthly husband still insists on doing all he can to beget such children, he breaks the law of Borderland, and will be led deeper and deeper into the mire of sensuality, and at last, perhaps be deceived by a subjective hallucination of devils whom he will be told are his children. If he presses for information, he will probably receive a more explicit truthful statement: i.e., that his spirit bride is unable to bear children on the Borderland of two worlds. But should he fail about this time in some detail of moral duty, or clear-headedness, and especially should he insist in sowing seed where no harvest can be reaped, he will most certainly be misled by all sorts of fantastic excuses. For such is the occult law. The psychic who, whether ignorantly or willfully, is unworthy, loses his grip on the lines of communication, and his own ill-regulated subliminal consciousness then steps in with its ingenious excuses—such as, perhaps, that his celestial partner is abnormally constituted as a woman, or that she kills their children as fast as they are begotten, etc., etc. And thus, through the failure of the earthly husband to observe the laws of marital self-control on the Borderland, one more tradition is launched upon the world about the devil-bride who seduces men and begets demons and kills children.

That she should be credited with being the author of "evil night-dreams" shows how prone the partners of spirit brides have been to subjective hallucinations. We do not find any such wholesale charge brought against spirit *husbands* of portraying evil dreams as is brought against Lilith. The imaginations of men's hearts must indeed have been evil in those days, and their brains beclouded, or the difference between a materialized spirit bride and the subjective phantasm of an amorous dream would have been more sharply defined. The psychic who confounds two separate planes of existence has forsaken the path of self-control and clear-headedness, and has entered upon the path whose end is insane delusion.

In the supplement of *Littré's Dictionnaire* (1877) occurs a suggestive etymology of the word *lilac* (or as it is in French, *lilas*). The writer connects the root of this word with the Persian *nil*, indigo, and calls attention to the various Persian words, *nilah, niladj, liladj, lilandj, lilang*, all relating to indigo. He connects the word *lilas* (French for *lilac*) with these words and also with the diminutive *lilak* (bluish, as fingers blued by the cold)—a tint which perfectly characterizes the flowers of the lilac of Persia which are of a pale purple. May there be some philosophical connection between this palely purple flower *lilas* and the ghostly "Lilis" or "Lilat" or "Lilith?"

Lilith figures in a text of Isaiah: but we have to go both to Mohammedan and to Ancient Greek folklore to find the connecting link between this text and the Lilith of Rabbinical traditions. The text refers to the destruction which the Lord threatens will befall Eden, and reads:

> And thorns shall come up in her palaces, nettles and thistles in the fortresses thereof; and it shall be an habitation of jackals, a court for ostriches. And the wild beasts of the desert shall meet with the wolves {or howling creatures}, and the satyr {or he-goat} shall cry to his fellow: yea; *the night-monster* shall settle there, and shall find her a place of rest.[134]

The word "night-monster" is, in Hebrew, "Lilith." The King James version translates this word "screech-owl"; the Vulgate, "Lamia"; in Luther's Bible, "Kobold." *Lamia* or *Lamya* is found in the Great Bible, and in Coverdale's, Matthew's, Beck's and the Bishop's Bible.

Now a Lamia is a mythical serpent-woman of a demoniacal character. Philostratus, in his *Life of Apollonius of Tyana*, gives a memorable instance. A young man on the road near Corinth met a charming woman who invited him to her house in the suburbs of the city, and said that if he would remain with her, "he would hear her sing and play, and drink such wine as never any drank, and no man should molest him; but she being fair and lovely would live and die with him."[135] The young man was, as Burton in his *Anatomy of Melancholy* puts it, in giving the account, "a philosopher, otherwise staid and discreet, able to moderate his passions, though not this of love," and he "tarried with her awhile to his great content."[136] At last he married her. To the wedding came Apollonius, and he at once recognized her as a Lamia, and declared that all her furniture was but illusion. She wept and begged Apollonius to be silent, but he persisted in exposing her, whereupon she, her house and its content vanished.

This is probably a Beauty and the Beast myth on the masculine side, Apollonius playing the part of the outsider who separates the lovers by harping on the things which are illusory and monstrous in the young man's psychic

134 Isaiah 34:13–14, Revised Version. (ICC note)

135 Quoted in Robert Burton, *The Anatomy of Melancholy* (London: Chatto and Windus, 1883), p. 494.

136 Burton, *Anatomy of Melancholy*, p. 494.

manifestations. It is worth noticing in this connection, that the young man had been living a temperate and self-controlled life when he was first approached by this Lamia or Lilith, so that he was evidently found worthy to taste the joys of affectionate connubial intercourse with his mysterious bride. Here evidently, the young man is not strong enough to endure the training required to consummate Borderland wedlock. He also, evidently, does not have his subconsciousness well under control, but allows it to run away with him. Mastery of self in every possible aspect—physically, intellectually, morally, affectionally—is one of two requisites for sustained marital relations on the Borderland; the other requisite being steadfast aspiration to personal communion with the Divine.

The Mohammedan Idea of the Evil Church Yard: Lilith Crops Up in Ireland

> The ancient Churchyard of Truagh, county Monaghan, is said to be haunted by an evil spirit, whose appearance generally forebodes death. The legend runs, writes Lady Wilde,[137] "that at funerals the spirit watches for the person who remains last in the graveyard. If it be a young man who is there alone, the spirit takes the form of a beautiful young girl, inspires him with an ardent passion, and exacts from him a promise that he will meet her that day month in the churchyard. The promise is then sealed by a kiss, which sends a fatal fire through his veins, so that he is unable to resist her caresses, and makes the promise required. Then she disappears, and the young man proceeds homewards; but no sooner has he passed the boundary wall of the churchyard than the whole story of the evil rushes on his mind, and he knows that he has sold himself, soul and body, for a demon's kiss. Then terror and dismay take hold of him, till despair becomes insanity, and on the very day month fixed for the meeting with the demon bride, the victim dies the death of a raving lunatic, and is laid in the fatal graveyard of Truagh."[138]

In Capt. Richard F. Burton's translation of the Arabian Nights occurs a story of a female desert-monster, called Ghulah, who devours human flesh. Captain Burton, in a footnote, remarks:

---

137 Jane Wilde, *Ancient Cures, Charms and Usages of Ireland* (1890), p. 84. (ICC note)
138 Dyer, *The Ghost World*, pp. 344–345. (ICC note)

> The Ghúlah (fem. of *ghúl*) is the Hebrew *lilith* or *lilis*; the classical *lamia*; the Hindu *yogini* and *dakini*; the Chaldean *utug* and *gigim*, (desert-demons) as opposed to the *mas* (hill-demon) and *telal* (who steal into towns); the ogress of our tales and the *bala yaga*[139] (Granny-witch) of Russian folklore. Etymologically *ghul* is a calamity, a panic fear; and the monster is evidently the embodied horror of the grave and the graveyard.[140]

In its more usual spelling of "Ghoul," this graveyard monster will probably be familiar to most readers.

> The female *ghul*... appears to men in the deserts, in various forms, converses with them, and sometimes prostitutes herself to them.[141]

Here we see the (1) spirit bride, degraded to the level of a harlot, (2) vague and unreasoning terror, (3) loathing and horror of the spirits of the deceased all meeting under one name. So far has Lilith, the Borderland bride, fallen from her rightful estate by reason of the befogged imaginations of mankind.

> The *shiqq* is another demoniacal creature, having the form of half a human being (like a man divided longitudinally); and it is believed that the *nasnas* is the offspring of a *shiqq* and of a human being. . . . The *nasnas* is described as having half a head, half a body, one arm, and one leg, with which it hops with much agility.[142]

This is another form of the giant progeny of Borderland unions—a form so fantastic as to show that its origin is a subjective hallucination, and not an objective reality. In other words, the Mohammedan *shiqq* and *nasnas* are both of them probably the subliminal invention of some imperfect earthly psychic in the centuries agone, who broke the Borderland law in his or her relations with a spirit bride, or a spirit husband, and who was grossly misled, in consequence, by his or her own subliminal self. That others since then claim from

139 Error in Burton's original, should be *baba yaga*.

140 Richard F. Burton, *A Plain and Literal Translation of the Arabian Nights' Entertainments, now Entitled the Book of the Thousand Nights and a Night* (Benares: Kama Shastra Society, 1885), vol. 1, p. 55.

141 Thomas Patrick Hughes, *A Dictionary of Islam* (London: W. H. Allen & Co., 1885), p. 137 (s.v. "Genii").

142 [Hughes, *A Dictionary of Islam*, p. 137.] (ICC note)

time to time to see these fantastic creatures does not prove that they exist. In psychical matters nothing is more common than for people to see ghosts at a given time and place when their imaginations have been worked up to the expectation of seeing one then and there, of a certain predetermined type.

The Mohammedan Paradise as well as its Borderland recognizes love between the sexes. And in this it differs from the Christian Paradise as popularly conceived—although as I have elsewhere shown, the statement by Jesus that we shall be, after death, as regards marrying, like "the angels in heaven," when taken in connection with the next in Genesis about the sons of God who wedded earthly women, shows pretty conclusively that the Christian Scriptures admit the existence of sex and marriage in the world beyond the grave. Nevertheless, the Church has chosen to flatly contradict the teaching of both the Old and the New Testament in this, with the result of blinding Christians utterly to these potent Scriptural truths. Mohammed, on the other hand, was sufficient of a seer to venture on restoring the ancient doctrine.

Heaven, as is well known, abounds in love-making; beautiful women called *houris* attending upon the risen soul of the male Mohammedan as he reclines at feast. It is true that apologists have suggested a figurative sense in which the accounts of Mohammed's Paradise are to be taken.

On the contrary, it is not at all remarkable. It was precisely because Mohammed was at that time living a fairly well-ordered and self-controlled life that he was enabled to learn sufficient of the world beyond the grave to assert that love between the sexes survives death and is one of the potent factors in social life there, as here. It is true that, being an Oriental, his "revelations" would inevitably conform to his cast of mind, so that the glitter and luxurious abandon of a feast presided over by *houris* might seem to him the acme of ideal bliss. But beneath and permeating all this voluptuous imagining breathes the mighty truth of sex-love in Paradise: that love which mutually strengthens and mutually uplifts as no other love in all the world can strengthen and uplift. I take it as the chief reason for its existence—the propagation of the species being of necessity incidental, therefore, secondary. But there is also a third reason which, unfortunately, is known to but few. Nor is it likely to be understood as it should be. The third reason for the marital union is that, for those who are worthy, it is, whether on the Borderland or the earthly plane, the surest and safest method of seeking union with the Divine Heart of the Universe and becoming one with all God's world. Only in giving joyful thanks to God, indeed, should that relation ever be entered upon. This, not only because it is fitting to give thanks to God, but because it is beautiful at that time, and because only those who have experienced the bliss of taking God into the marital partnership in its most intimate relation can be said either to be truly wedded or to truly realize what it is to love God, and be in return beloved by Him. This applies in earthly as well as Borderland wedlock.

Trite and commonplace as may seem this suggestion to give thanks to God in this relation and share one's joy with Him, it nevertheless appears to be the inner, sacred truth of all religions on their esoteric side, and of all mysticisms and forms of occult teaching, the world over—a truth which has been jealously hidden away from the masses. It has been concealed for several reasons, probably.

First, it is not a matter to be attained at once, but requires systematic and careful training in self-control. And some degree of intellectual and spiritual insight is necessary to rate this training at its just value, as well as to respect the sacredness of the idea which underlies it. There are three degrees to be passed in this training, of which I will speak later on.

Second, inasmuch as it enhances, instead of extinguishing, connubial pleasure, while at the same time it puts the begetting of children absolutely under the control of parents—and this, without violation of either civil or natural laws—its initiates evidently feared lest it be turned to base uses by the unscrupulous and licentious. A needless fear, this, however; as to the libertine, the game will never seem worth the candle; while, should he persevere in the training so as to become an adept in the third and last degree, he will be no longer a libertine.

Third. There is a belief among some occultists that an earnest wish, breathed at that time when husband and wife are one, will not fail to be granted. This opens, it is said, the door to those who practice what is called "black magic," and enables them to work harm upon other human beings. What foundation there is for this belief as applied to the magicians I do not see. If it really be that a wish is granted then more readily than when the seeker is in any other mood, it is probably because the occultist who attains the second degree has to exercise such supreme self-control at that moment that he is complete master of his subconsciousness. And if he has attained the third degree, he is in rapport with Spirit throughout the universe, so that his desire is granted because he desires only what is in harmony with Good and Right. That a black magician should be able at such a moment to enter upon harmonious relations with the universe by breathing a curse seems to me very unlikely. I am of the opinion that this belief is due to the mistaken idea that correct living and clear thinking are unnecessary to establish lines of accurate communication with the unseen world. And, because occultists have usually assumed the nearness of a world of devils, rather than of a world of angels, and because they have assumed that depravity and prejudice offer no bar to communication with the unseen, whether good or evil, it was a most natural conclusion that it would be dangerous to entrust the secret of the third degree to a "black magician." But, so long as a man is a black magician, he will fail to enter upon the third degree. This last degree is, I am firmly convinced, impossible, whether in earthly or Borderland wedlock, for either man or woman who does not live a pure life in self-control and aspiration to the Divine. And the occultist who seeks to attain to the third degree must first become a white magician.

Nevertheless, as I have said, the initiates in the third degree have guarded this secret most jealously, and apparently for the reasons I have assigned.

The first and second degree, however, seem to have been taught publicity in symbolic rites—such as for instance in that much misunderstood dance at the Columbian Exposition—the Danse du Ventre. It was noticeable that the Oriental men, one and all, viewed that dance with serious and at times reverent gaze. This fact was brought to my notice by two ladies (school teachers) who knew absolutely nothing of the Sex Worship symbolism of the dance, but who had concluded, simply from thoughtful observation, that there must be some religious and pure-minded motif back of it all. Nevertheless, most Americans and Europeans, whether men or women, failed to penetrate beneath the surface of this markedly symbolic dance, owing to the Occidental habit of thought which sees naught but impurity in the most important and sacred function of our nature. In Oriental countries, however, despite their being "heathen," sex is looked on as holy; in this connection, our phrase, "Give God the glory," takes on itself a vaster significance than is ever taught from our pulpits.

It is no wonder, then, the Oriental occultists should have penetrated at an early date to the underlying principles of marital relations on the Borderland. From their lifelong habits of thought, they viewed sex as simply and naturally as we should view the circulation of our own blood—as a curious phenomenon of absorbing personal interest. With no false shame to overcome, they were fitted to receive the higher truths concerning this subject, whereas our Occidental mediums, for the most part, receive words of impurity or are misled into a loose life. The difference is due to the exact antipodal standpoints of Occidental and Oriental psychics on the subject of the holiness of sex.

I have said that the initiates of the third degree seem to have made this the inner secret of their mysteries, the world over, and that they have always jealously guarded this secret from the masses. I am inclined to think that in the beginning it may not have been so, but that this jealous care may have been the result of a bitter lesson learned of the unwisdom of throwing pearls before swine, not because the swine turn and rend one—for the earnest teacher of truth never gives his own danger a second thought—but because the swine are too apt to soil the pearls by trampling them in the mire.

If it be asked in amazement how this teaching of "Giving God the Glory," and sharing with Him the supreme joy of the marital relation, could become so degraded by swinish human beings as to cause its teachers to withhold it in future from the masses, I answer:

By turning it into a commercial transaction with God.

The piggish, greedy man, learning by hearsay of the connubial bliss attending the Triune partnership with God, pressed eagerly forward with one thought uppermost: "I will pay God cash down for so much of my pleasure, and I mean to drive a close bargain with him."

The voluptuary, seeking to enhance his physical sensations, likewise pressed forward, saying to himself in an outburst of generosity: "God shall receive from me every whit as much as He gives me."

The sentimental but selfish mystic, ever yearning for a new subjective experience, likewise pressed forward, thinking: "I shall get acquainted with God on intimate terms by dividing up my pleasure with Him."

Be not deceived: God is not mocked: Whatsoever a man soweth he shall reap. And each of these types failed to get what they expected in pleasure, because it cannot be secured by any means but by love.

Now, these would-be initiates not only failed to get so much physical pleasure for so much tithing paid over to Him, but they [were] tempted by that very failure to enter upon what we may call (to put it euphemistically) a bargain.

The nervous system had been wrought to too high a pitch not to insist upon a purchase in some market—if not in God's market, then in the Devil's. Hence, I fancy, too often abnormal vices and abominations of ancient Sodom and Gomorrah, of the Orient today and the Roman Empire, when Christianity first turned its purifying (though salty) current through the Augean stables of latter-day sex-worship.

For this the initiates who held the whole truth, among other reasons no doubt, usually shrank from revealing even glimpses of it to anyone who had not passed a long probation. According to the Talmud, the ancient Hebrews had three names to express the idea of God, the first of which was interdicted to the great number. Sages taught it once a week to their sons and their disciples. The second was at first taught to everybody. "But," said Maimonides, "when the number of the ungodly had increased, it was entrusted only to the most discreet among the priests, and they repeated it in a low tone to their brethren, while the people were receiving the benediction."[143] The third name for God "contained," says Jacolliot, "the great secret of the universal soul, and stood for, if we may so express it, the highest degree of initiation."[144] Regarding this last, Maimonides says:

> It was only taught to a man of recognized discretion, of mature age, not addicted to anger or intemperance, a stranger to vanity, and gentle and pleasant with all with whom he was brought in contact.[145]

"Whoever," says the Talmud, "has been made acquainted with this secret and vigilantly keeps it in a pure heart, may reckon upon the love of God and the favor of men; his name inspires respect; his knowledge

143 J. Louis Jacolliot, *Occult Science in India and Among the Ancients, with an Account of their Mystic Initiations, and the History of Spiritism* (New York: John W. Lovell Company, 1884), p. 167.

144 Jacolliot, *Occult Science in India*, p. 167.

145 Jacolliot, *Occult Science in India*, p. 167.

> is in no danger of being forgotten, and he is the heir to two worlds, that in which we live and the world to come."[146]

All of which applies to the earthly partner of a celestial bride or bridegroom, when the laws of correct living and clear thinking are obeyed. Those who know this secret and vigilantly keep it in a pure heart are indeed the heir of both worlds, for they dwell upon the Borderland, harmoniously adapting their lives to both planes of existence; and, being at one with God, they can each say, "If God be for me, who can be against me?" Nor is the reward for making a proper use of this Great Secret confined to Borderland wedlock; its Kingdom may come on the earthly plane itself to worthy neophytes.

It was probably to keep the knowledge of this secret from the unworthy that the ancient mysteries of Isis and of Eleusis were designed. For this purpose, also, the sacred scriptures of all religions—not excepting the Hebrew and the Christian—seem to have introduced stories and aphorisms which should convey one meaning to an outsider, and quite another to an initiate.

> Woe to the man who looks upon the law as a simple record of events expressed in ordinary language, for, if really that is all it contains, we can frame a law much more worthy of admiration. If we are to regard the ordinary meaning of the words, we need only turn to human laws and we shall often meet with a greater degree of elevation. . . . Every word of the law contains a deep and sublime mystery.[147]
>
> If the law were composed of words alone, such as the words of Esau, Hagar, Laban, and others, or those which were uttered by Balaam's ass or by Balaam himself, then why should it be called the law of truth, the perfect law, the faithful witness of God himself? Why should the sages esteem it as more valuable than gold or precious stones?
>
> But every word contains a higher meaning; every test reaches something besides the events which it seems to describe. This superior law is the more sacred, it is the real law.[148]

146 A. Franck's *La Kabbale*. (ICC note) [Quoted in Jacolliot, *Occult Science in India*, p. 168.]

147 A. Franck's *La Kabbale*. (ICC. [Jacolliot, *Occult Science in India*, p. 104.]

148 Jewish Cabalists, quoted by Jacolliot, *Occult Science in India*. (ICC note) [Jacolliot, *Occult Science in India*, p. 105.]

The following occurs in the Book of the Pitris[149] with whom communication has long been held, after the fashion of modern Spiritualism, and with the same attendant phenomena.

> The sacred scriptures ought not to be taken in their apparent meaning, as in the case of ordinary books. Of what use would it be to forbid their revelation to the profane if their secret meaning were contained in the literal sense of the language usually employed?
>
> As the soul is contained in the body,
> As the almond is hidden by its envelope,
> As the sun is veiled by the clouds,
> As the garments hide the body from view,
> As the egg is contained in its shell,
> And as the germ rests within the interior of the seed,
>
> So the sacred law has its body, its envelope, its cloud, its garment, its shell, which hide it from the knowledge of the world. . . .
>
> You who, in your pride, would read the sacred scriptures without the Guru's assistance, do you even know by what letter of a word you ought to begin to read them—do you know the secret of the combination by twos and threes—do you know when the final letter becomes an initial and the initial becomes final?
>
> Woe to him who would penetrate the real meaning of things before his head is white and he needs a cane to guide his steps.[150]

The closing paragraph becomes significant, when we reflect upon the danger which the initiates feared would accrue to those still in the heyday of manhood's passions, if they proved unworthy of the Great Secret. The expression "The secret of the combination by twos and threes" has probably a double meaning here—the esoteric meaning turning upon the two kinds of marital partnership known to the initiates, husband and wife being the "combination by two" (in the second degree), and husband, wife and God—three in one, a sacred trinity in unity—being the "combination by three" (in the third and highest degree). And they who have once realized the blessedness of this triune partnership will move heaven and earth to make it renewable at will—so

---

149 Pitris, according to Jacolliot, is the name applied in India to the spirits of the dead. (ICC note)

150 Quoted by Jacolliot, *Occult Science in India*. (ICC note) [Jacolliot, *Occult Science in India*, p. 103.]

much sweeter and more helpful in every way is it than the mere "combination by two."

Now, because sex is distinctly emotional in its manifestations, there is always a tendency, with failure to reach the highest, to allow the emotions to slump down, as it were, to a lower level. Few natures are so supremely self-controlled as to say, at a critical moment, "the highest—or nothing. I will wait for that!" And so, the types I have mentioned above as failure—the piggish man, the voluptuary and the sentimental, selfish mystic—when, because of the delicate balance required of the initiate who would enter on the third degree, they slipped off their pivot, fell quite outside the circle of what is lawful, sure and normal, to [what is] chaotic, unlawful and horribly vile. From this dates much of the black magic. And this was the controlling subjective influence which made witchcraft a very real, objective terror to the victims of the witches during the Middle Ages. There is little doubt that many of the witches did practice a sorcery of the most diabolical type—a sorcery based upon the principles of hypnotic suggestion, and of the willful projection of the astral or double; a sorcery whose object was to cause evil, and which did cause evil in many cases where the victims were not protected from occult mischief—working by living pure and upright lives; a sorcery, finally, whose impelling motive was due to insane hallucinations, resulting in a very large number of cases from having violated the laws of right living in sex relations on the Borderland. It is probable that many of these witches passed the second degree, while few, if any, gained the third—the inner degree where aspiration in mingled purity and passion to union with God is [the] chief factor. Some of the attributes of a witch (we need not enumerate them all: the literature of the subject is voluminous) were:

1. That she sustained or was supposed to sustain occult sex relations with the Prince of the Powers of the Air, Yclept the Devil.

2. That she received on some part of her body a devil's mark or stigma, which was his seal of authority over her and which seems to have been hypnotically rendered insensible to pain. There were men, who did a business in discovering witches by pricking a suspected woman's body all over with a pin until they found some place insensible to the pain of the prick, when they would triumphantly announce this to be the "Devil's Mark."

3. That the Devil or one of his imps at times visited her in the guise of some animal—a dog, a cat, even a huge butterfly, to suck some part of her body, and that, whatever the part of her body chosen, it and no other spot was always resorted to by the impish creature thereafter. Sometimes witnesses testify to seeing these animals familiar, as in the case of a witch ill in bed who was being closely watched.

The witness, who was on guard, testified with much detail of circumstance to having seen a huge "fly," like a miller, which buzzed in among the hair of the sick woman and after a while flew away, when the witch called to the witness to lift up her hair, that she might show a sore place on the scalp which she said was where the Devil, in the form of a fly, was wont to suck her.

4. That she could work harm to people at a distance by what appears to have been hypnotic suggestion, and that she usually was wickedly and viciously inclined to do this, at will.

5. That she could appear in what seems to have been her double, or astral form, to her victims.

Now, regarding this last, the extremely critical and level-headed Society for Psychical Research have collected some three thousand cases of apparitions of living doubles at the present day, all of them well-attested by witnesses. Most of these apparitions (some of which were so like real flesh and blood as to be taken for the person himself), according to the Society's records, were spontaneous, only a few being deliberately self-induced—a fact which indicates that the projection of the double is probably a normal power and that it ought to be, therefore, not so very difficult for an illiterate old woman to acquire. A few apparitions of doubles seem to be due mostly to one of the following causes:

1. Violent shock, as a runaway accident, danger of drowning.

2. A state of health indicative of approaching death, so that the astral forms (is this the soul, the body of the immortal spirit?) seems already poised for flight.

3. The moment of separation of soul and body, especially if caused by drowning, suffocation, contusion on the head, wounds received in battle, etc.

4. Falling into "a brown study": gazing fixedly at an object in an abstracted

way (self-hypnotization); listening abstractedly to a continuous and monotonous sound.

5. Falling asleep with an earnest desire fixed in one's mind to visit such or such a person or place.

Any of these may be induced accidentally and, so far as we know, without the conscious will of the ego.

6. Deliberately willing, under some of the above circumstances, to have one's double appear at such and such a place. This act may or may not include—according to the extent of the psychic's training—an after-memory of the event.

From the above it will be seen that the apparition of the double, whether spontaneously or deliberately induced, seems to be brought about by a sudden focusing of mental force. I am inclined to think that some of the surest vouchers for the material objective substantiality of the world beyond the grave will be found among the phenomena attending the appearance of the double; inasmuch as the double, when most clearly manifesting, comforts itself like an earthly being with earthly necessities, and if this double be, as appears, identical with the soul-body which quits our mortal frame at death, we have only to collate and compare instances of the earthly double, and acquire the art of projecting our own double intelligently and without loss of memory while in earth-life, and we shall know beyond all doubt what its habits of thought, its appetites and necessities are likely to be beyond the grave.

In the witchcraft days, what is called repercussion was a common phenomenon. That is, the witch who appeared in astral form to her victims, if wounded with a knife, might be afterwards found to have sustained a similar wound in her physical body. This carries out the idea of the Theosophists and other occultists, that thought has power over matter, and that our physical frame is in reality molded by the spirit and soul which inhabit it. Col. Olcott[151] gives an interesting account of repercussion in his own case.[152]

Instances are not wanting where the earthly double has shown that its sex capacity remains apparently unaffected by temporary separation from the

151 Henry Steel Olcott (1832–1907), co-founder of the Theosophical Society.

152 Henry Steel Olcott, *Old Diary Leaves: The True Story of the Theosophical Society*, vol. 1 (New York: Putnam's; Madras: The Theosophist,1895), p. 388.

body. The following case, though probably founded on the falsehood of a clever woman, shows with what serious respect the phenomenon of the double was viewed some three hundred and fifty years ago.

> In the *Dictionnaire Infernal*,[153] . . . there is, *s.v. Fécondité*, a report of a trial before the Parliament of Grenoble, in which the question was, whether a certain infant could be declared legitimate which was born after the husband had been absent from his wife four full years. The wife asserted that the baby was the offspring of a dream, in which she had a vivid idea that her wandering spouse had returned to love and duty. Midwives and physicians were consulted, and reported on the subject. As a result, the Parliament ordained that the infant should be adjudged legitimate, and that its mother should be regarded as a true and honorable wife. The judgment bears date 13th February 1537.[154]

The following incident was told to me by a gentleman who had heard it from the lips of one of the parties. For obvious reasons, I suppress localities:

> A gentleman who was intensely dark, of a Spanish type, was in love with a girl of the true blonde type. They never married but later on she married someone else and moved to another part of the country. One night this gentleman had a very vivid dream, in which he fancied himself to be her husband. So real seemed the experience that he could scarcely convince himself on waking, that he had not actually just come from her presence. Several years later, he happened to be in that part of the country, and bethought himself of hunting up his former lady love. He found her husband to be a decided blonde, like herself. A little child, a decided brunette, ran up to him, exclaiming joyfully, "Papa, Papa!" "Well!" laughed the host, "I am glad that she has found someone to call 'Papa,' for she steadfastly refuses to recognize me as such." Whereupon the lady appropriately fainted. The visitor learned afterwards by making inquiries of her, that she had had a dream similar to his at the same time, and just nine months previous to the birth of the child.

153 J. Collin De Plancy, *Dictionnaire Infernal* (Paris: Sagnier et Bray, 1845), p. 213.

154 Thomas Inman, *Ancient Faiths and Modern: A Dissertation upon Worships, Legends and Divinities in Central and Western Asia, Europe, and Elsewhere, before the Christian Era* (1876), p. 265, footnote. (ICC note)

Was this a case of repercussion? Did his double meet her double (but not her physical self) on the astral plane, and was that thought-world more powerful in molding her child than was her physical environment as a wife? Or was it merely a telepathic impression conveyed from his mind to hers with sufficient vividness to "mark" the child? I may here remark, that I do not consider the theory that he was the physical father of the child, as it seems to me that that would be a violation of the natural laws of Borderland. Nevertheless, if he really was the physical father, the stories would only be in keeping with the stories of the giant progeny from angelic fathers, and the stories of women confined in high towers and yet becoming pregnant by a celestial visitor. In the case of Danae, her visitor materialized as a shower of gold—quite after the fashion of modern apparitions of spiritualistic séances where the spirits often materialize as floating masses of radiant mist. At recent séances, too, trained scientific observers have perceived the medium's double (I now speak of mediums who are not fraudulent and who are willing to submit to experimental tests) partially or wholly dissociated from the medium's physical self. Col. Olcott gives an interesting account of his double oozing through the walls of Mrs. Blavatsky's room on its way to the sitting-room to add three words to a MS. on which he had been busily writing just before retiring. Both the earthly double and the celestial spirit appear to possess this faculty of oozing through blank walls. May they not be one and the same? In that case, we see how easy it may be to confound spirit bridegrooms from the world beyond the grave (who cannot beget children on the Borderland because this would be a violation of natural law), and astral doubles of earthly lovers who can stimulate the begetting of children upon the astral double of an earthly woman so vividly as to mark the child of her lawful husband and herself with the likeness of the astral lover.

At this point it may be objected that such information as I am here giving should not be spread broadcast, lest unscrupulous libertines take advantage of this power of projecting the double to get innocent girls into their power, since high towers and bolted doors appear to offer no barrier to the double's entrance. It is precisely for this reason that this information should be widely circulated, in order that these possibilities may be made known to the general public and guarded against. The present flood of Theosophic and other popular occult literature, as well as the published records of the S.P.R., have already placed the knowledge of this power within the reach of the libertine, if he chooses to avail himself of it. When he can have this for the asking, it is high time that the general public know something of it also, as well as of the fact that correct living and clear thinking will always protect us from evil induced by occult means. It is an interesting question, however, as to whether children could really be begotten by a double upon a virgin, or, as in the case tried before the Grenoble parliament, upon a married woman whose husband is away. I am inclined to think not, since the double is for the time being on a different plane of matter from the physical body of the woman—being, in fact, in the same world as it will be after death—so that it must obey the law of the Borderland quite as much as if it were an angelic bridegroom, which is to sow no seed, inasmuch as no harvest can be reaped therefrom. But in this case, what becomes of the scientific basis of such stories as Danae and other virgins who become the mothers of children by a Borderland lover—whether earthly double or heavenly angel? There is but one way, so far as I see, by which a Borderland bridegroom could beget a child by an earthly woman. The woman must live each moment in strict obedience to the laws of her earth-life, and also of his heavenly life. She must be capable of appreciating the intellectual thought of his advanced world. She must understand and live in accordance with the higher code of ethics current in his realm. She must neglect no earthly duty; she must be conversant with the intellectual thought-world of her earthly associates; she must not crush out a single instinct of her nature, but properly use every physical appetite and passion to round out a symmetrical earthly life. When emergencies arise on either the earthly plane or on the Borderland, she must never make a mistake, for to do so will cause the lines of communication to waver and presently to part. In short, her life—judged not only by the highest earthly standing but by the more advanced standard in the world beyond the grave—must be absolutely perfect if she is to conceive, gestate for nine long months and give birth to a child begotten by a Borderland father; that is, she must be psychically on the same plane with him, and at the same time fulfill the laws of both planes, and that without a single break. Only thus were the laws on the Borderland obeyed.

The Roman Catholic Church, in its dogma of the Immaculate Conception, claims perfection for the blessed Virgin Mary. In so doing, it shows its wisdom. Though I am by no means a Romanist, I emphatically say that, from the occult standpoint, the immaculate life of Mary, for a long period prior to the Annunciation and until at least the birth of Jesus, is the only foundation upon which the possibility of the mysterious conception of Jesus as a Borderland child can rest. Having once attained this high plane, it is unlikely that she would ever descend to a lower plane afterward: so that, accurately speaking, the Roman Catholic doctrine of her immaculate life must have been absolutely perfect on all points, or she could not have conceived a child by the spirit of God; for God does not break his own laws. Nor is it likely that the heavenly bridegroom would break his laws in order to beget a child upon an earthly woman, provided that woman were suitably trained for some time for the occult espousal, and provided that God has a tangible form, as He appeared to Moses to have when He had Moses remain in the cleft of a rock while He passed by. (Exodus 33:21,23.) This is the strength of the one Catholic doctrine concerning Mary's stainlessness of life; and from the Apocryphal Gospels, it appears that Mary had had the advantage of being brought up as an orphan in the temple under the eyes of the priests. It was customary for her to see and talk with angels and to receive food from them before her espousal to Joseph. My own idea of it, however, is that such a conception—if conception there were—would require Mary's mentality to rise not only to the standard of an angel but to the omniscience and all pervading tenderness of God, in order for her to be so thoroughly his spouse on the Borderland as to conceive and bear a child to him. On the other hand, it is interesting to note, in connection with this, the record in the Apocryphal Gospels as to the appearance of an angel visitor to Mary in the guise of a handsome youth, and the opinion expressed to Joseph by the virgins left in charge of her during Joseph's absence, that it was the angel who had made her pregnant.

Perhaps when we come into harmonious rapport with the mystical theory, popularized by the school of Divine Science and other mystics, that each one of us is a part of the universal mind, and that that mind may know all things in the universe, we might allow even this on the Borderland. However, the Roman Catholic Church has seemingly provided for the high standard of mentality required from a spouse of Divine Science on the Borderland by ascribing to Mary not only the name, but the attributes, of "Mother of God."

In *The Perfect Way, or the Finding of Christ,* written by Anna Kingsford and Edward Maitland, occurs a remark about "the notion, far from uncommon, that by abjuring the ordinary marriage relation, and devoting herself wholly to her astral associate, a woman may, in the most literal sense, become an immaculate mother of Christs."[155] It is needless to add that the authors deprecate this, but their remarks show their total misapprehension of Borderland sex-relations, since it is only between husband and wife that those relations can exist objectively; all else is but subjective illusion. And, therefore, the command of Mary's Heavenly Bridegroom that Joseph was not to approach her as a husband until after the birth of the mysteriously begotten child would be strictly in keeping with Borderland laws, because it is the highest ideal of both worlds.

The mediaeval witch, as well as the Blessed Virgin, had her chance of Borderland nuptials on a high plane; but, unlike Mary, she failed to pass those ordeals which require correct living and clear thinking on the part of the earthly psychic. In the first place, the witch (poor woman) lived in days when the physiological relations of husband and wife occupied a far lower place in popular estimation than it did in the days of Mary, and moreover, in the Orient, Mary's home, the relation of husband and wife had then, and still has, a holiness on its physiological side which is foreign to European or American habits of thought. When the peculiar psychical experiences of the witch set in, therefore, she naturally jumped to the conclusion that, first, they were sinful; second, that, being sinful, they were the work of Satan. These assumptions were a departure from clear, unprejudiced thinking, and from that moment began her diabolical illusions, and she saw monsters, hobnobbed with imps, was lashed by scorpions, etc., etc., to the full extent of her willingness to receive these illusions as objective realities. The poor creature indeed had not our advantages in the perusal of records of hypnotism and of the Society for Psychical Research, and would have been sadly puzzled to draw the line

155 Anna Kingsford and Edward Maitland, *The Perfect Way, or the Finding of Christ* (London: Hamilton, Adams & Co., 1882), p. 83. Kingsford (1846–1888) and Maitland (1824–1897) were briefly Theosophists, but broke from the Theosophical Society to form the extremely small and short-lived but influential Hermetic Society, which influenced S. L. MacGregor Mathers and others.

between subjective illusion and objective materialization. Nevertheless, her angel lover was with her when she thought him the Devil. He comforted her in her poverty and loneliness (many of these witches, remember, were old women, whose lives had been the bare, dreary lives of the terrible poor), and he promised her such influence among her neighbors as she longed for most. This was an ordeal, had she but known it, which, if passed successfully, would have brought her a higher and sweeter pleasure. Some there were, here and there, who seem to have chosen the better part, and to have become "white witches," capable of clairvoyance, of healing human beings and cattle of strange diseases, forecasting the future and the like. But usually, these poor old women had been so embittered against selfish or heedless neighbors, that the influence they longed for most was to pay back their wrongs (real or supposed) with interest. Here again, they broke the occult law which calls for correct living on the part of the psychic, and trod the downward path of hatred and diabolism. In many cases, no doubt, the psychical experiences of a witch started from this fierce desire to be revenged upon those who had slighted her. She probably began with some simple form of self-hypnotization imparted to her by a neighbor who had already acquired some proficiency in the art. Once she had accomplished this, the astral world lay open wide before her with all its illusions or all its realities, according to how she proved worthy of one or the other. Sometimes, no doubt, she struggled upward to benevolent thoughts and prayers for help in resisting temptation and was accordingly rewarded with true occult power, and with union with her angelic mate, who was both her husband and her guardian. That she thought him the Devil partially interfered with the physical strengthening and psychical happiness which that union brought; while he, on his part, kept steady watch over her infirmities, always ready to help the slightest impulse of her spirit to rise to higher things, seeing, as only angels see, beneath that misshapen earthly body, the soul—the astral body which, despite the temporary disfigurements caused by evil thoughts, is ever young and fair—and waiting patiently throughout her poor, stumbling, sinful life, as only a man who truly loves a wife can wait, for the time when she will live down her mistakes, and see as clearly as himself.

If it be objected that this occult wedlock with an angel whom she ignorantly mistook for a Devil brought her misfortune, I answer: Not unless she broke the law of correct living by trying to turn her occult powers to base purposes, or failed to keep clear-headed.

But in that case?

In that case, also, her guardian angel took her through the deep waters and along the rugged, toilsome mountain path for her evolution, that she might be made perfect through suffering. Are we not all convinced that that is what God means by putting us, who are not witches, in a world where each of us has to wrestle with adverse circumstances in bitterness of spirit? In our inmost being we recognize God's wisdom in our being taken through sorrows, temptations and conflicts, for thus only can we grow strong and rise to our full stature as made in His likeness. And to the witch, Heaven was no less merciful than to us, in that it forced ordeals upon her which, when she passed them, brought her happiness, but which, when she failed to pass them, brought her suffering.

It is noticeable that most of the witches who came to grief, and who confessed to intercourse with the Devil, referred to certain ceremonies customary at each "Sabbath," although records of witchcraft point rather to subjective illusions of performing abominable rites, which symbolized abnormal vices. For details, the reader may refer to almost any work on witchcraft. He will there see, that with all the fuss made by the judges and persecutors about this intercourse with Satan, there was very little of real impurity, and what there was seems to have been entirely subjective—the illusion of an insane imagining. In short, the witch, as well as other brides of angelic lovers, was evidently far from impure-minded by nature at the start, and this, too, in an age of vulgar expressions, coarse ideas, and from which even the genius of a Shakespeare did not escape without contamination. Yet these women were mostly illiterate and miserably poor. It is probable that their poverty, however, had been their educator in ascetic deprivation and in bearing up under slights from more fortunate neighbors, and so had laid the foundations of that stern control of self which is absolutely necessary in the true occultist. That this feature—their feelings under slights received from neighbors—played an important part in their thoughts and consequently in their development, is shown by the fact that many of their attempts (real or supposed) at bewitching date from an unkind refusal of a neighbor to give them a bowl of soup or an old shirt. Ill-temper, then, morose broodings over wrongs, general sourness of spirit, were not the least important of the causes which turned those earthly partners of angelic bridegrooms into devil-handed witches.

Another cause seems to have been their failure to think clearly and without prejudice. Poor creatures! They were nearly all of them prejudiced (i.e., "prejudgers") from beginning to end. They prejudged angels to be the Devil; they prejudged the monsters imagined by their own subconsciousness to be real; they prejudged the wedlock into which they entered on the Borderland to be sinful; they prejudged their mysterious visitor to be a tempter to lead them away from religion and the church; they prejudged him as requiring unhallowed rites—dimly remembered survivals from the ancient Sex Worship, too often on its vilest side; they prejudged him as the means of ignoble satisfactions of their hatred and their animal desires. And thus they sank to diabolism.

There was yet another cause—not so much of evil as of illusions. This was the "Devil's Mark," that special mark of his with which they supposed themselves stamped on some part of their bodies. With this, we may classify the spot at which the Devil or one of his imps was said to suck them, and also the peculiarity that their bridegroom, in his marital relations, chilled them as though with ice.

There are many phases of occult sensitiveness. The ear for the clairaudient, the eye for the clairvoyant, the easily-swayed arm and hand for the writing medium, are the three physical organs through which communications usually reach us. But for the wife of a heavenly bridegroom, the nerves of touch, it is evident, must be the chief focuses of occult sensitiveness. Now, in order that the delicate balance of nerve sensation be maintained, it is important that such a psychic distinguish readily between real touches and illusory touches, between objective realities impinging upon the ends of her nerves and hypnotic suggestions, either self-induced or induced by an outside intelligence, say by her spirit bridegroom. And not only must she learn to distinguish thus between real and unreal sensations, but she must also learn to resist all hypnotic suggestion to feel sensations which do not exist or which are unlawful. No psychic can be considered thoroughly self-controlled who has not acquired this power of resistance to hypnotic suggestion of unlawful touches or of unreal things as real. No psychic's testimony can be considered reliable so long as she fails to distinguish between genuine and illusory touches. So long as she is lacking in any of these essentials to the wife of a heavenly bridegroom, just so long will her guardian persist in putting her through a course of training—a training which she must undergo until she passes her examination and is promoted into a higher class, there to take up still more advanced lessons in psychic discrimination and psychic self-control.

Now, the "Devil's Marks" and the "sucking" were both, so I hold, illusory sensations which the witch failed either to classify or to conquer, but to which she mistakenly succumbed. When the supposed Devil's imp showed nonsensitiveness to pinpricks, it was probably a case of autosuggestion—or, in the case of some, a hypnotic dulling to pain caused (oftentimes in mercy) by the angel guardian.

Of the same illusory character is that phenomenon which has so puzzled all the writers on witchcraft—the icy chilliness of the sperm. This experience is entirely subjective; because it is forbidden by Borderland laws to evoke a nervous energy for no definite result; and, as a harvest in offspring on the Borderland cannot be produced, it is breaking Borderland laws to sow the seed. The very fact that the Devil, who is supposed to be a deity of fire, [appears] cold in the Borderland marital union, ought to have shown his earthly partner that it was an illusion. And the psychic who expects or thinks to enact a forbidden experience on the Borderland, has only her own ignorance to thank for the illusion.

Incubi and succubae, evil spirits who were supposed to force themselves as lovers upon both men and women, played an important part in witchcraft days. Deformed children were supposed to have sprung of such a union. Luther believed implicitly in this. Virtuous women seemed to be especially subject to the attacks of incubi, and this was looked on as attesting the cunning of Satan, who thus aimed at those noted for purity of life. It rarely, if ever, seems to have occurred to people in those days that a virtuous woman, reasonably clear-headed, is a being who is under especial angelic protection, and that when such a woman was persistently singled out by a spirit for lover-like attentions, it must have been owing to the favor of Heaven, and not to the malignity of devils. That these attentions became a great annoyance at last was only because the woman either broke the moral law in some way, or became prejudiced against every such being as an emissary of Satan. In time, by the workings of the laws of Borderland, she who through natural curiosity and romantic sentiment at first hearkened to the angel lover, and afterward through the failure to live aright or think clearly felt bound to reject him as a devil, became subject to hallucinations, and also in some cases to annoying physical manifestations. Some picturesque stories have been told of such women to whom the spirit lover has appeared in the guise of a handsome youth, vainly wooing his earthly love night after night. The stories usually wind up with an account of fearful persecutions at the hands of the rejected lover, who thus by his malignity reveals himself as the Devil. Sometimes the priest is appealed to, but not always successfully. The Roman Catholic Church has a regular rite to exorcise demons, and is probably successful with the psychic through hypnotic suggestion. But in the case of a spirit lover who has once been received (whether as husband or by [a] communicating spirit), it would seem as though his hypnotic suggestion often outweighed that of the priest to still exorcise the fiend in cases of demoniacal possession. But I am inclined to think that the very lingering of these subjective experiences indicates that her psychic hallucinations were often not only due to hypnotic suggestions by her spirit lover, but were also the result—recorded in her subliminal consciousness—of a veridical phenomena which she at first encourages; whether through harmless curiosity, or through the romantic and tender sentiment of a pure heart, or through the grosser impulses arising from a luxuriant and untrained imagination, matters not. When her season of ordeals set in and she was obliged to distinguish between the illusory and the real, in order to maintain communication with her interesting visitor, she either grew alarmed at the phenomena of the ordeals or else rashly assumed the whole thing to be diabolical. From this time on, it were indeed strange if she should fail to see subjectively what she expected—i.e., the Devil. All in vain now was it for her to exclaim in terror or indignation, "I will have nothing to do with you!" Her angelic lover had indeed ceased to communicate; but her subconsciousness had not ceased to vibrate along the lines of psychical illusion; and unless she possessed great self-control and had her subconscious nature well in hand, time and time only could work a cure unless, indeed, she should implicitly submit her inner self to the priest or to some other earthly human being as her hypnotizer, in which case it was a change from the hypnotic control of a clear-seeing angel to that of a more or less blind fallible earthly man, who may or may not take undue advantage of the power placed in his hands over her mainsprings of action. When one (1) considers that every woman who enters a convent is pledged to a mystic union with a heavenly bridegroom, denominated Christ; (2) that the union, more often than the public is aware, becomes so objectively real that the confessor feels obliged to term it "*congressus cum daemonis*"; (3) that ignorance on the men's part of Borderland laws will render her experience fantastic or diabolical; (4) that her deliverance from these experiences may be secured by a change in the hypnotizer, from an unseen angel to a visible earthly priest: We see what a power resides with confessors to mold the minds of the nuns to carry out his hypnotic suggestions for the glory of the Church. For the person who has been hypnotized by spirits, and who has not acquired the power of resisting hypnotic suggestion, will more readily yield to an earthly hypnotizer. That the angelic lover should force himself upon her as an incubus against her will is contrary to Borderland laws; for in the world beyond the Borderland (the world beyond the grave), it is reckoned a sin for a woman to have aught to do with husband or lover save *for love's sake*; and hence the idea that women may be forced into a marital union on the Borderland is totally *incorrect*, inasmuch as the highest standards of social and ethical duty in both worlds must be lived up to by the two who meet upon the borders of the two worlds. Rationalists have tried to explain the spirit bride and spirit bridegroom as a nightmare arising from a plethoric condition of the body, an explanation which has force only when the spirit is an incubus and not a succubus and when the earthly psychic (man or woman) is asleep or dozing. But the clearest and most convincing manifestations of the objectivity of the heavenly bridegroom always come when the psychic is most clearheaded. It seems, indeed, that it is not even in a trance but only when the psychic is wide awake that the marital union takes place objectively. And this I think will be found to be the case with the witches. When their union with the supposed Devil was based on the faithful tender love of one woman for one man, and its reciprocity, in accordance with high moral standards, then was the union objective and natural. The gross rites of the Witches' Sabbaths, with their abnormalities and absurdities, were evidently the illusion of an insane imagination in great part—although it is also doubtless true that, as Professor Wilder says, there is little reason to doubt that these "witches' sabbaths" were formerly celebrated, and that they were, in some modified form, a continuation of the outlawed worship of the Roman Empire.

Early in the 17th century, a light dawned upon the horizon of these illusions and diableries. That light was the manifesto of a secret society of mystics called the Rosicrucians or followers of the Rosie Cross. In 1603 the sect became known; in 1623 it placarded Paris with mysterious announcements; but it professed to have existed long before. Who its members were, whether the society really existed, or whether the whole affair was a joke on the mystics, are questions which today remain still unsettled. But, whether a reality or a myth, the Rosicrucians were a factor in the literature and mysticism of their time, and a secret society of the same name still exists. They dealt a powerful blow at the superstition which assumed the spirit bridegroom and the spirit bride to be diabolical.

> They discarded forever all the old tales of sorcery and witchcraft, and communion with the devil. They said there were no such horrid, unnatural and disgusting beings as the incubi and succubi, and the innumerable grotesque imps that men had believed in for so many ages. Man was not surrounded with enemies like these, but with myriads of beautiful and beneficent beings, all anxious to do him service. The air was peopled with sylphs, the water with undines or naiads, the bowels of the earth with gnomes, and the fire with salamanders. All these beings were the friends of man, and desired nothing so much as that men should purge themselves of all uncleanness, and thus be enabled to see and converse with them. They possessed great power, and were unrestrained by the barriers of space or the obstructions of matter. But man was in one particular their superior. He had an immortal soul, and they had not. They might, however, become sharers in man's immortality, if they could inspire one of that race with the passion of love towards them. Hence it was the constant endeavor of the female spirits to captivate the admiration of men; and of the male gnomes, sylphs, salamanders, and undines, to be beloved by a woman. The object of this

> passion, in returning their love, imparted a portion of that celestial fire to the soul; and from that time forth the beloved became equal to the lover, and both, when their allotted course was run, entered together into the mansions of felicity. These spirits, they said, watched constantly over mankind by night and day. Dreams, omens, and presentiments were all their work, and the means by which they gave warning of the approach of danger. But, though so well inclined to befriend man for their own sake, the want of a soul rendered them at times capricious and revengeful: they took offense on slight causes, and heaped injuries instead of benefits on the heads of those who extinguished the light of reason that was in them, by gluttony, debauchery, and other appetites of the body.[156]

There is a book called *Sub-Mundanes*,[157] which in a vein of delicate humor deals with this belief of the Rosicrucians. It purports to be written by an acquaintance of one Count de Gabalis.[158] *Sub-Mundanes* refers to stories told of the Gothic Kings being born from a bear and a princess of Pegusians being born from a dog and a woman; of a Portuguese woman, who was exposed on a deserted island, having children by a large monkey. The author goes on to say that the sylphs of the Rosicrucians, seeing that they are taken for Demons when they appear, in order to diminish aversion, take the form of these animals, and accommodate themselves thus to the whimsical weakness of women, who would be horrified at the sight of a handsome sylph, but less so at a dog or monkey.

Sub-Mundanes tells a story of a hard-hearted Spanish beauty who repulsed a Castilian gentleman so effectually that he left her and set off to travel to

156 Charles Mackay, *Memoirs of Extraordinary Popular Delusions* (Philadelphia: Lindsay and Blakiston, 1850), vol. 2, pp.230–231. See also A. Reader, *Mysteries of the Rosie Cross* (London: A. Reader, 1891), pp. 20–21. (ICC note) ["A. Reader" was a pseudonym of Hargrave Jennings (1817–1890), British author of many books dealing with ancient phallic and sex worship.]

157 Villars de Montfaucon, and John Yarker, trans., *The Count De Gabalis; Or, the Extravagant Mysteries of the Cabalists Exposed, in Five Pleasant Discourses on the Secret Sciences*, vol. 1, subtitled *Sub-Mundanes; or, the Elementaries of the Cabala: Being the History of Spirits* (Bath: R. H. Fryar, 1886). Published by Robert H. Fryar (1845–1909), English bookseller, publisher, and associate of African-American spiritualist Paschal Beverly Randolph (1825–1875). Randolph is widely considered the spiritual father of 19th-century sexual occultism. Fryar was also a key figure in the formation of the Hermetic Brotherhood of Luxor in Great Britain, an occult group that incorporated Randolph's teachings on sexual magic. See Joscelyn Godwin et al., *The Hermetic Brotherhood of Luxor* (York Beach, ME: Samuel Weiser, 1995), p. 43.

158 Monsieur Bayle informs us that the *Count de Gabalis* was published at Paris by the celebrated Abbott de Villars (nephew of De Montfaucon) in the year 1670. (ICC note)

forget her. A sylph fell in love with her, took the shape of her absent lover, wooed her persistently and won her. A son was born; and when she was again pregnant, the earthly lover returned to Seville, quite cured of his passion, and hastened to call on her saying he should now displease her no longer, as he had ceased to love her. Result: a scene, tears, reproaches on the part of the young woman—parents come in and the whole matter is brought to light. The writer continues:

> And what part played the Airy-Lover (interrupted I) all this while? I see well enough (answered the Count) that you are displeased that he should forsake his mistress, leaving her to the Rigor of the Parents and to the Fury of the Inquisitors. But he had reason to complain of her: She was not devout enough; for when these gentlemen immortalize themselves they work seriously, and live very holily; that they lose not the Right which they came to acquire of Sovereign good: So they would have the person to whom they are allied, live with exemplary innocence.[159]

Sub-Mundanes also tells of a young Lord of Bavaria who was not to be comforted for the death of his wife, whereupon a sylph took her shape. The same story as told elsewhere, however, stated that it was his own wife who returned from beyond the grave. They lived together many years, and had children. But he "swore, and spoke lewd uncivil words." She reproved him vainly, and at last "she vanished one day from him, and left him nothing but her Clothes, and the Repentance of his not having followed her Holy Counsels."[160]

These two stories show what stress is laid by the spirit lover upon the necessity for the earthly psychic to keep the moral law.

Another story, unreal and fantastic as is the catastrophe, shows that bigamy is not condoned on the Borderland, and that no man can serve two mistresses without punishment when one of the earthly partners of one of these nymphs is his Borderland spouse. It appears that he

> was so dishonest a Man as to fall in Love with a Woman; but as he Dined with his new Mistress and certain of his Friends, there was seen in the Air the Loveliest Creature of the World; which was the invisible Lover,

159 De Montfaucon, *The Count De Gabalis*.
160 De Montfaucon, *The Count De Gabalis*.

> that had a mind to let herself be seen by the Friends of her unfaithful Gallant; that they might Judge how little reason he could have to prefer a Woman before her. After which the enraged nymph struck him dead immediately.[161]

But popular prejudice regarding the reality of witchcraft died hard. The Rosicrucians were charged with doing as did the witches—projecting their astral forms for selfish and lawless purposes.

> It was believed by the populace, and by many others whose education should have taught them better . . . that gentle maidens, who went to bed alone, often awoke in the night and found men in bed with them, of shape more beautiful than the Grecian Apollo, who immediately became invisible when an alarm was raised.[162]

But this seems rather unlikely, when we carefully consider the following *pronunciamento*, with which they placarded Paris.

> We, the deputies of the principal College of the brethren of the Rosie Cross, have taken up our abode, visible and invisible, in this city, by the grace of the Most High, towards whom are turned the hearts of the just. We show and teach without any books or symbols whatever, and we speak all sorts of languages in the countries where we deign to dwell, to draw mankind, our fellows, from error and to save them from death.[163]

Moreover, the Rosicrucians "maintained most positively that the very first vow they took was one of chastity, and that any of them violating that oath would be deprived at once of all the advantages he possessed, and be subject to hunger, thirst, sorrow, disease and death like other men. Witchcraft and sorcery they also most warmly repudiated."[164]

And the editor of *Sub-Mundanes*, in a footnote, refers to the Rosicrucian marriage with the elementary or Spirit-life, esteemed a duty by the sages and cultivated with fasting, watching, prayer and contemplation and acquir-

161 *Sub-Mundanes*. (ICC Note) [De Montfaucon, *The Count De Gabalis*.]
162 [Mackay, *Memoirs of Extraordinary Popular Delusions*, vol. 2, p. 228.] (ICC note)
163 [Reader, *Mysteries of the Rosie Cross*, p. 17.] (ICC note)
164 Reader, *Mysteries of the Rosie Cross*, p. 20.

ing thereby that condition of spiritual repose, only in which inspired visions occurred.

Why did these mystics call themselves Rosicrucian? Some writers have attempted to derive the name from two words meaning "dew" and "cross": but the usual interpretation is "followers of the Rosy Cross"—a cross with a rose being used as the society's symbol. Some derive the word from the name, Christian Rosenkranz, the reputed founder of the society: but in view of the fact that it is uncertain that he ever lived, and that the stories told about the opening of his tomb 120 years after his death have a decidedly mythical flavor, one may be pardoned for considering this personage a myth, invented as a convenient explanation to outsiders to throw them off the track of the real meaning of the society's name.

Now, the cross is an old, old religious symbol of the union of man and woman the world over, and dates from an unknown antiquity. The rose is a well-known symbol of love under its most ardent form. We have already seen that the Mexican Virgin, Sochiquetzal, was presented by a heavenly messenger with a rose when the annunciation was made that she should bear a mysteriously begotten son; that her name means the "lifting up of roses": and that this event marks the commencement of an epoch called "the age of Roses." We have seen that the Mexican Eve sinned by plucking roses—which elsewhere are called, apparently, "the fruit of the tree." We have seen that quite on the other side of the world, among the Mohammedans, is found a tradition that Christ was conceived by the smelling of a rose, and there is an Eastern legend that the burning bush in which the angel of the Lord appeared to Moses—a bush which burned without being consumed—was a rose bush. May not these roses be symbolically one and the same with the rose upon the Rosicrucian cross? If so, remembering the Rosicrucian teachings about the duty of chastity, the joy of nuptials with a being from the unseen world, and the obligation to enter upon that heavenly marriage with "fasting, watching, prayer, and contemplation"—we may well believe that they had learned the inner mystery of aspiring through passion to communion with God and of placing the rose of Divine Love upon the cross of marriage union in Borderland wedlock.

Although in a book entitled *In the Pronaos of the Temple of Wisdom*, by Franz Hartmann, occurs a list of Rosicrucian symbols followed by the significant remark: "He who can see the meaning of all these allegories has his eyes open."[165]

Many of these symbols are evidently phallic, and yield easily to the interpretation that they are symbols in the training of the occultist in the three degrees to which I have already referred.

But, despite the good work done by the Rosicrucians in lifting Borderland wedlock to a higher plane in the estimation of the public, it was not all plain sailing yet. The Church—that conservator alike of the useful and the useless things of the past—clung to the old belief of witchcraft days: When one of her mystics—either nun or priest—became thus espoused, the Church seems to have a middle course between the old and the new. Usually she termed such experiences "*Congressus cum daemonis*" and bent her powers to exorcising the evil one. But occasionally, as in the case of St. Teresa, the nun was a clear-headed woman of known integrity and purity. "*congressus cum daemonis*" was out of the question where such a woman was one of the parties to the union in these instances. By what one can only call an inspiration from on high, the Church promptly decided that the *congressus* was diabolical, but heaven-sent. And, since the nun was the professed "bride of Christ," what more natural than that her experience should be viewed as a mystical union with this Divine Bridegroom? In this, the Church acted according to her light, and I think it must be admitted she did fairly well, considering the ignorance and prejudice of the times.

Latin scholars will notice that the laws of Latin syntax require a word to be supplied in translating this phrase—a general term, such as the word "something," or "that which belongs to." As this grammatical construction was used by a very learned Catholic priest when discussing the matter with me, I cannot suppose it to be a slip of the tongue, as I should have supposed had the speaker been less of a scholar. This construction however, instead of obscuring, really sets forth the matter with clearer resemblance to the psychic's useful physiological experience, as will be seen by comparing it with the legends I have referred to regarding the finding of the body of Osiris by Isis. Only by comparing this Latin expression with the legends and their application will the phrase be properly understood.

165 Franz Hartmann, *In the Pronaos of the Temple of Wisdom* (London: Theosophical Publishing Society, 1890), p. 117.

It is noteworthy, however, that in St. Teresa's case, her confessor, after having her write out a detailed account of her experience, ordered her to burn a great part of it. Was it because the objectivity of her experiences did not harmonize very well with the mystical idea of "espousal to Christ"?

Where the earthly partner in these unions was a woman, and a nun at that, pledged to unfaltering obedience to her official superiors, it was probably an easy matter for her confessor to lump all her experiences—veridical as well as illusory—under one heading, that of subjective. A virgin is usually, by reason of her environment as a woman, so ignorant of the physiology of marriage that it is difficult for her as a psychic to distinguish what is real from what is unreal until she has been a Borderland wife for some time. But for the priest to whom the blessed experience of Borderland wedlock came in all its fullness, a different course of treatment must have been necessary; since, being a man, with the opportunities of knowledge open to a man, and to a priestly confessor of sinful men and women, he could not be hoodwinked by his superior into taking for subjective illusions these experiences which were distinctly objective. The records of witchcraft contain accounts extending over forty or fifty years of priests who were burned at the stake for a union of this sort, with a spirit assumed to be the Devil in the form of a woman.

Pope Gregory is known as Hildebrand, that pope who strove so persistently to purge the priesthood of simony and unchastity, and to emancipate the Church from interference by the temporal power. But what is done with priests nowadays who enter upon Borderland wedlock is not, so far as I can learn, revealed to the general public. From a French physician however, I learn of a custom among the Continental priests concerning their sleeping arrangements which suggest that more allowance is made nowadays than formerly for those who Heaven has thus singled out, and that the Church bows to the will of Heaven in this matter, and lays no blame upon the priest.

Théophile Gautier has written a novelette called *Clarimonde* which recounts the love of a beautiful vampire for a priest. She comes to him each night and they mount a horse and gallop away to her palace, then he returns at daybreak for his priesthood duties. The author represents the priest as struggling between his duties as a priest and what he considers the allurements of sin, and in consonance with the idea that punishment is visited upon the sinner. Gautier reveals her as a vampire sucking the blood of her lover while he sleeps.

It would seem as though the author, especially for a priest of God, were catering to the popular superstition that it is sinful to enjoy sensuous love. But if anyone in the world is entitled to the joys of true Borderland wedlock, it is surely a priest who has kept his vows of asceticism, and who is really pure-minded. If anyone in the world needs it, it is surely the priest who is supposed to stand midway as a bridge-builder, between earthly sinners and celestial beings of the unseen world beyond the grave, since it is pretty generally acknowledged that a well-ordered sex life is necessary to the development of a symmetrical character. For what mean the words "holy" and "holiness"? They mean "whole-ly," "wholeness." The man and woman who expect to be indeed "holy," must be "whole," i.e., symmetrical. In Old Testament times, Jehovah forbade any priest who was a eunuch to minister before Him, thus recognizing the importance of sex in the perfect man. The Rev. Arthur Devine, Passionist, in a book entitled *Convent Life, or the Duties of Sisters Dedicated in Religion to the Service of God*—a book which the title page shows is "intended chiefly for superiors and confessors," takes up the subject of nuns who are subject to visions and supernatural revelations. Considering the question as to whether such experiences are true visions or the results of deception and error, he mentions as one test the consideration of

> whether it {the revelation} contains anything false, because in this case it cannot proceed from the spirit of truth. Therefore, it is necessary to consider whether it is conformable to Scripture, to faith and morals, to theology and to the doctrine and traditions of the church. . . . Are they {these communications} accompanied by the cross and by mortification, and do they tend to the manifestation of the faith and the utility of the Church?[166]

From which it will be seen that a heavenly bridegroom who is not a good Catholic has every prospect of being classed as demoniacal, if he happens to have the same religious belief as herself (she being heretical). This is a case where religious prejudice furnishes the standard by which to test the com-

166 Arthur Devine, *Convent Life; or, the Duties of Sisters Dedicated in Religion to the Service of God* (London: R. Washbourne, 1897), p. 218.

munication, and it will be remembered that to start with; for, any subject, when dealing with occult phenomena, is certain to bring about occurrences of a fantastic misleading or diabolical character.

The *spiritus percutiens*, or "rapping spirit" conjured away by old Catholic formulae at the benediction of churches was brought forward by some of M. de Gasparin's critics. As his tables did not rap, he had nothing to do with the *spiritus percutiens* who proves, however, that the church was acquainted with raps, and explained them by the spiritualistic hypothesis.

A learned priest has kindly looked for the alleged *spiritus percutiens* in dedicatory and other ecclesiastical formulae. He only finds it in benedictions of bridal chambers, and thinks it refers to the slaying spirit in the Book of Tobit.[167]

The "slaying spirit" in the Book of Tobit, it will be remembered, was a so-called evil spirit who was in love with Sara and who objected to her marrying, and who slew seven successively earthly aspirants to her hand on their bridal night. He is always referred to as an instance of the incubus. But let us not forget that so-called incubi are angels, and are never evil; since in order to hold communication with the beloved earthly person they, as well as the psychic, are obliged to live correctly and think clearly. And what is evil on the Borderland is all subjective and never objective. And the number seven too, in regards to the husbands of a virgin who already has a spouse, has a suspiciously mythical, folklorish look.

That the Roman Catholic Church should take account of such a spirit in the benedictions of bridal chambers shows that it has had good reason to suspect the visits of incubi to the virgins of its laity, as well as to the virgins of its nunneries. Indeed, Tylor in his *Primitive Culture* tells us that the frequency of incubi and succubae "is set forth in the Bull of Pope Innocent VIII in 1484, as an accepted accusation against many persons of both sexes, forgetful of their own salvation, and falling away from the Catholic faith."[168]

The following, which I take from *Sub-Mundanes*, refers to one of the most noted instances in convent life of an incubus who was objectively, as well as subjectively, the spouse of a nun.

A little Gnome got into the affections of the Famous Magdalen of

167 Andrew Lange, *Cock Lane and Common-Sense* (1894), pp. 316–317. (ICC note)
168 Tylor, *Primitive Culture*, pp. 190–191.

> the Cross, Abbess of a Monastery at Cordova in Spain; she made him Happy, when she was but twelve years old; and they continued their *Amours Libres* for the space of thirty years; until an ignorant Director persuaded Magdalen that her lover was a Fiend; and forced her to demand absolution of Pope Paul the Third. Yet it is impossible that this could be a Demon; for all Europe knew, and Cassidorus Reniris has made known to all Posterity, the great miracles which daily were wrought in Favor of this Holy Woman; which certainly had never come to pass, if her *Amours Libres* with the Gnome had fallen so Diabolick, as the Venerable Director imagined.[169]

Another account, however, informs us that the abbess was accused by her nuns of magic—a very convenient accusation in those days when a superior was at all troublesome—and that she very cleverly anticipated them by going to the Pope to confess all and throw herself on his mercy. Inasmuch as he granted her absolution, one cannot help wondering if he did not read between the lines of this confession the occult truth and recognize her as a lawful Borderland spouse. Most of the accounts state that Magdalen's lover was the Devil, who appeared to her as a black man. Here we come upon the same root idea, doubtless, as that behind the black Madonnas, the black Krishna and the black Quetzalcoatl of Mexico, a symbolism due perhaps in part to the darkness of the unknown world whence they emerge, and in part to their folklore and occult aspect as deities of *night-time* and Borderland nuptials. "I am black, but comely," says one of the lovers in that mystical and passionate Song of Solomon.

I have already referred to the Song of Solomon as being interpreted by Christian comment and said to be a poetical statement of the rapturous union between Christ and his Bride, the Church. A side light is thrown upon the interpretation by a note in Kitto's *Illustrated Bible*,[170] which quotes Lane[171] as saying that the odes sung by Mohammedans at religious festivals were of a similar nature with the Song of Solomon, generally alluding to the Prophet as the object of love and praise. In the small collection of poems sung at Zikirs appears one ending with these lines:

169 De Montfaucon, *The Count De Gabalis*.

170 John Kitto, *An Illustrated History of the Holy Bible* (Norwich, CT: Henry Bill, 1872).

171 *Modern Egyptians*. (ICC note) [Edward William Lane, *An Account of the Manners and Customs of the Modern Egyptians* (London: John Murray, 1871), vol. 2, pp. 171.]

> The phantom of thy form visited me in my slumber; I said:
> "O phantom of slumber! who sent thee?"
> He said: "He sent me whom thou Knowest:
> He whose love occupies thee."
> The beloved of my heart visited me in the darkness of night.
> I stood to show him honor, until he sat down,
> I said, "O thou my petition and all my desire!
> Hast thou come at midnight, and not feared the watchman?"
> He said to me, "I feared: but, however, love
> Had taken from me my soul and my breath."[172]

Finding that songs of this description are exceedingly numerous, and almost the only poems sung at Zikirs, [and] that they are composed for that purpose and intended only to have a spiritual sense (though certainly not understood in that sense by the generality of the vulgar), I cannot entertain any doubt as to the design of Solomon's Song.

This religious mysticism finds a modern echo in a little publication recently issued by the Adi Brahma Samaj of Calcutta, as the first step in a new propaganda. It is entitled *The Religion of Love*. In its pages occur these words:

> Though these terms, Father, Mother, Friend, Husband of the soul, are all allegorical, they very aptly express our sweet relationship with God, and we have every right to use them. Among these allegorical designations the Husband of the Soul is the best.[173]

Zanchius wrote the *Excellent Traite du Mariage Spiritual Entre Jesus Christ et son Église*,[174] in which he drew a close parallel between earthly wedlock and the spiritual and divine marriage of Christ with the Church Universal. Among other things, he laid stress on that Scriptural saying of earthly husband and wife, that the twain shall become one flesh; and he said that, according to Scripture, it was neither God the Father nor God the Spirit who is Sponsor of his Church, but the Son, who was made of like nature with ourselves—like in all things to us, but without sin. He added:

---

172 Lane, *An Account of the Manners and Customs*, pp. 172–173.

173 Rajnarain Bose, *The Religion of Love, Intended for All Sects and Churches* (Calcutta: B.M. Press, 1894), p. 11.

174 Hieronymus Zanchius, *Excellent traité du mariage spirituel entre Iésus Christ et son église* (1594).

> His soul does not pervade all space, because it went out of his body when he died and consequently was not in all places, since going out of the body, it did not remain therein, afterwards being returned to the body {and} never was and never will be (any more than the body) in all places....
>
> In this spiritual marriage, all the person of each faithful one—that is to say, the body and the soul—is conjoined with all the person of Jesus Christ, and is made one flesh and one person with him.[175]

As to the method by which this combined fleshly and spiritual union of the Christian with Christ can take place, Zanchius seemed to think that the Eucharist in which one partakes of the body and blood of Christ is the sole appointed means.

Now the Eucharist, or the use of bread and wine in a sacred rite, was an old Pagan custom bound up with the idea of entering into blood brotherhood, of which Jesus made use to emphasize his own brotherhood with his disciples. The ceremony of the Eucharist was found in Peru when Jesuits first landed. In fact, it is a very, very ancient rite existing in widely separated countries. The Christian writer Arnobius rebukes in cutting terms the Pagan mock modesty which blushed at the mere mention of "bread and wine"—a matter which indicates some folklore connection between the Eucharist and sex; and if so, then between the Eucharist and the ancient mysteries of Phallicism. Inasmuch as by far the greater part of all that was pure and holy in Phallicism is bound up with Borderland wedlock, it is possible that the Eucharist may have esoterically a wider significance than either Arbnobius or Zanchius was aware.

Modern believers in the union with Christ have taken a less mystical and more practical view of it than did Zanchius. Mrs. M. Baxter of the well-known institution for Divine Healing, Bethlehem, London, issued a little pamphlet on that text of 1 Corinthians 6:13, "The body ... for the Lord, and the Lord for the body." In it, she says:

> One of the most successful devices of Satan has been his attempt to divorce our bodies from our souls in their relation to God. "Your soul is the Lord's of course, but your body is your own. You must serve the Lord with your soul, but enjoy yourself with your body." Such is

175 Original source of quote unknown.

> his counsel to those whose tendency is gross and carnal, such as easily become drunkards, fornicators, or prostitutes, and form the large class of fallen men and fallen women in our midst. To another class he comes and says, "You are religious; but it is your soul with which you can serve God; all you can do with your body is to punish it, and destroy it by slow degrees." Many look upon this as religious heroism; but it is as much a lie to the truth of God, as is the grosser misuse of the body for lust or appetite. God comes with his glorious claim. "The body is for the Lord and the Lord for the body."[176]

"Under the Divine Touch," a pamphlet written by Chester E. Pond of Philadelphia, contains the following recorded experiences, which, mystical as they may be considered from one standpoint, are singularly suggestive of the earlier experiences of the psychic who has entered on Borderland wedlock, but who has not yet learned to distinguish between subjective and objective touches—that is, between a touch which is material, tangible, real, and one that is only a hypnotic suggestion made by the Borderland spouse.

> For the last eleven months my whole being has been open more or less to the joys, delights and peculiar sensations of heaven. Recently the Lord has been giving me his choicest foretastes of heavenly blessedness just before I arise in the morning. During these eleven months I have been daily and almost hourly conscious of His positive and holy touch in some part of my natural body. But during these recent morning experiences His touch has been more sweet and more powerful than usual. These heavenly experiences when viewed from a human standpoint seem remarkable. But when viewed from a heavenly standpoint they seem perfectly natural. They have come to me very gradually. In every way they have been orderly and helpful. They seem just what might be expected to come to any devout Christian. For the Lord is no respecter of persons. In considering these experiences it should be borne in mind that Jehovah Jesus is in every way infinite, that He never makes two things just alike in the natural world, and that He never acts twice alike in the spiritual world. Hence, as might be expected, He touches my "natural body" through my "spiritual body" in an infinite variety of ways, and with infinite sweetness. But for convenience I will classify, and say that He touches me, first directly or immediately; secondly,

176 Mrs. M. Baxter. (ICC note)

He touches me through the medium or ministration of angels; and, thirdly, through the medium of His Written Word....

To my distinct consciousness the spirit of the Lord is that living divine, or divine substance which constantly proceeds from His divine person, somewhat in the same way and manner that rays of light and heat are continually proceeding from our natural sun. It is written that "God is love," and that "God is light," or truth. From this we learn that love and truth constitute the divine essence. And in the ordinary use of language heat corresponds to love and light to truth. We call a loving person warm-hearted and an educated person enlightened. Jesus Himself taught spiritual truths by natural symbols....

The Lord, in His mercy, tempers the inflowing of His spirit to our different states of receptivity.... If He had poured His divine love and truth into my soul and body one year ago, with the same degree of heat and power that He does now, I believe I should have been consumed.

My experiences are endless in variety. At times, when love seems to predominate over truth, the divine proceeding that streams forth upon me appears to my spiritual vision like the golden beams of an autumn sunset, but when truth predominates over love, they appear like streams of white light reflected from burnished silver.

At times I am consciously alone with the Lord. At other times I am consciously in the presence of angels. Since these touches of the Lord are infinite in variety, I can never tell one minute what will occur the next. As I now sit writing I am so literally full that every particle of flesh in my body feels as if it were alive and moving. This extreme fullness in the daytime does not occur every day. It will probably not continue more than eight or ten hours. While I am busy it is not excessively delightful. But if I were to lean back in my chair, or to go and lie down, I should soon be completely deluged with floods of heavenly glory, and be "lost in wonder, love and praise." The movings of the spirit are usually undulatory. When I am still, and sometimes when at work, they come like waves of liquid sweetness, and roll over me and through me in every conceivable direction, and with all conceivable variety.

Occasionally at night the Lord touches me all over alike for a few seconds. At such times I seem to be literally resting in and on the Divine. Sometimes He touches only a few fibers in some very small muscle, and through these He fills and thrills my whole being with unutterable divine glory. At times His holy touch is very delicate, tender and meltingly sweet. At other times He touches me with a power that moves the very foundations of my being, and that seems almost startling. Sometimes He moves very slowly, at other times so rapidly that it seems as if the next wave of glory would loosen my "spiritual body" from its present moorings in the "natural body." A few mornings ago while lying in bed under a divine influx that filled me with divine love and sweetness to the very utmost extent of my present capacity, I could but exclaim, "O Jesus, my dear heavenly Father! Thou alone art infinitely wise and infinitely holy! In Thy presence I am nothing, I am nothing! Before Thee I know nothing, I know nothing! These sweet touches of Thy spirit, these indescribable sensations, these angelic delights, these ineffable thrills of divine glory I cannot understand! I can now understand them no better than if I were a newborn infant lying at Thy feet! Such knowledge is too wonderful for me; it is high, I cannot attain unto it! Dear heavenly Father, I can no more understand how each divine touch can fill me with such holy sweetness and with such transports of joy, than I can understand how Thou canst create a world! O Thou eternal Word, by whom the worlds were framed! I can no more comprehend Thy present movings within my own little body, than I could have comprehended the ancient movings of Thy spirit upon the face of the great deep if I had been present when Thou didst say, 'Let there be light, and there was light.'" . . . .

Through the loving touch and conscious presence of an angel, be it a man or a woman, the Lord can fill me with celestial delights and sensations that are similar and almost equal to those produced by the direct inflowing of His own holy spirit. The difference between the two is easily discernible, but not easily described. Both are immeasurably superior to any soul or bodily delight we ever experience in the ordinary planes of Christian life. As near as I can describe it the difference between the two is this: When waves of glory are produced by the direct touch of the Divine Spirit they seem to have, as it were, a golden tinge, a delicate crest of holy sweetness, which does not accompany those produced through the touch of an angel . . . .

The angels are so thoroughly honest, so perfectly free from all false modesty and pretended humility, and are so free from all formality and human ceremonies, that the presence of an angel is always elevating and refreshing. . . .

The Lord touches me consciously now through the medium of His Written Word . . . .

When I read the Scriptures my whole "spiritual body" can feel the touch and power of the Living Divine that flows through its words and sentences, just as plainly and unmistakably as my natural body can feel the touch and force of the wind. And at times the "Spirit of Truth" flows all through me, and all over me, so forcibly that I feel as if I were literally "in the Truth." At these times the Eternal Word shines through the Written Word with such illuminating power that various human theories and speculations are scattered to the four winds. And under such illumination "it is given to know the mysteries of the Kingdom of God." . . . I can learn more in one hour under such practical tuition, than I ever have learned in a whole year at Yale Theological Seminary. In religion theories have their uses, but the school of experience is the only school that can be relied upon for instruction in the mysteries and deep things of God. It often seems to me as if the Christian world, ministers included, were looking more to their creeds, and to one another, for their theology, than to the Word and the Spirit . . . .

Before anyone can become personally acquainted with the Lord, and with the true meaning of His written Word, he must necessarily forsake every known sin and he must know what it means to live up to every known requirement and privilege of the Gospel. He must also ask for and receive a tender conscience, an enlightened reason, and a sanctified common sense. Then he will no longer be afraid to use his own reason and his own good sense. I have recently received from the Lord as I believe the following unsectarian motto:

"Love everybody, learn of everybody, and follow nobody but the Lord Jesus Christ."

To obtain and retain constant Divine guidance and tuition I find that my higher nature must bear complete and easy sway over my lower nature; that the "old man" must be wholly put off and the new man wholly "put on"; that the affections and thoughts of my "upward man" must have easy and complete control over every appetite, passion, and desire of my "outward man"; and that I must keep myself so full of the Lord, that I can live "a heavenly life upon earth," in all places and under all conceivable circumstances, just as easily and naturally as I can breathe the sweet air of heaven . . . .

This loving and indescribable union with God is no longer a mere matter of faith with me, but it is a matter of actual knowledge and sweet experience.

While enjoying these heavenly experiences the Lord has given me better health than during any eleven months for the last twenty years.

> And he has dealt more tenderly with me than any human mother ever dealt with a helpless infant....
>
> I sincerely hope that the love and goodness of the Lord, so bountifully manifested in giving me such large foretastes of heaven while yet in the body, will prove helpful and encouraging to every honest-hearted reader. But since the ways of the Lord are infinite in variety let no one look for an experience precisely like mine. I have prayed for years that the Lord would make me just as pure, just as holy and just as useful as lay within the scope of human and Divine possibilities. He is now taking His own way to answer my prayers.[177]

In the following experience, it will be seen that this so-called Divine touch reveals itself as that of a Borderland bridegroom. It is taken from a letter written by a lady, a devout and pure-minded Christian, as will be noticed. Her experiences occurred at a well-known summer resort in the United States where a cottage for divine healing had been established. But as the letter was shown to me by a third party, I do not feel at liberty to mention the town, lest some clue be given to the writer's personality. Indeed, it was only upon this condition that the person who showed me this letter allowed me to make use of it herewith:

> Dear Sister:
>
> Since learning from Miss _________ that you know the experience which is mine, I have thought I should write you.
>
> At first, as the newly married Bride, I shrank from exposing the secrets of my *Love*. They were sacred between my Beloved and myself. Now, it has shown me that this wondrous truth, as well as all other truth, must be acknowledged, and that a most glorious part of my high calling is to cooperate with Him in calling his Bride unto Himself....
>
> For myself, I had not time to question; the truth was sprung upon me unexpectedly, and I just went under. The fears and questionings came afterwards; but blessed be my God! He did not let me parley long with the foe, but Himself strengthened me to shake off his power, and, coming fully under the shelter of *His love*, press on—until He has fully established me, and I impelled by His mighty Spirit within

177 *Under the Divine Touch*, by Chester E. Pond, 1432 Chestnut St., Philadelphia, Pa. First published in the *Mount Joy Herald*, Mt. Joy, Pa., under dates of April 8th and 15th, 1882. (ICC note)

me, reach eagerly forward to the glorious unfoldings of His *love* and *power* that lie beyond . . . .

Suffice it to say, I am in great and abundant fullness and blessing, alike in my physical and in my spiritual nature, and that His own abounding life flows in power through my whole being . . . .

I would have . . . *fully understand* that this is the fulfillment of the marriage relation between Christ and the body—that as he has been recognized in the soul as Lord over it, and also over the other parts and organs of the body, so now must He be recognized and accepted in the organs of generation as Lord over them; and *His life* must be allowed to come in, where, through fear of evil, the emotions of life have heretofore been suppressed. Satan is bound to beset the soul with fears, it may be the most terrible, and to whisper, perhaps, dreadful things. The only way is to remember the faithfulness of Him who has led us these many years—*never* betraying our *confidence.* Standing upon the written word, and casting ourselves in complete abandonment upon Him, let Him have His way in every part. The life abundant must flow into every part of His *purchased possession,* ere we are *fully* redeemed.

Inasmuch as we withhold from Him one part or organ, we are robbing God of just this much. God has given us no idle words in his written Word; *EVERY PROMISE* is to be realized by us, as we follow on, and enter into the experience portrayed in each particular position of the word . . . .

"The Body, the Temple of God." I These. 4:3, 4; I. Cor. 3:16–19;

"The Living Sacrifice." Rom. 6:11, 12, 13; 8:10–13 ; Rom. 12:1 ;

"The Bride and Husband." Isaiah 26:9; 54:5; Cant. 3:1; Eph. 5:29–32; 22, 23; 2 Cor. 11:2; 1 Cor. 12:21–23; Col. 1:25–27; Ezek. 26:25; Hos. 2:14–16; John 17:23; Hos. 19:20; Hos. 6:3; Rev. 19:7–9; Rev. 21; Ezek. 13, to end.

The Song of Solomon was not to be a dead letter but meant by the Holy Ghost to be experience of the *Bride of Christ.* I find now in wondrous reality in His written Word. The meaning, hitherto unknown, of different passages, stands out clear and distinct—and Living Word within me, throbbing and thrilling and permeating my whole being with His glorious Presence, bears witness of the written truth . . . .

One day, I read in the Word, being led to it, the assurance of the angel concerning Mary. Perhaps that day—or very soon after—the Spirit brought to me, as I was preparing dinner, "Fear not, that which is conceived within thee is of the Holy Spirit." Such a rapid and powerful witness to the word went through and through me, beginning at the organs of generation, going all through, that I was in great weakness, physically. The tempter had been busy about this time, casting fear upon me lest the flesh were in the matter. Thus the Spirit gave him answer—with the revelation came the thought, "I am with child!"—but so sure was the witness, that instead of being greatly alarmed—*praise* the *Blessed One*, a great *joy* swelled up within me at the thought of such a possibility.

A *glorious victory*, afterwards. He showed me that it meant that this precious truth of the marriage relation between us was, "that which was in me was of the Holy Ghost." *Praise the Lord!* He has made me willing to do—to bear—to suffer anything for Him. He is making me fearless and filling me with His own desire for the spread of *all* His *truth*—though I feel more especially the desire to win souls for Him. I am assured that this, His most glorious and satisfying revelation of Himself *must* be acknowledged as He shall call upon us to do so, or we shall come into darkness indeed, and distress. Shall the chosen and honored wife shame to confess her husband when He would woo others, through her, to the same high place?

When we enter into this union, He is, as never before, the Life within us, and how shall we seek to suppress the Life that has entered in to displace our own old self-life, and to manifest Himself in and through us, in *whatever way He wills*. He must be permitted to speak through us—and as I constantly pray, to love, through me. Oh! with us there must be no question but one, viz: "What wilt Thou, my Beloved?"—and ready response, opening up to meet His blessed will. "As Thou wilt"—"no longer I, but *Christ*." No more *my* will, in the slightest particular, but the honorable will of my Beloved.

Reading Madame Guyon in *Spiritual Progress*, Part II, on "Union with God," I find the experience into which I have entered . . . .

We have, in these last days, by the . . . been realizing, as we did in the earlier days, the Presence and power of Him whom *we love*. God comes upon us as we meet together from 6 to 7 o'clock in the morning, to wait in silence before Him—at the table, before and after meals; as we partake of the food He gives. We meet Him in our rooms, and bow down before Him. As I go about my work, ofttimes, His Presence so fills me—or I hear the sweet wooing of His Voice, until I am constrained to step aside, where I may—to be *alone* with my *Love*, and fall at His feet in adoring worship . . . .

One asks, how is this Baptism obtained? In the *same way* exactly that all other of His gifts are—if we are in the condition to receive them, that is, by faith. He says, "Thy Maker is thy husband," and "in that day thou shalt call me—Ishi." . . . .

I would say, whatever you do, do not question, lest distress and perplexity come in; but immediately go to Jesus, accepting Him as Ishi—with the words I have given—"be it unto me as Thou wilt." He will do the teaching afterwards. Then again, lest one should make of it too scriptural a truth, separating it entirely from the physical, it should be plainly understood that the *union* is as the sexual intercourse of husband to wife.

If we expect this when the sensation comes, we will not be alarmed, but willingly and freely give those parts to our Divine Husband as the Bride would naturally do.

I have written very plainly, because, first, I know it is the way He would have me write; and secondly, because I would seek to save from distress and fear, that would harass, if the whole truth is not understood, viz: If one looks for one kind of manifestation (spiritual), and finds physical and animal.

Let me hear from you both, when the Lord leads.

Lovingly in Him.[178]

The same friend who showed me the above letter also showed me letters from a gentleman who is the editor of a religious newspaper, giving a similar experience upon several occasions in his life but with more circumstance of detail. Nevertheless, he regarded it as entirely a union with Christ, the Bridegroom of the Soul, and spoke of it reverently.

Madame Guyon[179] has left us memoirs of her rapturous union with the Divine Bridegroom of the Soul, and verses concerning His love and watchful tenderness which are rare specimens of pure and delicate sentiment. Yet,

178 For convenience of future reference let us call the authoress of this letter Mrs. R. S. T. (TS note)

179 Jeanne-Marie Bouvier de la Motte-Guyon (1648–1717), a French Roman Catholic mystic and follower of the Quietist heresy founded by Miguel de Molinos. She was imprisoned by the Church from 1695 to 1703 and her books banned.

so little was Borderland wedlock understood by the learned of those days, that Bossuet made a coarse joke about her marriage with the Child Jesus; and another French bishop, says Arthur Little, wrote what might almost be called an episcopal lampoon. One couplet will be enough:

> Par l'epoux quelque foi une jeune mystique
> Entend un autre epoux que celni du Cantique.[180]

From which it would seem as though the Roman Catholic Church admitted that there might be objective realities in Borderland wedlock (so far at least, as appears on the surface) which eschew objective phenomena on the Borderland and tries to keep her mystics entirely in the realm of subjectivity—a realm where illusions arise through the ease with which it is confounded with objective planes and where a well-trained mind is needed to distinguish between that which is suggested or thought hypnotically and that which actually occurs. And yet, it is for a Divine Bridegroom on the Borderland that the Church has long trained her nuns in the life of ascetics. For in various forms of austere self-denial, asceticism as well as total suppression of the sex-nature is an absolute preliminary step to Borderland nuptials, though only for a time. The question arises however: who is this Divine Spouse of the purified and ascetic nun? Is it Christ? Or is it an angelic lover? The Church says Christ when the union is uplifting and insists that the relation is entirely mystical and not at all objective. I think, from the testimonies in which I have adduced from Church writings, an angelic bridegroom is not impossible. And it is quite conceivable that, where a nun believes that Christ is the only Borderland Spouse, her prejudice may result in her lover's appearing to her as Christ, just as the mediaeval witch who believed that her Borderland spouse could only be the Devil was pretty sure to see him with horns and hoofs and to be whisked away (subjectively) to a Witch's Sabbath of diablerie.

Madame Guyon, indeed, admits that "the vision is never of God himself nor scarcely ever of Jesus Christ, as those who have it picture it to themselves: it is an Angel of light, who, according to the power which is given to him by God for this purpose, causes the soul to see his representation, which

180 "A young woman who is mystical understands another spouse than that of Canticles." (ICC note)

he himself takes."[181] (That is, the vision is subjective, probably a hypnotic suggestion induced by the angel.)

The following stories of saintly Catholic women who became espoused to a Borderland bridegroom show that they were untrained in distinguishing subjective from objective phenomena. No wonder then, if they should mistake an angel for Christ himself.

> The following is from the Act of Canonization:
>
> "St. Mary Magdalene, born of the illustrious house of the Pazzi at Florence . . . burned with so great a heat of divine love, that she would at times exclaim . . . 'O love! I can bear thee no longer!' and she used to be forced to cool her bosom with a copious sprinkling of water. . . . By Christ she was *wedded with a ring* . . . and crowned with a crown of thorns; whilst by the blessed Virgin she was covered with a most white veil, and by St. Augustine she had twice written upon her heart: 'The word was made flesh.' Being rapt out of her senses whilst embroidering, she used, though the windows were closed up and her eyes veiled, yet to proceed with her work, and finish it most accurately. . . . She was canonized by Clement IX in 1669."[182]
>
> We will now look at the Legend of *St. Rose of Lima*, whose festival is observed on August 30.
>
> "The first flower of sanctity from South America was the Virgin Rose, born of Christian parents at Lima, who even from the cradle shone with the presages of future holiness: for the face of the infant being wonderfully transfigured into the image of a rose, gave occasion to her being called by this name; to the which afterwards the virgin Mother of God added the surname, ordering her to be thenceforth called the Rose of St. Mary. At the age of *five she made a vow of perpetual virginity* . . . .
>
> "Having wondrously familiar intercourse, by continual apparitions with her guardian angel, with St. Catherine of Sienna, and the Virgin Mother of God, she merited to hear these words from Christ—' . . . Rose of my heart, be thou my spouse.' At last being carried to the Paradise of this her Spouse, and glittering with very many miracles, both before and since her departure, Pope Clement X enrolled her with solemnity in the Catalogue of Holy Virgins."

181 Jeanne Marie Bouvier de La Motte Guyon, *Autobiography of Madame Guyon* (London: Kegan Paul, Trench, Trübner and Co., 1897), vol. 1, pp. 69–70.

182 Lewis Hippolytus Joseph Tonna, *Nuns and Nunneries: Sketches Compiled Entirely from Romish Authorities* (London: Seeleys, 1852), pp. 37–38. (ICC note)

The following are extracts from the Bull of her canonization:

"... At this time she was favored with the following revelation: There appeared to her in her sleep an extraordinary person, beautiful above all the sons of men, habited like a first-rate sculptor on a festival-day, and he seemed *to court her as a lover.* Before Rose would *consent to his proposal,* she set him a task, namely, to carve a piece of marble; and she bade him return again shortly, when the sculpture should be finished. At the return of her spouse, the virgin blushed when she perceived the task she had assigned him was accomplished in a manner beyond his strength; and he opened to her his workshop, where were a number of elect virgins, working like men at carving and polishing marble. She discovered that they were his espoused, by the style and beauty of their nuptial dresses; they were moistening the stones, and preparing them for cutting by their tears, which dripped upon them. Rose perceived that she was to be dressed like one of them, and prepared to be advanced to a like espousal.... The mystery was disclosed to her thus: On Palm Sunday, when Rose was absorbed in meditation, in the chapel of the Blessed Virgin of the Rosary, *her lover* thus addressed her: 'Rose of my heart, *be my love.*' The virgin trembled at the sweet voice of her Divine Spouse, and at the instant she heard the voice of the Mother of God, *wishing her joy,* and saying, '*Rose, it is no mean honor which this my Son proposes to you.*' After this revelation, Rose began to torture herself more than ever.... When her Spouse did not appear to her at the accustomed hour, she used to admit an angel (who was always *visibly* present with her as her guardian) to her confidence, as his footboy or valet!!! (*ut pararium aut veredarium.*)[183]

Various miracles were said to have been wrought through St. Rose of Lima such as, for instance, the materialization of bread and also of honey in her father's house in time of scarcity; also, in answer to prayer, the payment of a debt of her father's by a stranger who appeared at the house, bringing the money wrapped up in a cloth.

"These are the assistances which her divine Spouse promised to the parents of Rose, that he would give her as a dowry, *when he wooed her* in the character of a heavenly sculptor."[184]

183 Joseph Tonna, *Nuns and Nunneries,* pp. 38–41.
184 Joseph Tonna, *Nuns and Nunneries,* p. 42.

In this last, we seem to be getting back to these angelic bridegrooms spoken of in ante-Nicene Christian literature, who materialized gold and other precious articles for beloved earthly spouses.

But, it may be asked, are these unions with a heavenly spouse mere marital unions with angels, and does God (or Christ, as His human manifestation) play the part in them? By no means. God is a party to Borderland wedlock in its highest aspect, whether that wedlock be an objective marriage union as in earthly wedlock, or subjective and mystical blending with a divine invisible intelligence. Madame Guyon was right in saying that her love toward God and God's love toward her was the blissful feature in Borderland experience. There are lower aspects of Borderland wedlock than that which includes union with God; which are subject more or less to illusions, fantastic or diabolical. Only when the earthly partner aspires to the Divine Soul of all things, does the supreme bliss of union with the angelic mate transpire. At such times one is fain to apply such a conception as that of Mrs. Gillen,[185] a London teacher of Divine Healing, which is:

> The Universe consists of three factors—a Thinker, outward Expression of His thought, and the realm of Mentality which lies between that Thinker and His Expression, and which is the means by which the Untreated shapes what it thinks into Expression in physical, material forms. If we conceive this Great Thinker (God) as the central nucleus of a great circle[186] which embraces the Universe, his Expression of thoughts, motives, feelings, will be on the rim of the large circle, and the sphere of Mentality, where those thoughts are being molded into shape previous to Expression, will be the zone lying between the nucleus, or Central Thinker and the outer rim of His all-embracing circle. Each living creature, as part of this great circle, is a sector of the circle—thus:

185 Alma Gillen (b. 1864), a proponent of Divine Healing and editor of *Expression: A Journal of Mind and Thought*. Divine Healing (or Divine Science) taught that illness originates in the mind, and that health and prosperity may be obtained by cultivating a positive attitude. It was a direct predecessor of the New Thought movement, which gave rise to Science of Mind (also known as Religious Science) founded by Ernest Holmes (1887–1960). The "Law of Attraction" popularized by the 2006 film *The Secret* also originated from New Thought.

186 This should be, of course, a sphere, and it is thus that Mrs. Gillen prefers to conceive the Universe. But a circle, being flat, is easier of comprehension by non-mathematicians when divided into sectors, and I have therefore adopted Mrs. Gillen's method of this easier representation. (ICC note)

> Such a sector consists, as does the entire circle, likewise, of three factors,—(1) that which thinks; (2) mentality, where thoughts are shaped; (3) the body, the material life, where spirit finds expression as outward form. Nos. 2 and 3—mentality and the bodily form—are but the instruments of the spirit, the thinker within us. The thinker within us is part of the Great Thinker at the center of the circle of the Universe.[187]

So that, according to Mrs. Gillen, it is incorrect to say "I have a spirit." We should say "I am spirit": i.e., "I am part of God." When the zone of our mentality is kept unclouded between our material, bodily form and that within us (up at the point of the sector)

which thinks, we are, as will be seen, in unbroken communication with the Great Thinker, God, who is Himself all in all: for our thinking self is part of Him. The application of this conception, from Mrs. Gillen's point of view, is that when that zone of mentality is unclouded by dislike or other antitheses of love, then disease and other mundane annoyances no longer exist for us; since, being part of God, and being one with Him at the heart of the Universe, we have His power to create outward circumstances.

From my own point of view, this conception has a bearing on the third and highest degree in the mysteries of Borderland wedlock. But before enlarging this, it may be well to begin with the preliminary training necessary to render one the Borderland wife or husband of an angel, and to set forth the three degrees in order with such detail as may be allowable in a work like this, which is intended for the general public. The reader's hope to

187 Alma Gillen, unknown source.

profit by these instructions for personal development, inasmuch if one can persuade one's earthly partner to try, with one's self, to live the life which is obligatory for Borderland wedlock, brings the Kingdom of heaven into earthly relations.

The preliminary training necessary may be summed up by the admonition: Live a correct moral life, according to our own highest standard (a standard, by the way, which should never be fixed, but always moving onward to still greater excellence) and to strive to think clearly and to form accurate conceptions of ideas, to express conceptions of ideas, to express conceptions with exactness, and to follow Truth, wherever she leads, and whatever your previous convictions upon any given subject. Especially you must have high and clean thoughts about sex, that you can think about it, read about it, talk about all the details without agitation, without grossness of thought, and with as impersonal a state of mind as if you were discussing the circulation of the blood. And you must learn to recognize the educational value of sex attraction in the evolution of humanity from savagery into civilization. Chiefest of all, learn that sex is holy before God and the angels. During this preliminary training, all sex union must be refrained from absolutely. The nervous energy which has hitherto been evoked for expenditure in this direction must no longer be expended, but, by continual self-mastery, be returned to the system for its upbuilding. Gradually, as the neophyte who has habituated himself to a pure-minded and idealistic conception of sex becomes accustomed to thus maintaining self-poise, no matter what the temptation, there will spring up in him a joy in his own power which will amply repay him for all his struggles.

This process may take months, or it may take years. The Hindus have a saying that he who seeks a Borderland spouse must have known no women for seven years. But whether the process be long or short, whether the partner be sought by Borderland or on the earthly plane, it must be perfected before the first degree can be entered upon. For those who would like to have at hand some textbook to help in passing this preliminary training, I would recommend a little pamphlet entitled *Practical Methods to Insure*

Success.[188] It is written from such a standpoint that it can be placed in the hands of young people, and it is suggestive rather than exhaustive of the subject under consideration. But it has nothing to do with Borderland wedlock, and, so far as I can tell, it seems to make this training—which I call preliminary—almost the ultimatum. It also advocates, incidentally, one or two ideas such as astrology and the necessity for occasional fasting, the truth of which, it seems to me, remain to be proven. But apart from these things, it is so admirably written that it will furnish a safe groundwork for any neophyte to build up his ideal sex life upon, and therefore I earnestly recommend its perusal. The first degree should not be entered upon, as I have said, until the neophyte is proficient in this preliminary training.

The first degree embodies the teaching of what is known as Alpha-ism. Its principle is: "No sex union except for the distinct purpose of begetting a child." The bearings of this principle will be discussed in my forthcoming treatise on "Psychic Wedlock."[189] Suffice it to say here that the staunch adherence to this principle has uplifted and brightened the lives of many husbands and wives who had begun to find the marriage state a hell on earth. But it is a mistake to consider this the most advanced teaching regarding the marital relation. It is beautiful, helpful, and necessary to acquire for those who would live the life of the truly wedded: but it is only the first of the three steps which lead husband and wife up to the ideal relation. In *The Christian Life*, a journal edited and published by Rev. J. B. Caldwell, Chicago, the teaching of Alpha-ism will be found set forth clearly and reverently.[190]

Following this should come another pamphlet called *Diana*, written by

---

188 Published by the Esoteric Publishing Co., Applegate, Placer Co., California. It will be sent free on receipt of postage. (ICC note) [Hiram E. Butler, *Practical Methods to Insure Success* (Applegate, CA: Esoteric Publishing Co., 1893). These "practical methods" include eating only bland foods, leaving open a window for fresh air while sleeping ("no matter how cold the weather"), bathing every morning in cold water, fasting, and regular enemas. Butler (1841–1916) was an astrologer, sex magician, and founder of the G.N.K.R. (Genii of Nations, Knowledge, and Religions), which emphasized sexual continence as a key to spiritual progress. The GNKR (along with the Hermetic Brotherhood of Luxor) was denounced by Blavatsky in 1889. See Godwin, *The Hermetic Brotherhood of Luxor*, p. 213.]

189 See chapter 3.

190 *The Christian Life* was the organ of the National Purity Association, which advocated coition only for the purpose of procreation. Its president, a Christian minister named J. B. Caldwell, was arrested in 1890 for violation of the Comstock law by publishing an article on "marital purity" the year before. Although the moral stance of the NPA was compatible with Comstockian values, writing openly about sex, even to proscribe it, was not. In any event, his arrest was probably politically motivated, due to *The Christian Life* printing a criticism of the government's conduct in another obscenity case. His case was dismissed eventually.

Prof. Parkhurst, the astronomer.[191] This pamphlet is unfortunately marred by being printed in the reform spelling, but one forgets after a page or two. It is a psycho-physiological essay, intended for husbands and wives, written from a high standpoint, and in refined language. *Diana* will furnish the initiate with a bridge between the first and second degrees, and it is one of the most important and helpful contributions to the sex question that have ever been published.

It is evident that this first degree is likely to prove a stumbling-block to those who degrade this beautiful principle of Alpha-ism (a principle embodied in the Scriptural command, "Be fruitful and multiply") into an excuse for sowing more seed than is needed to produce the harvest. The man or woman who, whether in Borderland or in earthly wedlock, thus persistently distorts the above Scriptural command into a permission for something very different from what was intended, will never get beyond the first degree of the marriage relation. To create children is not only a high and holy joy to every right-thinking husband and wife, it is a solemn duty imposed upon them by the laws of their own being. And the psychic who shirks this duty in Borderland wedlock, although maintaining marital relations by the angelic spouse, will be misled by all sorts of fantastic or diabolical illusions. Conversely, whoever wedded on the Borderland to an angel holds fast the thought of the duty of the married to create (*under suitable conditions*), will ere long be shown the truth—i.e., that between two people dwelling on entirely different planes of matter, while the marital relation is possible, lawful and beautiful, to beget a child is impossible until the earthly partner shall have crossed to the world beyond the grave.

The principle of Alpha-ism must be mastered by those who aspire to the second degree, whether on the Borderland or the Earthly plane. The second and the third degrees have this principle for their cornerstone. In none of the three degrees is it allowable to sow the seed except for the distinct purpose of begetting a child who has been reverently and prudently planned for at just that time. Nor is it ever allowable to waste the seed by throwing it away (and

191 Published by the Burnz Publishing Company, New York, price 25 cents. (ICC note) [Henry Martyn Parkhurst, *Diana: A Psycho-Fyziological Essay on Sexual Relations for Married Men and Women* (New York: Burnz & Co., 1882). Parkhurst (1825–1908) was an astronomer and advocate of a reform movement that sought to simplify English spelling along phonetic lines. Like Ida, he had published a book on stenography.]

with it the psychic energy). The second degree launches the initiate upon the perilous water of sense-gratification. If his previous training has enabled him to build a staunch craft for the voyage, well and good; otherwise he may be swamped at the first wave, or, if he rides its crest, and the crests of succeeding waves, he may rashly venture too near the fatal rapids and be engulfed. It is possible that was the error into which Josephus says the "giants" fell when they trusted in their own strength. The second degree was practiced in the Oneida Community for thirty years, and was obligatory upon all its male members. The result was highly satisfactory despite the society's unsavory practice of community of women. They do not seem, however, to have seen the necessity for a similar training of female members. The author of that popular novel, *The Strike of a Sex*, has been preparing a book called *Zugassent's Theory*, which is intended to deal with this method from a popular standpoint.[192] I have not seen the work (which I believe is now going through the press); but from what I know of the author's reputation and his efforts hitherto in the cause of social purity, I feel that the book is likely to be judiciously worded and to be an aid in mastering the second degree. I doubt, however, if it deals with the training of the feminine partner. But the principles underlying the training of the man may be studied out from such a work and applied by the woman. The author is George N. Miller, 59 Murray St., N.Y.

The second degree is the most difficult of the three degrees to acquire physiologically speaking, inasmuch as it exacts supreme self-control at a crucial moment. Those who have never attempted this degree, when told of it, are apt to either declare it impossible, or to scorn it as undesirable. But those who have once mastered this degree would no more forego the power which is now theirs, than a freed prisoner would voluntarily return to his dungeon. This way lies the path of liberty and life, and joy, and they who have once trodden it in the perfect fullness of magnetic union with a dearly-loved spouse will never care to stumble along the old paths. The Oneida Community, despite its social mistake of promiscuity, has made the human race its everlasting debtor, in that it has left a thirty-year scientific experiment on record detailing the methods and attesting the value of this second degree.

192 George Noyes Miller, *After the Sex Struck; or, Zugassent's Discovery* (Boston: Arena Publishing Company, 1895). Miller (1845–1904) was a member of the Oneida Community and cousin of John Humphrey Noyes.

But let it never be forgotten that this second degree must be built upon the first degree, Alpha-ism. To make use of it as a means to increased sensuality is to degrade it, and to do so effectually bars the initiate from entrance upon that third and highest degree, where all joys—physical, mental, emotional and spiritual—reach an intensity beside which the joys of the first and second degree pale as a candle-flame in the radiance of sunlight. Moreover, if this degree be thus degraded by the initiate, it is almost certain to bring nervous diseases of a very distressing character in its train.

On the third, and highest degree, no book has yet been written, so far as I know. The teaching seems to have been handed down orally or else by pictured symbolism or mystic rite, understood only by the initiates of this degree. I am now compiling notes for my work on "Psychic Wedlock" which I hope will take up the projected three degrees in more detail than is possible in this treatise. For the present, I can only lay down a few general principles, and these principles cannot be fully grasped by any except those who have mastered the first and second degrees.

The Hindus have the theory that God can enjoy food, drink and in fact all sense-pleasures, but only through the offering of an earthly devotee. Therefore, the devout Hindu offers God a share in all his gratifications of appetite—thus living out, indeed, the Christian Apostle's admonition of "whether we eat or drink, do all to the glory of God." Too often, it is true, this doctrine is perverted into an excuse for sensual excesses, the debauchee soothing his conscience by an offering to the god whom he worships. Thus has this sacred inner mystery become degraded by the unworthy. But even the tried and staunch initiate of the first and second degree, unless he holds grace as he enters upon this third degree, unless he holds fast to the teaching: "Aspire to the highest." Only in reverent and earnest aspiration to the Divine, to the Source of all things, to the Eternal Energy of the Universe, may this third degree be entered upon, either in Borderland or earthly wedlock. The more intense the emotion, the more absolute the necessity for aspiring with all one's faculties to union with the Divine. Every element of selfish desire must be eliminated; one must aspire at that time, because it is right and beautiful to bring one's holiest and tenderest and most ecstatic emotions into the presence of the Great Thinker, in order that they may there be purged of all dross and be a worthy expression of our own best self. That is the first half of this highest degree. The second half is entered upon when spontaneously—not from selfish desire—it dawns upon us that to offer God a share of our pleasure at the moment may give him pleasure. When singleheartedly, and in all sincerity and benevolent feeling toward God, we invite him to become the third partner in the marital union, then, indeed, do we understand what it is to love and to be loved. We enter thus into a personal relation with God in which, Impersonal Force though He be, we realize vividly that we are one with Him, and with Him one with all the universe. For that in us which thinks—the apex of our particular sector of the circle of the universe, is on the one hand, in unclouded relation with our physical self on the outer rim, and on the other hand, it is merged into the Great Thinker, the Great Nucleus who is at the center of all creation. From that moment, we are able to say to this Pantheos, Great Thinker, to this All-Pervading Energy, "My *friend!*" (And inasmuch as God is love in the fullest possible sense of that expression, the connubial bliss of Borderland lovers is increased tenfold.) From that moment, we know what it is to truly love God. This divine trinity in unity must be the final goal of Borderland wedlock, if such wedlock is to be permanent.

It is in this sense, I am inclined to think, that Mme. de Guyon, St. Teresa, and other mystical Spouses of Christ received the Divine Bridegroom. Subjectively mingled with this rapturous union with Deity, no doubt, were the experiences of union with the angelic husband, of whose very existence as such they were unaware, confounding him with the Impersonal Deity who was the third element in their union. Then, too, we must remember that these women, intelligent as they were, were untrained in the nice distinctions of subjective and objective, hallucinatory, veridical, automatic, telepathic, subconscious, etc., [states, as] evolved by the modern Society for Psychical Research and other recent investigators of the occult. Moreover, there are psychical experiences in Borderland wedlock which are subjective while they seem to the untrained occultist to be objective. Of such a nature (apparently) was the experience of a Philadelphia lady, a Spiritualist, who told me of her spirit husband. She was a widow, and this spirit was a deceased lover from whom she had been separated in youth by a misunderstanding. He returned from the world beyond the grave to explain matters, and to reclaim his lost love, and finally proposed that she should consider herself to be his wife from that time on, assuring her that it was so recorded in his land. Thereafter, on several occasions, she experienced (when she was by no means prepared) a series of galvanic shocks extending upwards through her body. These were doubtless hypnotic suggestions to prepare and train her for experiences of a more objective character. The manifestations, however, were interfered with by the return of a chronic complaint of the liver with which she had suffered at intervals for years.

If it be asked how a misty, vaporous being, such as a ghost is popularly supposed to be, can sustain an objective marital union on the Borderland, I reply that the ghost is not mist-like in reality, but only appears so because he is in a new world of matter, with a more extended scale of vibrations per second for the various forces of sound, heat, light, and electricity than obtain upon our earthly plane. Beyond the last faint violet ray of the spectrum, science has demonstrated that there are rays of color to which we are blind, but which so lowly a creature as the ant can perceive. Dogs can trace a scent of which we have no perception. Many people are so color-blind as to be unable to distinguish a red from a green light—a fact brought out some years since very markedly in an examination for railway service in England. An astigmatic person is almost, if not quite, blind to a fine line running in some one direction. Recent experiments by Galton[193] have shown that cats and birds are sensitive to a whistle which is inaudible to the human ear. If our inferiors in the animal kingdom reveal such marked superiority to ourselves in sensitiveness to vibrations, is it unlikely that our former equal and our superior, the deceased human being who has passed out of earth life into a wider realm, shall also acquire sensitiveness to a wider range of vibrations? The ghost probably senses all things on our plane, plus a great many more things on his own. Our sensations are included in his, but his extend far on each side of our own. Therefore we cannot perceive his form or hear his voice in all his material relations, because he is in a world where forms, colors, sounds which we are physically incapable of perceiving—except in the exalted condition of the clairvoyant or clairaudient—are part and parcel of his daily life. When we see him, we see only through the narrow range of our own limited scale of

193 Sir Francis Galton (1822–1911) was an English anthropologist, inventor, and polymath.

vibrations: so that we see him but in part, and therefore mistily, or hear his voice but faintly, or perhaps not at all, as it may cover a range of vibrations per second quite one side or the other of our own scale of sound vibrations. For this reason, he is often obliged to speak to the psychic by the interior voice—a hypnotic rendition, apparently, of his voice through the medium of her subconsciousness. For this reason, because his voice is not audible, as a rule, to her physical ears, the psychic must learn to discriminate accurately between this interior voice and the voiced imaginings of her own subconsciousness, which will utter themselves quite as audibly as does the interior voice if the psychic has not acquired the faculty of holding her subconsciousness well under control. With experience, however, the discrimination comes in time to be made inerringly, as St. Teresa has stated.

Through the interior voice, a Borderland mystic may be wooed and won as a wife if she be clear-headed and keep the moral law with scrupulous care. She does not need to be clairaudient to hear her lover's voice interiorly. Nor does she need to be clairvoyant, if she be willing to go it blind, so to say. She is then in the condition, however, of a person who is totally blind; and who is almost totally deaf. She needs to be on the alert quite as much as if she were dependent on an ear-trumpet, in order to make no mistake in catching the remarks made by the interior voice. Nevertheless, even people who are blind and people who are deaf may fall in love with someone on this earthly plane and marry despite the defective means of communicating ideas. Fortunately there are other means of transmitting ideas than by the interior voice or by the eye or the ear. In this connection the following article by Paul Tyner[194] on "The Sixth Sense and How to Develop It" offers a suggestive thought:

> I have said that I regard psychometry as the key to the development, on rational lines, of the sixth sense. Psychometry itself seems to be a development on the psychic side of that physical sense, which is at once the finest, the most subtle, the most comprehensive, and the most neglected of all the five senses—the sense of *touch*. While

194 Paul Tyner (b. 1860), an itinerant social worker and a key figure in the New Thought movement, edited the New Thought journal *Arena* from 1898–1899. He was a close associate of Freeman B. Dowd (1825–1910). Dowd was a member of the Hermetic Brotherhood of Luxor, founder of the Temple of the Rosy Cross in Philadelphia in 1878, and a successor to Paschal Beverly Randolph. See John Patrick Deveney, *Paschal Beverly Randolph* (Albany, NY: State University of New York Press, 1997), p. 499.

> distributed over the whole surface of the body, through the nervous system, this sense is more delicate and sensitive in some parts than in others. The marvelous possibilities of its development in the hands are shown in the cases of expert silk buyers and of coin handlers. The first are enabled, merely by touch, to distinguish instantly the weight and fineness of a score of different pieces of cloth hardly distinguishable to the eye. Girls employed in the mints, while counting gold and silver coins at an astonishingly rapid speed, detect at once the minutest difference of overweight or underweight in the coin passing through their hands. The remarkable sensitiveness developed by the blind in the tips of the fingers, under such scientific cultivation as that provided in the Perkins Institute, of which Laura Bridgman in the past and Helen Keller in the present are such conspicuous examples, is familiar to most readers.
>
> It may not be so generally known that recent *post mortem* examinations of the bodies of the blind reveal the fact that in the nerves at the ends of the fingers, well-defined cells of gray matter had formed, identical in substance and in cell formation with the gray matter of the brain. What does this show? If brain and nerves are practically identical, is it not plain that, instead of being confined to the cavity of the skull, there is not any part of the surface of the body that can be touched by a pin's point without pricking the brain? It shows, moreover, I think, that all the sensations generally received through the other physical organs of sense may be received through the touch at the tips of the fingers. It proves that a man can think not alone in his head, but all over his body, and especially in the great nerve centers like the *solar plexus*, and the nerve ends, on the palms of the hands and the soles of the feet. The coming man will assuredly perceive and think in every part, from his head down to his feet. Need I suggest the importance of remembering, in this connection, how much in our modern life is conveyed by the hand clasp, or the deep delight that comes to lovers in caressing touches, when impelled to pat the hands or cheek of the beloved one, or to stroke her hair? It is through the emotional life that our sensitiveness is led from the physical to the psychic plane of sensation.[195]

It is through the nerves of touch that Borderland wedlock becomes objective. The lover may remain forever invisible, as in the fairy stories, material-

195 [Paul Tyner, "The Sixth Sense and How to Develop It,"] *The Arena*, Boston, June 1894. (ICC note)

izing only at night, and then only to the touch of those nerves most capable of sensing his tangibility. But, ghost though he be, it was the testimony of Reginald Scot in his *Discoverie of Witchcraft* that the Witch "hath more pleasure that way, they say, than with anie mortall man."[196] The angelic bridegroom, as well as this earthly partner, must live a correct moral life and think clearly; and this means that he must exercise a tenderness, a considerate regard for his wife's comfort and happiness, and also a marital self-control of which too many earthly men are ignorant. No wonder then, that on the plane of sentiment, she should prefer this ghostly spouse to "anie mortall man." And on the plane of physiological relations, I think I have already shown that the husband who is an initiate in the third degree, who has trained his wife therein, can assure her of connubial bliss which is perpetual. The Borderland bridegroom has this advantage, too, over the earthly bridegroom; being able to read his partner's thoughts, he can adapt himself to her most delicate fluctuations of sentiment at a moment's warning, and so never fail to be truly her companion.

"If one could prolong the happiness of love into marriage," wrote Rousseau, "we should have Paradise on earth."

In my own case, Paradise—the Kingdom of Heaven—has come into my earth life, and it has come through my heavenly bridegroom.

196 Reginald Scot, *The Discoverie of Witchcraft, Being a Reprint of the First Edition Published in 1584* (London: Elliot Stock, 1886), p. 44.

Postscript: from Ida's Diary[197] (1895)

Thursday, January, 3rd, 1895.

I have not been making entries lately, because (1) I have been going to bed too late to get much of anything; (2) Iases seems to have been choosing to use what psychic strength I had to issue instructions regarding the work on *Heavenly Bridegrooms*—a work which I think I can truly say, is much, much more due to his directing intellect than I should have ever dreamed possible for me as a psychic. The more I think about the way that "Heavenly Bridegrooms" has been put together, the more I am amazed. Certainly, I, by myself, should never have been able to concoct it as it now stands. That is not saying, of course, that it is going to be a suitable work for the public, although I trust it may be. But the great wonder of it all to *me* is that an outside intelligence seems to be running the machine, so to speak, and I am little more than amanuensis for him, —or it, whatever one may call that intelligence. Of course, I am, I trust, a fairly intelligent amanuensis, so that I have no hesitation about making corrections promptly of the matter given to me, when such corrections seem to be needed. But oftener it is the other way round, and Iases corrects *my* work. Many of the theories and explanations which I have put into "Heavenly Bridegrooms" I never, to the best of my belief and knowledge, had thought until the command came from him to write so-and-so at just that point in the treatise. But, when they were written, they commended themselves to my reason and common sense, and so I allowed them to stand, sometimes modifying them with a "probably," or "it seems likely," and so on, so as not to commit myself as holding such and such views implicitly. The quotations and authorities I have, of course, looked up myself in the first place. But Iases has arranged these quotations in such order as suited him best, I acting, as I have said, as a secretary for him. Many, many quotations which I had laid aside for this work, he emphatically rejected, as overloading the treatise, or as being calculated to shock the public and bring me into danger of

197 In January of 1895, Ida Craddock recorded the following account immediately after the writing of *Heavenly Bridegrooms*. This account was intended only for the man who had financed her during her researches in the British Museum. (TS note) [From an unpublished typescript, originally intended to form part of an introduction to Schroeder's publication of *Heavenly Bridegrooms*. The "man who had financed her" was W. T. Stead. This version has been corrected and conformed to Ida's original diary entry.]

legal suppression by the obscenists. From first to last, his great insistence has been that the book should be "suited to the general public," and that it must not contain anything upon which the obscenists could lay a finger.

In some cases this has been a great regret to me, as I have had to leave out one or two important arguments—for instance, arguments which would have included the phrase, "mental masturbation," a term which explains, I have reason to believe, much that goes under the name of "spirit communications" in these matters. Then, again, I begged, and begged, and begged that I might explain the exact English meaning of the Roman Catholic phrase, "*congressus cum daemonis*," but Iases objected every time, insisting that it was risky in *this* edition. You will observe, by the way, that the phrase as I have here written it and also in the treatise, is "*congressus cum daemonis*" whereas, in speaking with you, I have always used *daemonibus*. I have changed the expression for the following reason—which, as Iases has forbidden me to put it in the treatise, you may be interested in seeing here. I have never seen this phrase in any of the books which I have so far come across, and have heard it only once—from a Catholic priest with whom I was discussing my experience, and who was trying to frighten me by telling me that my husband was a demon. As I didn't believe in demons, and didn't believe that any evil-minded person who had passed to the world beyond the grave had power to communicate, much less harm me, I simply laughed at what he said. He afterwards said to a mutual acquaintance that I was—I forget the exact word he used, but it meant "invincible, unbreakable." Well, he at first told me there was a great deal of literature written on the subject; my experience was nothing, as similar experiences had been known for centuries in his own church, and the whole thing was very evil; there had been enough written on the subject to fill the room where we then sat. At once I asked, eagerly, would he please tell me the names of some of the books, so that I could read up on the subject? This was more than he bargained for, and he at once changed his tactics, and tried to make me think that I had misunderstood him in this last remark; what he had meant to say was that all that had been said on the subject could easily be crowded into that room. And from that moment I could get nothing out of him save that my experience was by no means unique, and that it was entirely evil, and the work of a demon. He several times used the phrase, "*congressus cum daemonis*" as the term applied by the Church to such unions. Afterwards I looked up the declension of the word "*daemon*," as it seemed to me there must be something wrong, grammatically speaking, about that phrase. As *cum* ("with") governs the ablative, and his expression was *daemonis*, which is the genitive, I concluded (rashly, as I am now convinced) that he had made a slip of the tongue, and that he must have forgotten his declensions, and have thought that *daemon*, which is really a noun of the third declension, was a noun of the first declension, whose dative and ablative plurals end in *is*. And so I always used it afterward, in speaking to you, as "*daemonibus*." But when I came to write it out in my treatise, I saw there was still something wrong about it, for that would make the phrase literally "congress with demons" whereas a psychic usually claims congress only with one, and not with a plurality of spirits. But before this idea had struck me, I had set myself to work to look up every possible exception to *cum*'s government of the ablative. I found, in a note, that sometimes the word which *cum* governs is omitted, and only the genitive dependent on the missing word appears. So that the phrase "*congressus cum daemonis*" would be quite correct, provided some missing word were understood—a word of an indefinite meaning, such as "that pertaining to," "the things of," etc. This would make "*congressus cum daemonis*" mean literally, "congress with something belonging to a demon."

Do you see the exquisite nicety of that rendering? Evidently, the psychics to whom that term was applied, had experiences just like mine, insofar as the fact that only "something belonging to" the spirit—i.e., his phallus—materialized; so that their "congress" was literally with "something belonging to" him. Compare this with what I have told of the two legends relative to Isis finding the pieces of her husband's body, in one case, all except the phallus, and in the other, none of the pieces except the phallus, from which solitary member she reconstructs the deceased husband. I did put in the legend of Isis, and wanted awfully to put in this about the "*congressus cum daemonis*," but Iases wouldn't let me. The priest who used this phrase was a very intelligent man, with quite a passion for book study, so that, you see, it really is very unlikely he should make this grammatical slip—in this language of all languages, which is *the* vernacular of the Catholic priesthood.

Chapter 3

Sexual Mysticism

In *Heavenly Bridegrooms*, Ida Craddock described a system of sexual mysticism having three degrees. The first degree, which she called "Alpha-ism," required strict sexual abstinence, the only permitted exception being for the purpose of procreation. The second degree, referred to as "Diana," allowed for sexual intercourse, but without ejaculation on the part of the male. Only after mastery of the first two degrees could the third degree be attempted, which involved inviting God to become a mystical third partner in a couple's lovemaking, thus providing them with access to divine consciousness. These degrees were succinctly set forth and elaborated upon in an essay entitled "Psychic Wedlock," which Ida began assembling during the writing of *Heavenly Bridegrooms* and completed the following year.

Ida's system has some intriguing similarities with that of the most well-known occult organization to practice sexual mysticism, the Ordo Templi Orientis ("Order of the Temple of the East" or "Order of Oriental Templars"). Formally established by high-ranking German Freemasons in 1906, the O.T.O. also had three degrees of sexual mysteries, originally developed by Carl Kellner[198] around 1895. The first degree of Kellner's system called for sexual chastity as well. In spite of these similarities, however, it is unlikely that Kellner was directly influenced by Craddock, or vice-versa. Although completed in 1895, neither *Heavenly Bridegrooms* nor

198 Carl Kellner (1851–1905) was an Austrian industrialist, Freemason, and Theosophist whose wealth allowed him to travel widely. He studied tantric mysticism during an extended stay in India.

"Psychic Wedlock" were published during Ida's lifetime; they were circulated only directly by her to a very limited audience of close associates. The O.T.O.'s teachings were also unpublished and made available only to initiated members. Nonetheless, a later leader of the O.T.O., Aleister Crowley, credited Ida with having "initiated knowledge of extraordinary depth" and "access to certain most concealed sanctuaries." He even speculated that her revelation of those secrets contributed to her untimely demise.[199] Apparently she had hit pretty close to the mark.

It has also been suggested that Craddock and Kellner were inspired by the same source.[200] Kellner may have been a member of the Hermetic Brotherhood of Light founded in Boston in 1895, which incorporated the occult sexual teachings of Paschal Beverly Randolph dating from the 1870s. The influence of Randolph undoubtedly found its way into the O.T.O.'s system of sexual magic, and the O.T.O.'s 1906 Constitution explicitly acknowledges its origins in the Hermetic Brotherhood of Light. In *Heavenly Bridegrooms*, Ida cites works by two individuals with known connections to Randolph: Robert Fryar, publisher of *Sub-Mundanes* (from which she quotes) and the main purveyor of Randolph's works after his death; and Paul Tyner, editor of the *Arena* and follower of Randolph's successor, Freeman Dowd. She also made notes from *In the Pronaos of the Temple of Wisdom* by Franz Hartmann,[201] an associate of Kellner and one of the founding members of the O.T.O. But she didn't cite Randolph directly until she wrote "The Marriage Relation" in 1900, quoting from *The Ansairetic Mystery* about the need for men to pace themselves to allow their partner time to orgasm.[202] By this time, the details of her three-degree system of sexual mysticism had already been worked out in full.

Furthermore, there are key differences between Ida's system of sexual *mysticism* and Randolph's and the O.T.O.'s teachings on sexual *magic*. In *Heavenly Bridegrooms*, Ida acknowledges the potential of her third degree to be used for magical purposes, noting that "an earnest wish breathed at that time . . . will not fail to be granted." She dismisses this, however, as a mere side effect of the operator's requisite self-control and harmony with

199 See Appendix.

200 See John Patrick Deveney, *Paschal Beverly Randolph* (Albany, NY: State University of New York Press, 1995), p. 252.

201 Franz Hartmann (1838–1912), a German physician, author, and Theosophist.

202 It is possible that Ida was exposed to the writings of Randolph by Henry and Belle Wagner, members of the Hermetic Brotherhood of Light who were active in Denver at the same time Ida was there working on "The Marriage Relation."

the universe; or, in the absence of these, as "black magic" destined to fail.[203] For Ida, the ultimate aim of sexual mastery is the mystical experience of union with the divine. This is in fundamental contrast to Randolph's teachings, which emphasize the attainment of magical powers through the sexual act.[204] Furthermore, Randolph insisted that "it is absolutely essential that the neck of the uterus be bathed in and by the husband's prostatic lymph and ejected semen *every time* they know each other,"[205] exactly the opposite of Ida's injunction against male ejaculation.

So although Randolph's works were certainly known to Ida, at least by 1900, they probably didn't play a significant role in the original formulation of her teachings. If that is the case, then where *did* they come from? We can confidently answer this question through careful examination of the evidence found in *Heavenly Bridegrooms* and in her diaries at the time of its writing. The name of Ida's first degree, "Alpha-ism," provides the first clue. The term is undoubtedly derived from E. B. Foote's 1882 book, *Dr. Foote's Replies to the Alphites*. Foote, whom Ida knew well through their Freethought connections, coined the term "Alphites" to refer to members of the Social Purity movement, which promoted the idea that sex should be undertaken only for the purpose of procreation. A prominent spokesperson of this group was Dr. Caroline Winslow,[206] who published a journal called *The Alpha*; thus the term "Alphites" denoted her followers. The debate raged on through the 1880s between Winslow and Foote, both medical doctors who advocated their positions from the standpoint of public health. Although politically and personally Ida would have been more sympathetic to Foote, she nonetheless recognized the value of the Alphite doctrine within the scope of her first degree, and cited another advocate of Social Purity, Rev. J. B. Caldwell, in the text of *Heavenly Bridegrooms*.

Ida's second degree, however, was a distinct departure from Alphaism, because it specifically inculcated sex for non-procreative purposes. Ida called this degree "Diana," after a work she cited in *Heavenly Bridegrooms* entitled *Diana: A Psycho-fyziological Essay on Sexual Relations for*

203 Nonetheless, according to her diary for September 16, 1897, Ida made use of sexual magic with her husband Soph to "bless and strengthen" W. T. Stead, who was suffering from ill health at the time.

204 Paschal Beverly Randolph's *Ansairetic Mystery* (1873) enumerates 122 of them.

205 Randolph, *Ansairetic Mystery*.

206 Caroline B. Winslow (1822–1896) was a physician, woman's suffragist, and advocate of sexual continence.

Married Men and Women. This curious pamphlet was written by a professor of astronomy, Henry Parkhurst, who had previously been a court stenographer.[207] The practice of Diana (named for the Roman goddess of chastity) was essentially Noyes' Male Continence, sexual intercourse without ejaculation. Parkhurst believed that this was a refinement of the Alphite doctrine, which made it practicable for ordinary men and women who would otherwise not have the discipline to carry it out. From *Heavenly Bridegrooms*, then, we can identify the sources of Ida's second-degree teachings as Parkhurst, Noyes, and George N. Miller (*Zagussent's Discovery*). In "Psychic Wedlock," Ida also introduces Alice B. Stockham's *Karezza*,[208] which differs from the others in that it advocates continence on the part of the female as well, requiring *both* partners to refrain from orgasm. This recapitulated her own view, set forth in "The Danse du Ventre," that the woman's self-control during coitus was just as important as the man's.

In "Psychic Wedlock," however, Ida introduces a second level to the second degree. At this level of mastery, the male obtains the ability to experience orgasm fully, but without ejaculation.[209] She notes that "this is a step beyond the teaching of even the Oneida Community, and I cannot refer the reader to any books upon the subject. But there are today men who have acquired even this power." This statement suggests that Ida acquired knowledge of this ability personally rather than through her library research, most likely from Westbrook.[210] She also describes a similar process for women, in which orgasm is repeatedly approached but not fully indulged until the partners are able to climax together, "in self-control and aspiration to the highest."

For the third degree of her system, Ida provides no citations. In *Heavenly Bridegrooms*, she states that no book has been written about it, but its

---

207 An interesting coincidence, considering that Ida had also started her career as a stenographer. Parkhurst was also an advocate of the Spelling Reform movement, an attempt to simplify American spelling to make it more phonetic, hence "fyziological" in the title of his pamphlet.

208 Published as *Karezza: Ethics of Marriage* (Chicago: Stockham Publishing Co., 1896). Alice Bunker Stockham (1833–1912) was a Chicago obstetrician-gynecologist and author of *Tokology* (Chicago: Alice B. Stockham & Co., 1886), a popular guide to childbirth and motherhood.

209 This ability is described in ancient Taoist literature, and was observed by Kinsey in the 1940s. For a modern discussion of this technique see Mantak Chia and Douglas Abrams, *The Multi-Orgasmic Man* (San Francisco: HarperCollins, 1997).

210 In an 1896 letter to E. B. Foote, Jr., Ida described a man who had mastered this level; although she did not name him outright, her description matched Westbrook precisely.

lessons have been passed down only through verbal, symbolic, or ritual means. Turning to her diary for the period, we find that, indeed, this was the case with Ida. In her entry for October 1st, 1894, she wrote:

> Mr. Harte called to see me yesterday, and we walked in Kensington Gardens, and had a long and interesting talk. One thing on which he laid emphasis was the Hindu idea that a god can enjoy only through a mortal, and that mortals ought to share their delights with the gods, or with God; and that the difference between the pious and the impious man was that the impious man forgets God, while the pious man remembers Him, and offers him a share of all his earthly enjoyments. Last night was the appointed time for union with Soph, and, as the union progressed, and the usual time came for praying to be united with God, I fell to thinking of Mr. Harte's remarks, and I thought how beautiful his idea was. I at once longed to give God the pleasure which my husband and I were having. I would here remark that I was playing Venus to his Adonis,[211] and that I knew it would probably be the last night before *tapu* time; and I felt, doubtless for that reason, more passionate than usual. At all events, I tried my best to be passionate and voluptuous and self-controlled, and at the same time to offer my enjoyment—I should say, *our* enjoyment—to God, as the all-pervading Spirit, the final Force with which all forces, material and spiritual, correlate; and I offered it, not as a mere scientific experiment, but out of love for God. I think I was never so near to feeling what it is to love God. And all the while, too, I was loving my husband, and striving to give him some of my magnetism, so that he could pursue his studies successfully with more ease, and also I was rejoicing with my husband over his promotion, and longing to make our union a sort of festivity for that occasion. In short, I felt many, many things at the same time; and the more I longed to give to God, the more I had to give. I cannot describe the deliciousness of the physical union, the passion, the voluptuous delight, far beyond any religious delight I ever had, of offering to God something that He really cared for. Oh,

211 I.e., she was lying face-down with him lying on top of her.

> if sensualists did but understand the joy of self-control, of aspiration to God in the very midst of one's ecstasy, and still more, the joy of sharing one's delight with God—well, they would turn with loathing from their present methods of performing the "act of kind"! I am so glad, so glad, to have had this experience, even if I never manage to again on earth. *It is the only right way, I know, I know, I know it.*

In her October 27 entry, she also noted:

> Of late, since I have learned actually what it means to share our joy with God thus, there are times when I feel that God, the All-Pervading Force, is my personal friend. Not, by any means, as a human incarnation; it is as a *Force*. And I feel as though I had a sort of claim upon him for help at trying times, and for protection in my gospel work. I feel that I can turn to him, as to an earthly friend, and say, at some special moment, "Do please help me." I think it is most wonderful and beautiful—this realization of the actuality of God at once as the One Sustaining Energy of the universe, and yet as my personal helper and friend, with whom I can interchange loving offices, giving pleasure *to* Him as well as receiving it *from* Him.
>
> And all this has come about from that first Sunday morning chat with Mr. Harte.

So who was this very helpful Mr. Harte, who orally transmitted the doctrine of the third degree to Ida? Undoubtedly it was Richard Harte (1855–1925), an American journalist living in London at the time, who was a long-time personal friend of Colonel Henry Steel Olcott (1832–1907), co-founder of the Theosophical Society. Harte had joined the Society early, within a few years of its founding in New York in 1875. He served as acting editor of *The Theosophist* journal for a time, and traveled to India in 1888 to represent the American section at the Society's headquarters in Adyar. But he eventually had a falling-out with Madame Blavatsky and, by 1893, was no longer active in the Theosophical Society. He remained in London, however, and was probably introduced to Ida by her patron, W. T. Stead.

Thus, all the pieces were in place for the writing of "Psychic Wedlock." Ida's teacher of Divine Science in London, Alma Gillen, provided the philosophy of "expression" and the terminology of the "Great Thinker" set forth in chapter 2. Albert Chavannes[212] was Ida's source for the concept of "sexual magnetism" exchanged by the partners in coitus as the true measure of satisfaction. Alpha-ism and Diana provided the basis for the first and second degrees treated in chapters 3 and 4, and Richard Harte inspired the idea, confirmed by Ida's own experience, of the third degree's "communion with deity" as described in chapter 5. This work represents Ida's full synthesis of a complete system of sexual initiation into the gnosis of divine bliss.

I have also included in this chapter a short piece by Ida that Theodore Schroeder extracted from her magnum opus, "The Marriage Relation," written in 1900. Schroeder titled it "Spiritual Joys" and submitted it pseudonymously to the occult journal *Azoth* in 1918 under the name "Cadi" ("Ida C." backward). I have restored two additional paragraphs from the original and included them here for the first time in print.

212 Albert Chavannes (1836–1903) was a successful American businessman and Freethinker, author of *Magnetation, and Its Relation to Health and Character* (Knoxville, TN: privately printed, 1899). Ida corresponded with Chavannes; one of his letters can be found in her surviving papers.

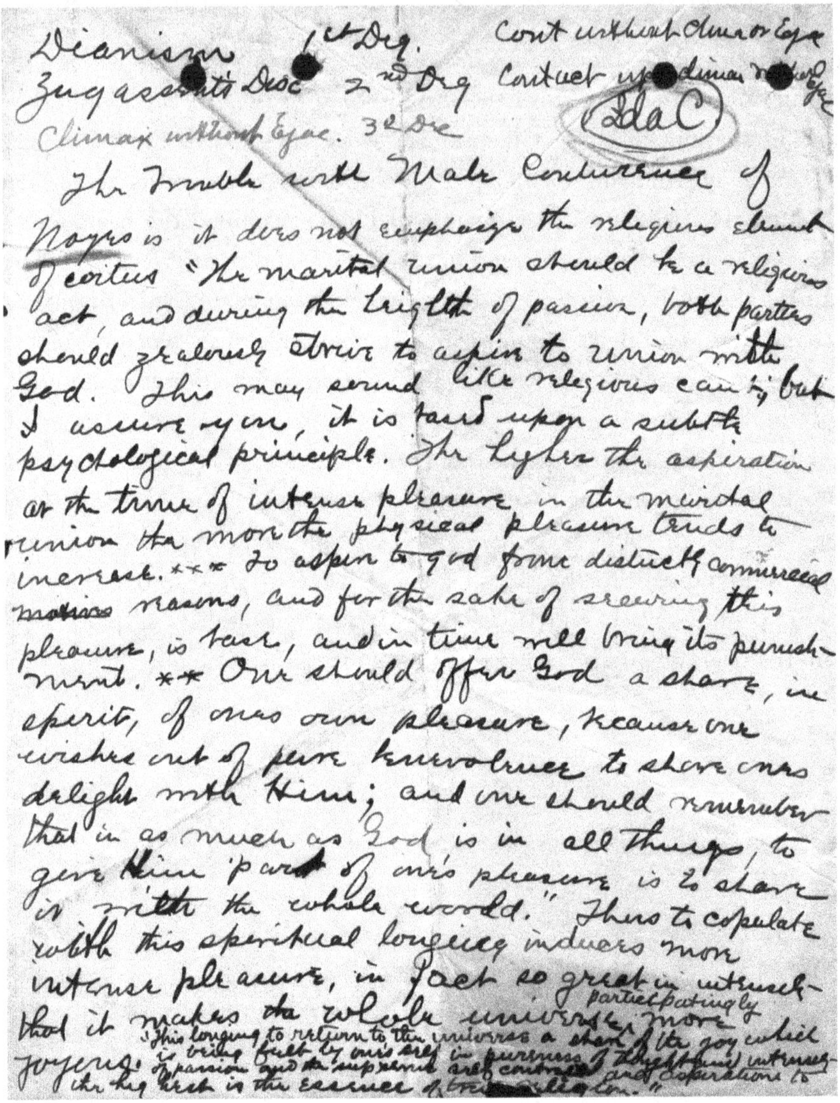

Dianism 1st Deg. Cont without climax or Ejac
Zugassent's Disc 2nd Deg Contact up to climax no Ejac
Climax without Ejac. 3d Deg

Ida C

The trouble with Male Continence of Noyes is it does not emphasize the religious element of coitus "The marital union should be a religious act, and during the length of passion, both parties should zealously strive to aspire to union with God. This may sound like religious cant; but I assure you, it is based upon a subtle psychological principle. The higher the aspiration at the time of intense pleasure in the marital union the more the physical pleasure tends to increase. *** To aspire to God from distinctly commercial motives reasons, and for the sake of securing this pleasure, is base, and in time will bring its punishment. ** One should offer God a share, in spirit, of ones own pleasure, because one wishes out of pure benevolence to share ones delight with Him; and one should remember that in as much as God is in all things, to give Him part of one's pleasure is to share it with the whole world." Thus to copulate with this spiritual longing induces more intense pleasure, in fact so great in intensity that it makes the whole universe participatingly more joyous. "This longing to return to the universe a share of the joy which is being felt by one's self in pureness of thought and intensity of passion and the supreme self control and aspirations to the highest is the essence of true religion."

Figure 5. Ida's notes on sexual mysticism, from the Ida Craddock papers, courtesy of SCRC.

Psychic Wedlock (1895)

Chapter 1: Introductory

Marital union takes place on three planes—body, mentality and spirit. In the perfect union, the amount of energy expended on any one plane is in exact equation with that expended on either of the others. But when the reverse occurs, the union is imperfect; and when the inequality is marked, the union has no claim to be called true wedlock.

Thus, when the energy expended upon bodily union is greatly in excess of that expended upon the mental and spiritual planes, it is called lust, and right-thinking people turn from it with a shudder.

When intellectual and artistic tastes are the chief basis of union between man and woman, we have a partnership in which mentality is in excess. Such unions are mutually helpful and bettering, for the two are then intellectual or artistic comrades. But if, as is too often the case, the body be ignored or despised, it is not wedlock, but Platonic friendship which really unites the two.

Union upon the plane of spirit in excess of either body or mentality is perhaps very rare. Like mental union *per se*, it has its peculiar raptures; but no mood of spiritual ecstasy can be permanently helpful if it fail to translate its raptures into an expression of energy upon the mental and bodily planes.

It is to suggest the duties and the joys of union in an exact equation upon all three planes that this little essay on Psychic Wedlock has been written.

There is a great deal of misapprehension today, among intelligent and refined people, regarding the relation which should exist between husband and wife. Sex union upon the bodily plane is too often deprecated as a concession to a degrading appetite; those who thus deprecate it, tacitly follow in the footsteps of St. Paul, who advised marriage as an outlet for uncontrollable passion, saying, "It is better to marry than to burn." The early Christian fathers almost universally chorused this idea, insisting that perpetual virginity in man and woman is the state which those should seek who wish to live the ideal life. Marriage was looked on as impure; and this idea crops up in the

Church and among the laity for several centuries, and is bearing fruit today in our social and religious customs. Christianity, so far as the writer is aware, is the only religion in the whole world which fails to give some teaching to its young people concerning their sex capacities and duties, so as to prepare them for the sacredness of the marital union. From whom, let us ask, do the prospective fathers of the race acquire their knowledge of sex powers? Usually from prostitutes, from gross-minded schoolboys, or from depraved men of the world. From whom do the prospective mothers of the race acquire their knowledge? Perhaps, at most, from French novels, or in the unhealthy atmosphere of girls' boarding schools, or from married women scarcely less ignorant than themselves. But usually their knowledge is acquired from the aforesaid prospective fathers, upon the wedding night. Can we wonder that the offspring from such parents tend more and more, as successive generations are born, to differentiate into two widely opposing types—on the one hand, the ascetic and the prude, who loathe the body as impure in all its sex relations, and on the other hand, the carnal-minded man or woman, whose thoughts about marital union relate chiefly to the body?

It is the prudish silence of the Church and of those whom she influences, which we in Christian lands have largely to thank for the marital unhappiness in our midst.

In savage tribes today, however ignorant, and in the old days of Paganism at its best—before Paganism had sunk into refined sensuality—we find a very different state of affairs. We find the dignity and holiness of the sex relation upheld by symbol and rite, by mythic tales and sacred dances. We find the medicine-man or priest instructing young men and maidens in the marital duties which they are about to assume—crudely, indeed, but with a mingled frankness and reverence for sex mysteries which we today should be a purer-minded people for imitating.

The ancient medicine-man has disappeared in civilized lands, having split up into three beings—the priest, the physician and the schoolteacher. But the old wisdom still survives in out-of-the-way places, and can be restored by the learned. And our wise men possess what the ancient Pagans and the modern savages did not and do not—a detailed knowledge of embryology, of many laws of sex physiology, and of certain aspects of psychology. Why should not the modern heirs of the old medicine-man—the priest, the physician and the schoolteacher—resume the position which is naturally theirs, of instructors of the young in that which all need to know who are likely to enter the marital relation?

The times are ripe for such a movement. People on all sides are eagerly seeking knowledge which shall lead them up, and not down, in sex matters. Will the Church, the medical fraternity and our academies of learning continue to neglect their duty?

Let us hope that all three will erelong awake to the vital necessity for some organized and systematic teaching to the people upon sex—teaching which shall treat frankly of those physiological matters which are expunged from our school-books; teaching which shall set forth in its true light the hygienic value of sex union for every normally constituted man and woman; which shall show the moral obliquity of those who, whether legally married or not, create children by accident, and not by intention; which shall insist upon the sacredness of the wife's person; which shall uphold the duty of union in self-control and aspiration to the highest, and which shall not blush to frankly add that such self-control and aspiration will result in increased pleasure to both husband and wife. Last, but not least, let us have teaching which shows how the path to that ideal life which we all of us hope and mean to live, lies *through the senses* to the Highest whom we variously term God, the Unknowable, the Ideal, Unconscious Energy, Law, Force, etc.

Meanwhile, however, since our natural teachers, the physician, the priest and the schoolteacher, remain silent on this vital question, we of the laity must do what we can to enlighten each other. And the present essay on Psychic Wedlock is an attempt to do this, in a small way. Such truth as I have discovered, I desire to share with my fellow-beings, hoping that they will add thereto, and pass our joint knowledge along to others.

It will be observed that this essay treats of three degrees of initiation into psychic wedlock. These three degrees seem to be bound up with the inner mysteries of pagan religions everywhere; but the second and third degrees in especial appear to have been jealously hidden from the people, and to have been imparted only to those who had passed certain ordeals, and had thereby proved themselves worthy. These things were also bound up with Borderland occultism under certain aspects. In ancient times, the people had not the public school; they were more ignorant of the natural sciences than is the merest schoolboy of today; so that there was a good reason then for keeping advanced sex mysteries carefully hidden from the masses. Moreover, the science of psychology (which we may here use as a convenient term to include all effects of mind upon mind) was then in its infancy. What Dr. Carl du Prel[213] terms "the displacement of the psycho-physical threshold of sensibility" through dreams, hypnotism, drugs, insanity, anger, strong emotion, etc., was in those days studied and understood only by the learned few, mainly the priests. The latter produced the "temple sleep" (nowadays known as the hypnotic sleep) in which the inner sensibilities of the hypnotized subject, exalted to an unusual degree, brought about remarkable results in prophecy, medical prescriptions, clairvoyance, telepathy, etc. Today, however, the science of hypnotism is exploited in medical and lay journals, so that any non-professional reader may inform himself of its wonders in detail; and the Society for Psychical Research has carefully collated hundreds of well-attested cases of thought-transference which indicate that the faculty of telepathy is a common property of humanity.

But even today, the realm of psychology contains vast unexplored tracts.

One of these as yet unexplored tracts is the psychic effect of mind upon mind during the marital union. People who would shrink from drugging themselves with liquor or opium, and who hold that yielding to so-called "spirit mediumship" is dangerous, will, nevertheless, recklessly abandon their self-control during the sex ecstasy. It is well established that a child conceived when the father is drunk will be mentally unbalanced, usually to the borders of idiocy. If intoxication—i.e., lack of self-control—at the moment of conception be produced by other means than by alcohol, is it likely that the resulting offspring will not be tainted thereby?

Now, the keepers of the ancient mysteries probably did not know what we in modern days know about physiology, embryology, and similar ologies.

---

213 Carl Freiherr du Prel (1839–1899), a German philosopher, Theosophist, and author of *Die Philosophie der Mystik* (Leipzig: Ernst Günthers Verlag, 1885); studied hypnotism, dreams, and spiritualism. Sigmund Freud called him "that brilliant mystic."

But they seem to have learned sufficient to realize the importance of never displacing the psycho-physiological threshold of sensibility during the sex union, except in a state of absolute self-control. And the acquirement of this self-control appears to have constituted the second degree in initiation. But because it puts the begetting or non-begetting of children entirely within the power of the parents, and because it intensifies the delight of wedlock, they probably feared that it would be a dangerous knowledge to place within reach of any but a worthy initiate. Hence it was and still is jealously guarded from the general public. But inasmuch as we of the nineteenth century live in an era of almost universal education, it would seem as though the time had come when this second degree, and also the third and final degree, may be more widely imparted.

The following are the three degrees treated of in this essay:

1st. Sex union forbidden, except for the distinct purpose of creating a child at that particular time.

2nd. Sex union enjoined in absolute self-control and aspiration to the highest.

3rd. Communion with Deity as the third partner in the marital union.

To those who wish to train themselves in these three degrees, I would say: *self-control* is the keynote. And in order that self-control may be acquired with as few setbacks as possible, I strongly urge that all liquor, tea, coffee, tobacco, opium or other narcotics be dispensed with from the first moment of entrance upon the training until the final acquisition of initiateship in the third degree. These things, one and all, displace the psycho-physical threshold of sensibility, each after its own fashion; so, also, does the emotion evoked during the sex ecstasy; and it seems foolish to wantonly increase the ordeal through which one must pass in acquiring the marital self-control of the second degree.

Another point which is of the highest importance in the preliminary training of the would-be initiate is, that he or she shall learn to look upon the human form divine with emotions which never degrade, but which always seek to idealize their object. Whatever the neophyte's opinion as to the wisdom or unwisdom of the nude in art, he must acquire the habit of viewing the human form, wherever and however *he* lights upon it, with chaste emotions, and without agitation. Until he can do this, he is not worthy to enter upon even the first degree.

He must also acquire the ability—if he does not already possess it—of hearing sex physiology discussed without undue agitation, and of discussing it himself upon a high plane. In short, he should strive to become master of his emotions, as a necessary preparation for entrance upon the first degree.

But asceticism should never be an ultimate aim. It is useful only as furnishing a gateway to higher, purer, more refined and more spiritual, as well as more enduring, sense-pleasures.

If we would conquer a fractious horse, do we do so by felling him to the earth? By no means. We control him by the bridle, and by gentleness; or again, we apply whip or spur, being careful to hold a tight rein; and at last we can guide him at our will. To kill him or even to stun him is not to truly master him. And to crush the sex nature out of existence is not to truly master it, either. We can bring our sex powers under our control only by applying similar methods to those which we should adopt with a high-spirited, full-blooded horse. Sex desire is nothing to be ashamed of; it is something to rejoice in, provided it be governed as absolutely as we govern an impetuous horse, allowing it to do nothing but what our higher self wills it to do.

And oh, the joy, the joy of self-control! Only they who have thus conquered can understand!

Chapter 2: The Individual and the Universe

To appreciate the highest aspect of psychical wedlock, and therefore of the inferior degrees which have the third degree as their goal, it is necessary to frame some philosophical conception of the relations existing between the individual and the universe. This conception should be one upon which Christian and non-Christian, Atheist and Theist can agree.

To seek to measure the infinite by the finite is, of course, absurd; but to deduce from the finite some of the laws of the infinite—i.e., from the known, a partial knowledge of the laws of the unknown of which that known forms a part—is both logical and satisfying.

The following conception will, I think, be found to have at least the merit of simplicity:

Every act of the individual is an *ex-pression* (something *pressed out*) from the inner to the outer. The process consists of three stages. Let us say that a man

(1) Conceives the idea of pushing a ball out of his path.
(2) He determines how the ball shall be pushed aside, with hand or foot, gently or powerfully, etc.
(3) At the command of his mentality, his body performs the act of moving the ball.

To produce the desired result, then, two factors concur:

First. The conception of moving the ball from his path.

Second. A definite thinking out of the method, and a transmission of the order to the body.

If the second stage be gone through with clearly within the man's mentality, the result in the third and final stage of the process will be an exact *expression* of his original conception, "I will push that ball out of my path." But if his method of pushing the ball aside be not planned out properly, so that his mind fails to exercise full control of the bodily muscles, he will find the inertia of the ball successfully oppose him, and he may stub his toe, or let the ball drop on his pet corn before he accomplishes his intention.

Clear-headedness, therefore, is of the greatest possible importance. Our mentality must be kept clear and unclouded, if what we may term "the thinker" within us is to have its orders correctly transmitted to our bodily selves. We may view the mentality which intervenes between the thinker within and the body without as an atmosphere through which rays of light stream from the inward self to the outer body. When the atmosphere is clear and colorless, the rays reach their destination unaltered. When it is colored by prejudice or clouded by ignorance or dislike of anything or anybody, they likewise become colored, or they are distorted, refracted, or almost entirely swallowed up in the mist, so that the few glimmerings which reach our intellect (that side of mentality which blends with the body) can but mislead. Were our inward conceptions conveyed to our intellects through an atmosphere of absolutely unclouded, unprejudiced and loving mentality, our outward lives would be godlike, for the thinker within each of us is godlike, and in truth desires to realize only the highest ideal.

What if we imagine all humanity as laid side by side to match, so as to form one continuous body, one continuous mentality, one continuous inward self? We might represent this blending of humanity as taking place in a circle, thus:

In this imaginary representation of humanity, each human being is a sector of the circle, and at the apexes of the sectors, where each of us is the godlike thinker, the blending must of necessity be perfect, however imperfect the blending and sharply defined the sectors may be on the mental and bodily planes. At the center of this imaginary circle, where our godlike selves join those of our fellow-creatures, we are blended into one godlike spirit which is really the directing spirit of humanity—its *Great* "Thinker," so to say. If in this circle we include each living creature, whether plant or animal, we blend upon the "Thinker" plane with the egos or inward selves of all animate nature. And, what with the recent theories of "fatigue in metals," "chemical affinities of atoms" and "sex in minerals," it would perhaps not be unwarranted to include inanimate nature in our representation of the circle and sectors. If the members of the mineral kingdom have no life (as we understand life), at all events, they are the result of law, and appear to be the expression of that law, so that it would seem as though they also should be included as sectors in our circle.

This circle, it will be seen, images the universe, not as a kingdom, with the Deity as a king who distributes his favors with the partiality and favoritism of an Oriental monarch; but as a republic, in which each sector, however tiny, has a vote in the General Council which directs the entire universe. In Scripture, indeed, we are told that God not only made man in His own image, but also that he breathed his breath into man in order to make man a living soul. In Scripture we are also told that we are heirs of God and joint-heirs with Christ; and Jesus himself, in the Sermon on the Mount, exhorts us to be *perfect*, even as our Heavenly Father is perfect. So that, from a Christian as well as from a philosophical standpoint, we may consider ourselves as like unto God, and one with Him in spirit. Within ourselves, at the apexes of our sectors, each of us is Creator, for there we are one with Him; there also are we love, wisdom, power, and can create our outward lives as we will—*provided that we keep our mentality clear and unclouded for the transmission of the godlike ideal of the spirit into the bodily life.*

In the circle, not only is each sector the equal of every other sector before the law; but each of the three planes has its part to play in the perfect whole, and is therefore of equal importance with the other two. It is true that, in the carrying out of a conception, the order is:

First. The conception of the thinker, on what is the plane of the spirit, which is subjective to mentality, although objective to the inward thinker.

Second. The molding of the thinker's conception into definite shape in the workshop of mentality, during which process the evoluting conception is objective to mentality, but as yet only subjective to the outward bodily life.

Third. The carrying out of that conception on the material plane of the body, at which time it is no longer merely a subjective thought, but an objective act in the world of matter.

This, as I have said, is the order. But we must not forget that great law: "reaction is equal to action, and opposite to it in direction." If spirit, through mentality, acts upon body, so, likewise, does body, through mentality, react upon spirit. And, also, the impulse to vibration being set up on the bodily plane, it is transmitted through mentality to spirit, resulting in a reaction from the apex of the sector outward again to the bodily plane.

Let us apply this philosophy to the marital relation. Where the three planes of body, mentality and spirit are in fairly harmonious adjustment, as they are in all normally constituted people who seek to live aright, the bodily sex relation with another sector and the spiritual sexual relation with that sector interact upon one another through mentality, for the good of the two creatures and the happiness of the entire universe. For, remembering that each of us is part of the Great Thinker at the apex of our individual sector, it will be seen that vibrations set up in our bodily life, and transmitted through mentality to our apex of spirit, must affect the universe on all sides.

But only the initiate of the first and second degrees in marital union can appreciate and act upon the suggestive and far-reaching conception of the relation of the individual to the universe, and of the universe to the individual.

Chapter 3: First Degree

Sex union forbidden,
except for the express purpose
of creating a child

In married life of the usual type, children are brought into the world with a strange recklessness. The Bible command, "Be fruitful and multiply," has been twisted into a sanction for immoderate sex union. So far as can be learned, men appear to be here the chief trespassers upon the privileges of the matrimonial state. But if men are the aggressors, their wives are too often accessories before the fact, in that they yield their bodies to marital excess without a murmur, inwardly assuring themselves that by so doing, they are obeying God's behest to be dutiful wives.

I recall a charming woman, whose husband is intelligent, refined and thoroughly devoted to his wife. Both are devout Christians; both abhor drunkenness, and are living lives of purity and aspiration, so far as an outsider can see. Yet this happily married wife, when discussing with me certain aspects of the marital relation, remarked, incidentally, "For my part, on going to bed at night, I am usually very thankful when my husband doesn't want me, and I can go quietly to sleep."

"When my husband doesn't want me!" Why should he ever approach her, unless *she* wants *him?* It is not the man, but the woman, who must be the best judge of when union is desirable; and for her to yield to a husband's solicitations when she does not desire union is a fraud upon him, since he finds only a corpse or a hypocrite in the place of a sincerely loving and tender marital partner. Moreover, it encourages him to think that, no matter what his wife desires, she is quite willing to serve at any time as a convenience for his lust; so that she confirms him in his selfishness, and degrades herself from the position of priestess in a sacred mystery, to become a mere cuspidor.

A cultivated Philadelphia lady, who lost her money and took up the profession of nursing for her livelihood, tells the following:

She was attending a young wife in her first confinement. The patient had been greatly lacerated in delivery. On the second day after delivery, while the nurse was attending to the baby, the husband entered, and requested the nurse to leave the room. "For God's sake, Nurse, don't leave me!" exclaimed the sick woman. But a look from the husband caused the nurse to obey him, nevertheless. Shortly after, she heard her patient scream, "Oh, he'll murder me!" Whereupon the nurse rushed in, and found the husband in the act of committing a rape upon his wife. The nurse seized his arm, and endeavored to pull him away; but he did not yield until he was ready, when he allowed himself, sullenly, to be led from the room, covered with blood. The wife meanwhile had fainted. When she recovered, she cried, "Oh God, would that my baby girl and I could die! That man promised on our wedding-day to honor, love and protect me; but every night since then he has used my poor body!"

This is doubtless an extreme case; but the wife who allows her husband to approach her whenever he wishes, regardless of her own desires, is the first term in a downward series of which this unfortunate woman is, alas! not the last, as many a physician can testify.

In Pagan lands and among the Jews, there are five days out of every twenty-eight when the woman is forbidden to the man; and those who violate this taboo period are looked on as law-breakers. Folklore and religion alike memorialize the abhorrence in which the violator of this taboo period is held, *everywhere except in Christian lands.* If the reader objects that no educated or refined man would fail to respect the five-day taboo period, let him inquire about this of some reputable physician with whom he is intimate, when he will learn how sadly numerous in our midst are the husbands who respect no physical condition and no night in the month.

Modern researchers have shown the impressionability of the embryo child during gestation. Napoleon the Great owed his remarkable military genius to the fact that, prior to his birth, his mother accompanied her husband through a military campaign. If the coming child be so impressionable during the nine months of gestation, it surely behooves every conscientious parent to see to it that no abandonment to passion shall occur during that period to stamp the embryo, even for one little moment, with lack of self-control. And, on the other hand, it would seem as though every act of mutual considerateness and every tender caress between husband and wife at that time must bear its part in making their coming child self-controlled, sweet-tempered and affectionate.

But not only should the nine months of gestation be free from the abandonments of sex passion. So, also, according to some authorities, should the nine months or thereabouts be devoted to lactation. The child that is suckling is a drain upon its mother's strength, and it is cruel, at least to the child, even should the mother desire it, to draw further upon her nervous energies at that time, and to probably render the milk feverish, by abandonment to sex passion. Among so inferior a people as the Zulus and Kaffirs, the wife's person is held sacred by the husband, not only during gestation, but also during lactation. It is true that these people have more than one wife. That is their way of dealing with this question. But will it be pretended that a civilized, high-minded white man cannot get along during his wife's pregnancy and lactation without indulgence, and that he must choose among polygamy, association with harlots, or violation of the person of a pregnant or nursing wife? If so, he should be prohibited by law from ever creating a child, since he cannot become a father without afterward committing a crime.

Some sex reformers hold that the creation of a child should not occur oftener than once in three years, inasmuch as a little child is entitled to the mother's personal care during its infancy—a care which is interfered with when the mother is passing through the delicate condition of pregnancy.

At all events, it cannot be denied that, were fewer children born to a family, those who are born could be better taken care of than they are at present. A poor man is not able to properly rear and educate a large family. Nor, indeed, can any but the very rich do this. So that, from a financial as well as from a hygienic standpoint, large families are undesirable, as being an undue tax upon their parents and also as rendering it unlikely that proper care can be bestowed upon each individual child.

But if large families are undesirable, so, also, are the usual preventive checks undesirable, being abnormal, unhealthy and immoral, whether by withdrawal or other methods. They are immoral, because they place no check upon passion, but allow it full range. They are unhealthy, because the psychic powers of both parties are depleted, without sufficient interchange of magnetism. And being a violation of the natural and healthy relation, they are abnormal.

The only lawful preventive to conception is self-control. *The seed should never be sown where no harvest is prepared for or desired.*

The wife is the one to decide when that harvest is to be desired. She should be queen of her own person, so absolutely as she was while still a maiden. She should never consent to sex union unless she desires it. Otherwise, she degrades her wifehood into prostitution, for she is then little, if any better than the courtesan who rents her body to a man for so much money a night.

The coming child should be deliberately, reverently, and prudently planned for. To choose a time when there seems to be least likelihood of conception is degrading the generative powers for purposes of sensuality. Moreover, the wife is less desirous of union at such times. Nature's appointed love-season is, almost without exception, during the day or days immediately following the monthly taboo period. Those who allow this natural wedding-time to pass, and who unite two weeks later, at the ebb-tide of the woman's passion, should not be surprised if she manifests only indifference or disgust, instead of tender affection.

Another thing:

It must be remembered that the seed should be sown with the honest intention of producing a harvest. When it has been sown, it behooves husband and wife to wait, it may be for weeks or even months, to learn, beyond the possibility of a mistake, whether the seed has germinated or not. And of course, when pregnancy is assured, no further seed need be sown.

This is the teaching of the First Degree.

Not until the initiate shall have grasped the teaching in its fullness, will he be worthy to enter upon the training for the Second Degree.

Chapter 4: Second Degree

Sex union enjoined
in absolute self-control
and aspiration to the highest

In sex union there are two functions concerned—love and parentage. Likewise, there are two sets of organs for the performance of these functions. The organs of parentage are, in the woman, the ovaries and uterus; in the man, the testicles and vesiculae seminalae.

The organs of love are those which contact during sex union; and through these, when the union is normal and on a high plane, an interchange of magnetism results which is helpful and strengthening to both parties.

To secure a thorough equipoise of the whole being, it is important that the love-function have healthy and normal exercise at frequent intervals. But the function of parentage should be very rarely exercised; and intervals of years may elapse, without detriment to the health and general well-being, provided that the love-function be exercised in moderation and upon a high plane meanwhile.

If the reader asks, incredulously, how, on the man's part, the love-function may be healthfully exercised without the wasteful scattering of seed supposed to be a necessary climax to each marital union, I would refer him to a little book called *Zugassent's Discovery*, written by Geo. N. Miller.[214] I would also refer him to the accounts of the Oneida Community, where for thirty years, this possibility was demonstrated. Also to *Karezza*, by Alice C. Stockham, M.D.[215]

If it be asked how this power of self-control is to be attained, I answer: by degrees, as one would acquire proficiency in any athletic exercise or any art. One should resolutely decide at the outset that no seed shall be scattered, no matter what the impulse may be at the moment, and should sternly abide by his self-registered vow, to the best of his ability. It is quite likely that one or two failures may result at first; but as the power of self-control is developed, it becomes more and more possible for a man to do here just what he wills. And no man who has once acquired this power will ever care to return to the old habit of abandonment to passion; for he will see that he was then a slave, whereas now he is a king. (Again, I would remind the reader that ascetic self-denial is Nature's appointed gateway to increased sense-pleasure.)

In India, the philosophy of sex relations reached this high standard centuries ago; and today, such power of self-control appears to be a well-nigh universal inheritance among the natives.

214 Published by the Boston Arena Publishing Company. Price, 25 cents. (ICC note)
215 Price, $1.00. (ICC note)

This is the first half of the teaching of the Second Degree—the ability to suppress at will the scattering of the seed.

Its effects are not only bodily, but psychic as well; and the husband who has acquired this power can frequently turn a passive, indifferent marital partner into a tender wife.

One reason why many women manifest indifference or disgust in the marital union is that women are usually slower in coming to the climax than are men. Affection, tender considerateness, gentleness and delicacy on the man's part, accompanied by the exercise of prolonged and absolutely self-controlled union, would transform many a merely tolerated husband into a welcome lover.

But the wife, also, has her part to play, and should look well to the management of her own sex powers. She must learn not to abandon herself to emotion, any more than she would willingly yield to a horse that is trying to run away with her. Let her act with her emotions as she would strive to act with such a horse—control with whip and bridle, and make herself absolute mistress of the creature. But let her also remember that to kill a horse is not to govern it.

When both parties shall have acquired this self-control, they will begin to understand somewhat of the beauty and joy of *psychic wedlock.*

An objection sometimes raised by men is that, on grounds of health, a bodily secretion needs to be gotten rid of at frequent intervals. That depends. In the case of tears, it is not so. We may go for months and years without suffering in health from not weeping; and yet, if occasion arise, the secretion is formed instantaneously in response to our need. Why should not other secretions which are evoked by occasional emotion be ranked in the same category as tears?

It will of course be understood that the above does not apply to any secretion in the nature of a mucous fluid which is intended by Nature merely for purposes of lubrication. The Second Degree prohibits only that which is ejaculated—i.e., the masculine creative seed.

A more reasonable objection, however, is that, after a secretion is formed, it cannot be returned to the system without detriment to health. But Dr.

Brown-Sequard[216] has asserted that repression at the last moment and restoring the seminal secretion to the system prolongs a man's life and adds to his vigor. Dr. Brown-Sequard, however, seems to have made the mistake of supposing that it mattered not by what means either the secretion or the repression of that secretion was induced. Hence his theory about obtaining the "Elixir of Life" at such a moment from guinea-pigs, bulls and other male animals in which the secretion had been artificially induced—a theory which careful scientific experiment duly exploded. His crucial mistake lay in his not grasping the fact that the excitation should occur in a normal manner, that the repression should be voluntary, and not brought about by any means but self-control, and that the strengthening value of the secretion consists in its being returned to the system to which it belongs.

Again I would remind the reader that the power evolved by the practice of the Second Degree is psychic, as well as physical.

Every ejaculation means a waste in psychic energy—a waste which may be counterbalanced in part by the exchange of magnetism in a tender marital union, but which can never wholly be made up.

I have said that the first half of the Second Degree consists in the ability to repress the ecstasy entirely, however prolonged the union. And this power should be acquired by the wife, as well as by the husband. The second half consists in going *through* the final ecstasy in absolute self-control, and with no ejaculation.

This is a step beyond the teaching of even the Oneida Community, and I cannot refer the reader to any books upon the subject. But there are today men who have acquired even this power.

In this stage, also, the woman should go through with a corresponding training in self-control. To use a figure of speech, one may compare the last half of the Second Degree to struggling through a mountain torrent. Again and again, as we strive to breast the dangerous stream, we are swept from our footing and nearly submerged; yet each time we manage to keep our head above water, and at last we emerge triumphantly on the other side, clamber

216 Charles-Édouard Brown-Séquard (1817–1894), a Mauritian-born physiologist and neurologist who studied epilepsy and spinal-cord injuries. He was also one of the first to postulate the existence of hormones in the blood stream, and conducted early experiments in hormone replacement therapy, which were derided at the time as an attempt to develop an "elixir of life."

up the steep bank, and go on our way, rejoicing in the consciousness of our strength.

The dangers attending the practice of this Second Degree by the unworthy initiate are serious. It may be made the means of sensual excesses which degrade the moral nature and break down the health. I am inclined to agree, it is true, with other writers on the subject, in maintaining that, to the selfish man and the libertine, the game is not worth the candle. Nevertheless, I should not be doing my duty by the general reader were I to fail to utter a word of warning, and to insist that only in moderation and aspiration to the highest may the Second Degree be safely practiced. Not only this. The Second Degree, without the Third and Final Degree, is not only imperfect, but is certain in time to become demoralizing, inasmuch as it deals chiefly with prolonged sense-pleasure upon the planes of body and mentality alone.

Let us, therefore, now turn to the consideration of the Third and Highest Degree, which is the one in which our spiritual natures find activity.

Chapter 5: Third Degree

Communion with Deity as the third partner in the marital union

In the chapter on the Individual and the Universe, a philosophical conception was set forth which represented the Great Thinker at the heart of the universe as consisting of the sum of minds which exist throughout nature. Reaction being equal to action and opposite to it in direction, we showed that although our inward spirit sends impulses outward through mentality into our bodily life, yet it is logical to infer that vibrations set up on the bodily plane will react through mentality upon our spirit; and since that within us which thinks may be considered to be part of the Directing Spirit of the universe, our bodily life, by transmission through our mentality and this Central Thinker, probably acts upon the entire universe.

If this hypothesis be accepted as logical, it would seem to be the duty of each of us to so live that our bodily acts shall result in help and happiness to the rest of the universe. The old-fashioned books tell us that we have within us a safe guide, called Conscience. Modern philosophy, however, has demonstrated that Conscience needs to be enlightened in order to be thoroughly reliable. Of one thing, nevertheless, we may be reasonably certain. If we endeavor, to the best of our ability, to keep our mentality free from prejudice, dislike and ignorance, so that the light from our higher, inward self shall stream through mentality uncolored and unrefracted, we shall be quite safe in following the guidance of that mysterious inner something which we term "Conscience."

This the Atheist would call living in harmony with law, inasmuch as it necessitates clear-headedness as its first requisite. The Theist would call it seeking to know the will of God.

Prayer is one of the ways of clearing our mentality, so that the vibratory impulses may be correctly transmitted from That Which Thinks, outward through our mentality into our bodily life. Prayer is also a means of transmitting through our mentality, to the Great Thinker at the heart of the universe, the results of what we do on the bodily plane, for the betterment of the entire universe.

When, under the powerful influence of sex emotion, the psycho-physical threshold of sensibility is displaced, an especially intimate communication is opened up, whether we wish it or not, between our bodily lives and the Great Thinker. If we aspire to act in unison with that Great Thinker at such a moment, the vibrations set up within us by the sex emotion must result not only in our own betterment, but in joy and help to all the world.

This is the first half of the Third Degree—the *duty* of aspiration during the sex ecstasy to communion with the Great Thinker.

And the second half of this degree is the *joy* accruing both to the Great Thinker and to ourselves through such communion.

The Hindus have a belief which many people would term a superstition, to the effect that a god can enjoy material pleasures, but only when his worshipper offers him a share. And so the devout Hindu offers his god a share of his food and drink and even of his debaucheries, believing that he may enjoy himself as he will, if only he gives the god a part. That is, of course, a degradation of what is really a beautiful and inspiring idea—the idea that God can and does enjoy the material world through our enjoyment.

The second half of the Third Degree is entered upon when we realize that perhaps it is possible for us individually, after all, to give to the Great Thinker a pleasure which no one else can, and when, out of sheer benevolence and good-will, and with no selfish desire to secure our own pleasure, we offer the Great Thinker a share in our delight, asking Him to become the third partner in the marital union. Pantheos, Personal God or Impersonal, Unknowable Force as may be that Great Thinker, nevertheless, if this offering be sincerely and reverently made, there will dawn upon the twain who are one flesh a realizing sense of the personal relation between themselves and the heart of the universe, which is obtainable in no other way. For the time being, they will know what it is to "love God" and to be loved by Him, and will be one with all the universe, in a rapture which is indescribable. And because at that moment the way lies clear and unclouded between their bodily lives and the Great Thinker, the initiates of the Third Degree will realize in all its fullness genuine psychic wedlock—i.e., sex union upon all three planes of body, mentality and spirit, in the exact equation which constitutes the ideal union of husband and wife.

I have tried to set forth, with such clearness as seemed admissible in a work intended for the general public, the fundamental principles of genuine psychic wedlock—the only sort of union, it seems to me, which men and women ought to seek in the sex relation. Having succeeded at times in living up to this philosophy myself, I speak of its possibilities as one who knows. And so I am sending out this little essay, hoping that others, both husbands and wives, with wider lives than mine, may be helped thereby to attain the ideal happiness of Psychic Wedlock.

Spiritual Joys (Excerpt from "The Marriage Relation," 1900)

An experience of sex union in which the controlled orgasm and sustained thrill by both husband and wife are passed through, with the Central Force of the Universe, the Impulsive Power of Primordial Matter, as the third partner, is an experience never to be forgotten; an experience which, once had, will be longed for again.

> "O to realize space!
> The plenteousness of all, that there are no bounds,
> To emerge and be of the sky, of the sun and moon and
> flying clouds, as one with them!"

So panted Walt Whitman. What he yearned for in those lines may at times be realized by the husband and wife who have learned how to enter into the self-controlled and ecstatic triune sex partnership with the Impulsive Power of Primordial Matter. I say "at times," for, as I have already stated, no two such unions with the Infinite Force are exactly alike; and the sexual thrills of delight which permeate one's entire being during such a union, physically, mentally and spiritually, now all at the moment, and again alternating with one another in successive vibrations of rapture, are never satiating.

It does not get to be an old story; there is a new delight at each union, and a wider apprehension of the pervasiveness of God's presence. Sometimes, indeed, it is as though "space" and "the plenteousness of all, that there are no bounds," for whose realization Walt Whitman so passionately longed, had begun to be understood. Again—and now I must speak rather in the figurative terms of the mystic, for it is well-high impossible to express subjective experiences accurately in spoken language—it is as though the Great Power Of All There Is held one by a firm, tender hand, detained in a secret retreat of exquisite beauty, where vivid colors and softly rounded forms are seen, and where, for some organizations, fragments of soul-stirring melodies rise and fall upon the inner ear, and where, for some other organizations, rhythmical waves of poetic measure may pulsate to and fro until, in ever wider and wider arcs, fragments of these, also, sweep up through the subliminal consciousness to the very threshold of the intellectual consciousness itself, and part of a poem is thus projected from the Infinite Heart of the Universe into the heart of the individual. And again it may be as though one were privileged to see into Chaos ere the formative period of the world began. Strange blendings of colors surge to and fro, without order or place; or purposeless vibrations of sound are heard; or vague shapes flit about one, now separate, now blending like storm clouds. Then, suddenly, as the individual exerts his or her spiritual self-control, these indistinct and purposeless shapes and colors and sounds begin to crystallize into that which is definite; and the trained mystic gets a glimpse in a way not to be expressed in words, of how the Purposive Center of All Thought-Force in the universe originally worked a Cosmos out of Chaos. Or, again, the onrush of sex passion in this triune partnership may appear to the inner senses as the rapids of a Niagara, into which no untrained neophyte may dare to enter, for he will be swept onward to destruction. But the husband and wife who have known the bliss of the controlled orgasm and sustained thrill in partnership with the Most High, tremble on the verge of these mystic rapids but for a moment, and then enter, to find themselves, as it were, at the very Heart of those forces which first sent the nebulous, unformed mass of our solar universe whirling into space. They are in Chaos, but a Chaos which is being evolved into a Cosmos. They struggle in the foaming rapids of sexual creative passion, they and God all one together; the impetuous current seems momentarily about to sweep them from their feet, and they breast the waves in a delicious, thrilling agony; yet all the while they know themselves to be so firmly God-centered that, sway to and fro in the whirl of sex passion as they may, to be swept to destruction will not happen. Suddenly, as an especially high and impetuous wave of passion is met and surmounted with the most intensely voluptuous thrill yet experienced in this triune partnership, they feel firm ground beneath their feet; they brace themselves for a final dash through the lesser rapids, and emerge on the farther bank, triumphant, serene, mutually uplifted; they climb with steady and tranquilized nerves the heights of affection and spirituality; and on that high plateau they walk in the lovelight of the Divine, blended soul and body in a wedded union whose happiness can never be expressed in words.

Sometimes during such a triune partnership or at its close, God is sensed as we were wont, when very, very small children, to sense our mother—a powerful, mysterious being of loftier stature than ourselves, in trailing robe, to whom we looked up with awe and to whom we clung as our protector; a being whose presence radiated a comforting soul warmth, whose hands showered blessings on us if we had been good children, and whose voice vibrated firmly, yet was tender with love; and nevertheless a vaguely understood and somewhat feared personality after all.

The closer one gets to God in a triune sex union, the more awful and glorious and majestic appears the Divine Impulsive Force of the Universe, and yet the more unspeakably tender.

At times it is as though one stood beside the Engineer who, with hand on throttle, guides the rushing, mighty train of Universal Nature, and one feels an inexpressible thrill of delight at being so close to the Heart Of All There Is.

And forever through and through these strange mystic experiences, be it remembered, bodily sexual desire and bodily sexual bliss rise and fall like the surging waves of the ocean.

The philosophy of the triune partnership is an old, old Oriental teaching, and lies at the base of all true occultism, although it is rarely taught to any but advanced students, and then usually under a pledge of secrecy. It is centuries upon centuries old; but when given forth, either orally or in writing, it has been hitherto presented in a veiled way, which only the initiate could understand; so fearful have the mystics been of this holy and precious truth being trampled underfoot or turned to base uses.

For the first time in the history of the race, this sacred inner truth is given openly to the public, in this book and in the more condensed but less philosophic pamphlets which have preceded it. It is fitting that this important teaching, so fraught with blessing for humanity, should come to the world with the dawning of the twentieth century and in the land where freedom of thought and the triumphs of modern material science and diffused popular education do most obtain. America and Americans are ripe for the teaching.

Chapter 4

Social Reform

Sometime during 1894, Ida and her mother were apparently reconciled. In her diary for June 20, Ida notes that her mother had come to London and helped her move into a nicer room. But it wasn't until the summer of 1895 that Ida felt comfortable enough to return to the United States. In July, she was back in Philadelphia, living with her mother again, although still wary, as her mother had threatened to burn all of her precious manuscripts given the chance. This kind of ambivalence was characteristic of Ida's relationship with her mother throughout her life; in 1889, she wrote to a friend that she would not live with her mother after returning from California, yet she always eventually found her way back to Lizzie Decker's house at 1032 Race Street in Philadelphia. In 1895, Ida wrote to her patron W. T. Stead:

> Poor Mother! It must be awfully hard lines for her, I feel sure. She would so like to have me conventional, and I can't be, in the way she wishes. But if she would only help me to work out my propagandism, I *could* get where she wants me to; but it would be later on, and upon a much higher plane than she now aspires for me. But she can't see it in that light.
>
> My constant prayer is, that I may speak my gospel to the world, far and wide, and *then, then,* if they want to chop me up into pieces, I shan't care. And if no other way offers, I shall (because I *must*) leave Mother's side, and do my work by myself.

At first, she did try to be conventional, as her mother wished, but the need to spread her "gospel" kept calling. She was convinced that her teachings about sex could solve many ills of society by increasing marital satisfaction, and thus reducing the incidence of divorce, prostitution, and venereal disease. She felt that her message was too important and its benefits too great for her to remain silent. Not wanting trouble from the law, in 1896 she met with the Inspector General of the Philadelphia post office, who informed her that according to the Comstock Law, it was illegal to send *any* writing about sex through the mail, regardless of the motives of the author. Discouraged, she wrote in her diary:

> Why should I remain here all my days, fretting my heart out, worrying to keep out of the clutches of the law? I long but for one thing—to preach this beautiful, uplifting gospel which sets my heart and my soul aflame. For that I would give my body gladly. And so, sometimes, it seems to me possible that to leave this land, and to go to the world beyond the grave might not be wrong, if only I give my life for the cause. If I might do as Arnold Winkelried[217] did—rush plump against the enemy, and, gathering a handful of spears of their phalanx into my arms, make a breach for the liberty of those who can come after me, I should feel that my life had told for the cause. The blood of the martyrs is the seed of the Church. And I care only for one thing—to give my life for this gospel. If I am to be stifled, gagged, prevented from preaching it out, I do not care to stay in this land. More that that, it seems to me a sheer waste of nervous energy.
>
> My husband has said to me that there is one thing to do—teach orally, and to women, by preference, rather than to men. Of course, the women are really the ones to be first converted, and they will then compel their husbands to do as they (the women) feel to be right. And women are less hysterical over sexual matters than are men, so that there is some chance of having women study up right sexual living in seriousness and from a high plane; whereas a majority of men are liable to have sexual hysterics while discussing the physiology and hygiene of sex.
>
> I *may* succeed in this. But Heaven knows what infernal laws may be brought into requisition to choke me off even here.

217 Legendary 14th-century Swiss hero who opened a breach in enemy lines by throwing himself upon their spears.

With these prophetic words, Ida took up her cause as a social reformer, managing to stay out of the clutches of the law by spreading her gospel directly to individuals, teaching and counseling them one-on-one. In 1897, she rented an office on Arch Street in Philadelphia, not far from her mother's house. She paid the rent by doing secretarial work for the Bureau of Highways at City Hall nearby.

During this time, Ida became exposed to the sexual concerns and complaints of a wide range of ordinary men and women who made up her clientele: young and old; single, married, and widowed; lawyers, doctors, schoolteachers, and housewives. She kept notes of her sessions with each client, which she later compiled into a series of eighty-seven case studies under the title "Records of Cases of Marital Reform Work," following the format of pioneering sexologist Krafft-Ebing's *Psychopathia Sexualis*.[218] She also developed a program of "Regeneration and Rejuvenation of Men and Women through the Right Use of the Sex Function," which required her clients to answer a ninety-eight-item "diagnosis" questionnaire, anticipating Kinsey by forty years. By listening to her clients, answering their questions, and dispensing advice, she fulfilled a badly needed function halfway between that of doctor and minister, drawing praise from members of both professions even though she had no formal training in either. (The nascent field of psychotherapy was just being developed by Freud in Vienna at the time.)

With the experience she gained through personal contact came a shift in Ida's writing, from the spiritual and ideal to the worldly and practical. The result was *Right Marital Living*, written in 1899 as a distillation of Ida's philosophy on marital reform. The cornerstone of *Right Marital Living* was still sexual self-control, consistent with her earlier writings, but the emphasis was placed more on its personal advantages to marital happiness and sexual satisfaction, and the resulting societal benefits of stronger marriages and fewer unwanted children. This was followed a year later by *The Wedding Night*, an even more practical pamphlet containing advice for the bride and groom about to undertake sex for the first time. Some further development of Ida's theoretical foundations may also be discerned in these works. *Right Marital Living* elaborates on the concept

218 Richard von Krafft-Ebing (1840–1902), an Austrian psychologist and sexologist, coined the terms "sadism" and "masochism". *Psychopathia Sexualis* (published in German in 1886, English in 1892) contained 238 case studies of sexual deviance, and quickly became a bestseller.

of "sexual magnetism" mentioned briefly in "Psychic Wedlock," quoting directly from Chavannes on the doctrine of "magnetation,"[219] and *The Wedding Night* manages to incorporate yoga, newly introduced to America by Vivekananda[220] whom Ida had recently read. The main thrust of both these works, however, remained practical instruction.

It may be difficult for us today to appreciate the true significance of the social changes Ida advocated in *Right Marital Living* and *The Wedding Night*. Of course, many of her views on sexuality were firmly rooted in the prejudices and misconceptions of the time. For example, she subscribed to the well-established beliefs that masturbation was unhealthy, male ejaculation resulted in a "loss of nerve energy," and a child conceived while its father was drunk would be born "mentally unbalanced." She also opposed all forms of artificial contraception (though this put her at odds with her Freethought colleague Dr. Foote), correctly pointing out that the methods of the time were both unreliable and illegal, but also considering them to be masturbative and morally degrading. These positions were still within the mainstream consensus of 1890s America.

Some of her other ideas were controversial for the time and remain so today. In 1893, she wrote a letter to the editor of the *Philadelphia Public Ledger*, commenting upon the case of a gang rape reported by the paper. She noted that imprisonment alone would probably not prevent the offenders from raping again after their release, and recommended thorough training in sexual self-control; until such training was available, however, she maintained that rapists should be castrated. In *The Wedding Night*, she went so far as to suggest infant female circumcision and even clitoral excision in extreme cases (for women who have an "abnormally long clitoris"), practices that were not unheard of in her time and that unfortunately continue today.[221]

---

219 Chavannes defined "magnetation" as "all forms of sexual magnetism made for the benefit of the actors and not for purposes of procreation." He borrowed the term from anarchist and free-love advocate J. William Lloyd (1857–1940).

220 Swami Vivekananda, born Narendranath Dutta (1863–1902), introduced yoga to the American popular consciousness through very successful speaking tours from 1893–1896 and his book *Raja Yoga* (New York: Baker and Taylor,1896).

221 It should be noted that Ida's mention of these practices was not an unqualified endorsement. In an 1895 diary entry, she wrote: "I remembered having read that there are some savage tribes who regularly circumcise the clitoris of the women--or, rather, cut it out. The castrated clitoris and the circumcised penis (to compel the man to prolong the union)--what barbarous devices these are, compared with the teachings of *Zugassent's Discovery* and my teachings of the Second Degree!"

In spite of her limitations, however, many of the things she wrote about marital sexuality were extremely progressive, to the point of being revolutionary for her time. Foremost was her contention that there are two physiological functions of sex—one for pleasure and one for procreation—and that both of these are naturally and morally independent. This was a direct challenge to the notion that the sole purpose of sex is reproductive, and that pleasure is a side effect merely intended (whether by God or by evolution) to encourage reproduction. The idea that sexual pleasure is subordinate to mating still has currency today; for example, it is often invoked in the debate over same-sex marriage. But for Ida, it was clear that the organs of the "love function" were able to operate independently from the organs of the "parental function" without threat to one's physical or spiritual health. By learning to control these functions separately, it would be possible to make conception a conscious decision for parents, not the hit-or-miss proposition that it usually was. Ida was concerned about the toll exacted by repeated childbearing on the health of women of the time, as well as the social problems created by having more children than a family could support. Maternal and infant mortality rates were extremely high in the late 19th century. Ida empowered couples to mitigate these risks and reduce unwanted pregnancies by teaching them to choose when to conceive. Although opposed to abortion, she was definitely "pro choice" when it came to conception.

Furthermore, Ida insisted that desire and pleasure were just as important for the female as for the male in a satisfying relationship.[222] She took a stand against the long-accepted assumption that it was a wife's "marital duty" to provide sex for her husband whether she wanted it or not, bluntly stating that the wife who submits to sex without desiring it herself was no better than a harlot—*worse* than a harlot in fact, because at least the harlot is paid for her compliance! She also recognized that a husband who sexually imposes himself on his wife against her will is guilty of rape, which was inconceivable in American society at the time. In fact, a husband could not be charged with the rape of his wife in most states until the laws began to change in the 1970s. Once again, Ida proved to be way ahead of her time.[223]

---

222 Also consistent with the prejudices of the era, the only sexual relationships contemplated by Ida were heterosexual ones, although there is some evidence that she was erotically attracted to women as well as to men.

223 In an unpublished paper entitled "Telepathy Between the Sexes" (1900), Ida gave several practical methods of self-defense against rape, including, if necessary, crushing the testicles of the assailant.

Some other radical ideas she advocated included recommending at least twenty to thirty minutes of foreplay (which she called "lovemaking") before intercourse, to allow time for the woman's lubrication and desire to build; encouraging pacing on the part of the man to ensure that the woman would have the opportunity to orgasm as well; suggesting a variety of sexual positions and passionate (but controlled) pelvic movements; and even allowing for sex during pregnancy, should the woman crave it. All of these prescriptions were extremely bold for the 1890s and 1900s, as they promoted sexual parity in the bedroom at a time when women were not even allowed to vote. But Ida's pamphlets were also radical for the simple fact that they were addressing sexual subjects at all. To her clients and supporters, among them respected physicians, her frank and direct handling of such specific subjects as how to deal with a tough hymen or a "matrimonial misfit" (even if today we might cringe at the "electrical treatment" prescribed to enlarge the male organ in such a case) were badly needed and unavailable anywhere else.

To crusaders of moral decency such as Anthony Comstock, however, any open discussion of sex was "obscene, lewd, and lascivious" and therefore illegal to disseminate. Ida was well aware of the risk, and took precautions like requiring orders for her pamphlets to be submitted on pre-printed professional letterhead. But she felt that her mission was too critical to be compromised by mere threats from the law, and she forged boldly ahead, counseling clients and distributing *Right Marital Living* and *The Wedding Night* to all who might benefit from her advice.

EUGENE W. SAWYER, M. D.,
HOMEOPATHIC SPECIALIST.

Cancers and Morbid Growths.

CHICAGO:
~~808— Stewart~~
NO. 1210-11 COLUMBUS MEMORIAL BUILDING.

1416 Masonic Temple.

July-16-1901.

Dear Dr.:

Your "Wedding Night & Right Marital living" ought to be in the hands of every American citizen, and if I had my way they would be....... The amount of ill health and misery that comes from ignorance of the subjects treated of in your little books is amazing, eve among the Drs!!!!! Enclosed please find a dollar and send me copies of each. I loaned mine and have forgotten to whom, andof course they have forgotton to return to them, but they my be circulating and doing good so it is all right....... If I could afford to do so would get a lot of them so as to give them to every one of my patients. What do you charge for them when taken in quantities Please send me another circular, as I can at least pass them around. I have given quite a number of your address, and suppose they have ordered the books, hope they hav at any rate...

Fraternally,

E. W. Sawyer

Figure 6. One of many letters of praise for *Right Marital Living* and *The Wedding Night*, from the Ida Craddock papers, courtesy of SCRC.

Right Marital Living (1899)

The following essay is an expansion of an article of mine upon this same subject, which appeared in the *Chicago Clinic*, for May, 1899. It is published in response to requests from physicians and others all over the country for a simple, clear presentation of my teaching which could be handed by physicians to their patients and circulated among men and women who desire to know how to live healthy, wholesome, chaste lives as husband and wife.

Among these correspondents a noted gynecologist of New York City writes to me as follows:

> If your method can be taught, it will almost entirely do away with adultery in either sex, it will aid in suppressing prostitution, and do many things that will make the world better and happier.

In the marital relation, there are two physiological functions—the love function and the parental function. These two functions are not always exercised conjointly. There are also two sets of organs for these two functions, respectively.

For the parental function, in the woman, the organs are the ovaries and the uterus (the womb); in the man, they are the testicles and the vesiculae seminales. The organs of the love function are those which contact—the erectile organ in man; the vulva (the external genitals) and the vagina in woman. The uterus, however, also seems to be with many women a love organ; for, during the final ecstasy, where the man's organ is not sufficiently long to touch it, the uterus frequently descends into the vagina, as though seeking contact. It is probable that the uterus is intended by nature to always take part in the culmination of the act; but this, it will be observed, is merely as an organ of contact. When the uterus becomes a receptacle, it is then a parental organ.

The love function may and ought to be exercised periodically, in order that both husband and wife may have a healthy, well balanced physique and mentality.

The parental function may remain for years unexercised, without harm to either husband or wife.

It is popularly supposed that the love function should never be brought into play without at least an abortive attempt at exercising the parental function. That is, when the love organs of husband and wife have been brought into contact, it is supposed that the man's creative semen ought to be ejaculated, even though a child begotten at that time would be brought into the world under the worst possible circumstances—circumstances which would result in its being born a pauper or an idiot, or predisposed to drunkenness or insanity or criminality. To this mistaken belief (namely, that an attempt at parenthood should always terminate sexual intercourse)—a belief rooted in the popular mind by centuries of wrong living—the well-being of the future generation is daily sacrificed.

Of course, preventives to conception are always wrong. And there never yet was a preventive invented which is certain. Moreover, they are all forbidden by law; and to sell a preventive, or to lend it, or to give it away, or to state where or how it can be procured, is to commit an offense which, if known to the authorities, renders the party liable to a heavy fine or imprisonment, or both. Most preventives are distinctly injurious to one or both parties at the time; many are said to injure the tissues of the woman later on. If used, they put no check upon passion; and they are, all of them, abominable and degrading. The condoms, womb veils and pessaries, by interposing a foreign tissue between the genital organs of husband and wife during the act, render the relations masturbative for both parties. So do the various suppositories, which, by dissolving, cover the walls of the vagina with a coating of foreign substance. The syringe, by driving the spermatozoa nearer the mouth of the uterus, often helps along the very thing it is intended to prevent; and some physicians claim that, as it must be used while the tissues are still engorged, the shock is injurious to the woman. It likewise detracts from the delicacy of the conjugal act, for people of refinement. Withdrawal is an act of onanism; it is unhealthy and morally degrading. And men who habitually practice it are apt to carry the sign of their unclean habit marked on their faces and in their manner, for all knowing people to read. The popular fourteen day period (two weeks after the menses) is decidedly not a sure preventive, as a woman can become pregnant at any time in the month; and it is unnatural to have intercourse at the time in the month when the wife least desires it. Such coition tends to make her loathe the performance of her conjugal duty.

All these methods are degrading; they all coarsen what should be a pure and exquisite attraction; and at any moment they may fail to prevent conception, and will then, through the wife, stamp the child with unwholesome tendencies, mental perversions, or physical deformities.

Yet, to refrain from exercising the parental function (the ejaculation of creative semen) during coition, and to exercise only the love function (that is, the function of prolonged genital contact which mutually refreshes, stimulates and upbuilds the entire nervous system) is popularly supposed to be either unhealthy or impossible.

This is because, for many, many centuries, men have been perverting the natural functions of their sexual organism, until that which is really the best way has come to seem impossible to the many, and unwise to the few who have learned that it is not impossible. I refer to the suppression of the ejaculation of the semen upon all occasions, except at the time when the creation of a child has been prepared for by both husband and wife.

Let us remember that the seminal fluid is bestowed by Nature upon man for one purpose only—the creation of a child. It is quite true that Nature, in order to secure the propagation of the race, surrounds the act of creation with all sorts of allurements. If it were not so, people would seldom take the trouble to beget children. But the semen itself is given, not for mere sensual gratification, but for a creative purpose. To turn it aside from its natural purpose is to live wrongly as a husband. Also, to create children at random and by the wholesale, or in an environment unsuitable for either the mother or the child, is a degradation of the holy power of fatherhood.

If, then, the semen has been bestowed by Nature on man for the one purpose of creation, it is wrong to sow any seed in a woman after the child has begun to develop, for it is unnecessary, and is a waste of precious material. Now it is usually necessary to wait for over four months after the seed has been sown, in order to determine with certainty whether or not it has germinated. It is true that physicians do sometimes make fortunate guesses much earlier; but it is safer to wait until four or four and a half months shall have elapsed, by which time not only will the child have quickened, but also it will have become possible for a physician, by means of a stethoscope, to hear the child's heart beat. The latter is held to be the one sure sign by which to determine the existence of pregnancy; and if the educated ear of the physician distinguishes the quick beating of the child's heart then, separate from the slower beat of the mother's heart, of course there will be no further need for seed-sowing at that time. To persist in sowing seed during the remaining months of pregnancy is a violation of natural law.

It is true that a woman is sometimes more amorous during pregnancy than at other times, owing to the swollen condition of the uterus, which induces excitement at the genitals, so that she craves sexual satisfaction. Just as when a woman, during pregnancy, craves a peach or other wholesome food, she should be allowed to have it, so if she craves sexual intercourse during pregnancy, she ought to be allowed to have it; but only in moderation, and with care not to press upon the uterus, either from without or from within, in such a way as to injure the growing child. Of course this should not be made an occasion for seed-sowing. Genital contact should take place only for the purpose of interchanging sexual magnetism.

During the nursing period, it is unwise to unduly excite the mother sexually, as it is apt to render the milk feverish, and this will injuriously affect the infant. And to render the mother pregnant while nursing, as is sometimes done, is cruel to her and to both children.

And, surely, a little child is entitled to the care of its mother during the first two years of its life, is it not? Now, everyone knows that the care of a mother for a young child is likely to be interfered with, if she be undergoing the nervous fluctuations of pregnancy.

This brings the time for a man's abstaining from ejaculation of semen up to two years and nine months—say, in round numbers, three years. But he may have sexual intercourse with his wife during that time, if he will refrain from ejaculating the semen.

> It is popularly, but mistakenly, supposed that the semen is an excretion which a man needs to get rid of periodically. But the reverse is the truth. "The male semen," says Dr. W. Xavier Sudduth,[224] a well-known nervous specialist of Chicago, "is an acknowledged tonic, ready prepared for absorption into the system." Every expenditure of semen

224 William Xavier Sudduth (1853–1915) was a well-respected American physician specializing in clinical microscopy and uro-genital diseases.

> means a loss of nerve energy. Instead of its being thrown forth upon the slightest emotional provocation, it should be reabsorbed through the lymphatic vessels which are so abundant in the walls of the vesiculae seminales and the vas deferens, in order that it may circulate in the blood throughout the entire body, nourishing the vocal organs which make a man's voice deep and masculine, nourishing the roots of the beard, building up brain and nerves, and intensifying his virility and manly bearing. Noirot[225] says: "the resorption of what Dr. Le Camus[226] called a mass of microscopical brains is a source of vigor and longevity."[227]

Jozan,[228] in treating of cases of obliteration of the epididymis and vas deferens, says:

> The seminal fluid, although it is yet secreted in this case, having no issue, is resorbed, as blood in a closed vessel would be resorbed. The individuals affected with such an obliteration are unfruitful, but not impotent. . . . It would seem that, all communication of the testicles with the vesiculae seminales having been interrupted, the man should be considered castrated, and bear the signs of that condition, that is, that the hair of his chin and of the member should fall, that the voice should assume the shrill tones of an old woman, that the muscles will become soft, and the forms rounded. It is not so; even if the testicles, although useless, exist in the body of a man, he will preserve all the exterior signs of virility, that is, the beard, the low voice, the angular form of the members, the firmness of the muscles. An experiment, repeated several times in Germany, confirms this fact. When the two testicles of a young cock are removed and immediately replaced in the abdominal cavity, they graft themselves on to the peritoneum, and, although they be separated from the organs of generation, the young animal continues to grow with the attributes of the male. His "ergots" lengthen, his crest develops, his voice becomes sonorous, and he remains the sultan of the yard; he claims its right with the same

225 Louis Noirot (1820–1902), a French physician and author of *L'art de vivre longtemps* ("The Art of Long Living," Paris: E. Dentu, 1868), the main key of which was sexual continence.

226 Antoine Le Camus (1722–1772), French physician and author of *Medecine de l'esprit* ("Medicine of the Spirit," Paris: Ganeau, 1753).

227 David V. Bush, *Practical Psychology and Sex Life* (rpt. Chicago: Huron Press, 1922), pp. 26-27.

228 M. D. Jozan was another 19th-century French physician preoccupied with the role of sex in longevity.

> pride and energy; only he has no posterity; while his young brothers, whose testicles were removed without being replaced in the abdomen, have the forms, voice and character of "chapons," and fatten peaceably, without desires or passions.[229]

From the above, it is evident that it is not the expulsion of the semen, but its secretion and circulation through the blood which renders the male virile.

Some years ago, Dr. Brown-Sequard discovered that the voluntary suppression of the ejaculation of the semen, just at the last moment, strengthens a man and conduces to long life. He wrongly inferred, however, that the strengthening effect of this suppression was due entirely to the semen, thus returned to the body; whereas it seems to be largely due to the mental act of self-control in accomplishing the suppression, which thus acts as a tonic for the nervous system.

An impression prevails among both physicians and the laity, that to exercise the organs of the love function without also at least an abortive attempt on the man's part at exercising the parental function, will be prejudicial to his nervous system, and, consequently to his health. That is, that it is dangerous to suppress the ejaculation of the semen during coition. This may be true, if the act of suppression be performed merely as a means for bodily, sensual enjoyment. It is *not* true, however, if the mentality (which, in its turn, as we all know, governs the nervous system) be kept in a state of serenity and exaltation, so that the inner spiritual forces may be brought into play.

It is a medical dictum that the nervous system regulates the bodily functions, and that these functions are perceptibly affected, for better or for worse, according as the nervous system itself is in good or in bad working order. Now, the nervous system is controlled by the mentality. And the mentality can be controlled by the inward self of the person—if he so desires.

Take the matter of blushing. A blush is caused by a mental state of embarrassment, of mortification, of exhilaration, or of passionate feeling. This mental state acts upon the nervous system; the nerves act upon the capillaries; the capillaries call the blood to the face and the face gets red. Children redden easily with very slight provocation; but, as they grow older and, with advanc-

229 Quoted in Kenneth Sylvan Guthrie, *Regeneration: The Gate of Heaven* (Boston: L. Barta & Co., 1897), pp. 28-29.

ing years, more self-controlled, they tend less and less to crimson uncomfortably under trying circumstances. People sometimes explain this by saying that a grown person has become "less sensitive." What has really happened is, that the grown person, little by little, has learned to resist any suggestion on the part of his mentality that there is something to get red in the face about. That is, he has found out how to control his mentality in this particular, and, through the mentality, his nervous system, and through the nervous system, the capillaries, so that he need no longer blush, when to do so would render him annoyingly conspicuous.

The self-control which people usually learn to exercise in the matter of blushing, may be extended to other bodily functions, in many surprising ways. But, in order to do this intelligently, one needs to understand how important it is to have one's mentality well under control. It is important, because it is impossible for us to issue our commands directly to our bodies. All commands must be issued to the Mentality, and, through Mentality, be transmitted to the nervous system, which, in its turn, regulates the bodily functions. Thus, if we wish our hand to move, we may say, "Hand, move!" and we may keep on saying this to all eternity, but our hand will never move until we *think*, "I wish my hand to move!" That is, we practically say to our Mentality, "Mentality, I wish my hand to move!" Thereupon, Mentality transmits, with more or less accuracy (according as we have trained it well or ill), our command to the nervous system; the nerves act upon the muscles; the muscles contract and the hand moves.

If we wish the hand to perform a difficult piece of music on the piano, we must earnestly and resolutely give instructions to Mentality over and over again, until Mentality gets so well trained, that our slightest suggestion is sufficient to cause Mentality to attend to the muscular exercise of our hands with thoroughness and nicety, like a well drilled servant, leaving our inward and higher self meanwhile free to occupy itself with other thoughts, if we so desire.

What can be done (through Mentality) in enabling the hand to master a difficult piece of piano music, can be done similarly with other muscles of the body, especially with those which participate in the sexual embrace; but it must be by controlling Mentality.

The orgasm, according to Dr. Sudduth, "represents the height of nervous tension; it is a mental and physical act combined, which it is impossible to accomplish on a purely physical plane."

Control Mentality, therefore, from the plane of the higher, inward self, and you can control the orgasm (the ecstasy, or final thrill) which is set going by Mentality.

How can this be done?

There are three steps in the process:

(1) Total suppression of the orgasm itself when it is still afar off.

(2) Going gradually nearer and nearer to the verge, and stopping at the last moment, without the orgasm, and consequently, without ejaculation of semen.

(3) Going right through the orgasm, with the controlled and sustained thrill, but without any ejaculation of the semen; unless it be desired to create a child at that especial time, when the semen may be ejaculated at will.

The first step (total suppression of the orgasm) is accomplished thus: just before the last thrill which precedes ejaculation, all motion on the part of both husband and wife should be promptly desisted from, and, on the man's part, the thoughts should be completely turned away from the bodily sensations, and fixed on something beyond and above the body.

If he believe in God, let him pray to God at that moment, not only consecrating his body to God and praying for strength, but also asking God to be the third partner.

If he be an Atheist and a Materialist, let him seek, in thought, to be in harmony at that moment with Nature, with the Ideal, the Beautiful, the True; with the Ultimate Force, the Unconscious Energy of the universe.

This last is strictly logical, from a Materialistic standpoint. For the Materialist insists that there is but one substance in all the universe, Matter, and that from Matter, every known force is produced, whether physical, mental, or emotional. Now, since it has already been demonstrated by physicists that certain physical forces, such as motion, heat, light, etc., may be transmuted, one into another, and that it is only a question of the difference of vibrations;

and since these physical forces, according to Materialism, are all of them manifestations of the Ultimate Force; and since, as we all know, the mental state of a person has a very important effect on his bodily condition: it logically follows, from the Materialistic standpoint, that if a given accumulation of thought force can be restored to the Ultimate Force of the universe, it may, under suitable conditions, be transmuted into some other force which correlates with the Ultimate Force—say, the force of physical vibration along the nerves of the body. That is, the man sends thought force into what may be considered the laboratory of the universe—the plane of Ultimate Force, of Unconscious Energy, of the Primal Cause—where it is worked over and re-issued to him on the plane of physical vibration. It went into the laboratory of Ultimate Force as thought vibration; it returns to him (provided he has sent it there under the right conditions) as physical thrills which intensify his bodily sensation and invigorate his entire nervous system.

I speak from the standpoint of a teacher of over six years' experience, when I insist to my pupils on the importance of aspiration to the highest during the marital embrace. Many a libertine stumbles upon this possibility of suppression of the orgasm, and, with it, the suppression of the ejaculation of semen, and practices it for awhile, only to find at last that he has wrought great harm to his nervous system, and has, possibly, also enlarged his prostate gland. But the libertine seeks mainly sensual gratification, and when he prolongs the act by suppression of the orgasm, it is with the thought of increased sensual, bodily pleasure distinctly in his mind. He would be the last person to think of praying to God at that moment, or seeking to enter into harmony with Nature, or trying to turn his thoughts, during sex union, resolutely toward the Ultimate Force or the Unconscious Energy of the universe. And so, being ignorant of the psychological law which works upon his body during sex union, he fails to establish healthy thought currents along his nerves. It is because the sexual orgasm is a mental, as well as a physical act, that it becomes so important at that time to have the mentality well under control of the inward, spiritual self—that inward self which all deeply religious people feel to be a part of God. I therefore most earnestly urge the masculine reader, when he takes his thoughts away from the bodily sensation just before the last thrill comes which precedes ejaculation, to fix them, not upon something on the bodily plane, but to lift his thoughts to that which he considers the very highest and grandest power in all the universe, call it by what name he will—First Cause, Unconscious Energy, Primordial Substance, Jehovah, Brahma, Allah, God, the Ultimate Force, the Divine.

This is not religious cant; it is not goody-goody talk; least of all is it idle sentiment. So far as my observations go, it appears to be a psychological *fact*, that only in aspiration to oneness with the impulsive power of the universe, whether phrased poetically as "Nature," or theologically as "God," or scientifically as "Ultimate Force," may the sexual orgasm be suppressed and finally controlled without harm to the health in the long run.

The first step—total suppression of the orgasm while it is still afar off—is quite easy, although it may seem difficult to the man who has never tried it. But he will speedily find, if he does take his thoughts away from the bodily sensation and aspire to the highest just before the last thrill comes which precedes ejaculation, that the tendency to ejaculate will subside. The erection will *not* subside immediately; and presently the movements may recommence.

The second step—going gradually nearer and nearer to the verge, and encouraging the orgasm, while he still suppresses the ejaculation of semen, and yet stopping at the last moment without an orgasm—is much more difficult. But the experience of mastery of the first step will help greatly in this. And let it be always borne in mind that the second step is merely a half-way house on the road to the controlled orgasm and the sustained thrill. It should never be considered as an ultimate act, but merely as a step in the training for self-mastery. Just in proportion as he masters this second step, will he be enabled to experience the controlled orgasm and the sustained thrill in a satisfactory manner. The second step is to be conquered in the same way as was the first step.

In the third step he should pass *through* the orgasm without ejaculating the semen, but with the full enjoyment of the final thrill, and in union with God, or Nature, or the Ultimate Force. It is to be mastered in the same way as were the first and second steps.

"The intense pleasure of the orgasm," says Albert Chavannes of Knoxville, Tennessee, a writer on psychological subjects, "is not, as is usually supposed, due to the ejection of the semen. While they are coincident, it is quite possible for men to prevent, by the use of will force, the emission of semen at the time of the orgasm. . . . The enjoyment of sexual intercourse is due to the generating of a current of sexual magnetism, created by a certain degree of affinity between the parties, and increased by friction. When this current has become sufficiently strong, and a certain amount of magnetism has accumulated around the sexual organs, an overflow—orgasm—takes place, which, in obedience to inherited tendencies, sends a magnetic current to the testicles and causes a discharge of the seminal fluid. It is Nature's method to procure conception."

> Magnetation is the application of the power which man possesses of controlling this overflow, preventing it from taking its usual course and causing the usual discharge, and compelling it to take another direction. That direction is the dissemination of the magnetism through the system of both the man and woman, the woman assimilating the magnetism of the man and the man that of the woman. Magnetation requires for its successful practice self-control, affinity and union of purpose, but under right conditions it permits the full enjoyment of the overflow without the weakening influence of the emission. . . . Magnetation is the art of regulating the course taken by the overflow of sexual magnetism. Uncontrolled, it goes to the testicles and causes an emission. Controlled, it diffuses itself through the organism.[230]

The cleaner the thought and the more aspiring the impulse which prompts a man to seek the sex union which culminates in what I call the third step, the more satisfying to him physically, mentally and spiritually will this third step be. Those who seek only sensual pleasure therein are likely to be disappointed every time. But those who resolutely lift their thoughts to the spiritual plane at this time will experience thrills of physical rapture which they can experience in no other way.

I am sometimes asked by pupils who are church members, if requesting God to be the third partner in the marital embrace be not sacrilegious. To such I reply as follows:

People who consecrate their lives to God, and then give him only the intellect and the heart, reserving the body for their own fleshy gratification, are failing to keep their contract with the Almighty. "The body is for the Lord, and the Lord for the body," says the Apostle; and elsewhere, when he is

230 Albert Chavannes, "Magnetation" (SCRC, 1899), p. 1.

exhorting his readers to "flee fornication," he asks, "Know ye not that your body is a temple of the Holy Spirit which is in you, which ye have from God?" In one of the two great commandments on which hang all the law and the prophets, we are commanded: "Thou shalt love the Lord thy God with all thy heart, and with all thy soul, and with all thy mind, *and with all thy strength*." How can a man obey the Biblical command to love God with all his strength, if he fails to love God during the sexual embrace, and at least as strongly as he then loves his wife?

At all events, a man need only live this doctrine for awhile, to know whether it be good to follow or not. Even the feeblest aspirations of a sensual man, during the marital embrace, to the mere fringe of God's attributes of purity, tenderness, unselfishness, will be rewarded by God with an outgush of love which the man will feel in the remotest fiber of his physical body, as well as mentally and spiritually.

The Hindus have a quaint superstition which is instructive at this point. The Hindu believes that the god whom he worships cannot experience bodily sensations of any sort, unless his worshipper shares his own sensations with him. Therefore, when the Hindu is about to drink a glass of water, he pours out a libation on the ground, so that the god (poor thing!) may not go thirsty; and when he is about to eat, he likewise scatters morsels of food on the ground, that the poor god may not be hungry. And when he is about to go on a debauch, he manages, in some symbolic way, to offer a share of his expected pleasure to the god, after which he feels that the intended act has been consecrated and is all right.

This superstition is probably a survival from an earlier teaching, such as I have set forth above, which may have been given, in the first place, to advanced initiates by wise men, and afterward corrupted and carelessly bandied about among the common people. There is at its core a beautiful suggestion—the thought that Deity may perhaps experience personal pleasure when we share our own enjoyment with Deity.

Indeed, if we view the Primal Cause as God, we must surely hold that everything, even the capacity for personal enjoyment, emanates from God, and so he must possess the capacity to love us personally and to reciprocate our feelings of goodwill toward him.

And from the Materialistic standpoint, it must certainly be admitted that, since everything in the universe is a manifestation of an Ultimate Force (the impulsive power of primordial matter), the capacity for personal enjoyment which human beings possess must be somewhat seething or vibrating in the bosom of that Ultimate Force; in short, since a product cannot be greater than its cause, the capacity for personal enjoyment and personal love must be an inherency of the Ultimate Force of the universe, or it could not be so constantly sent forth to be an attribute of human beings.

Take it as you will—Personal God, Impersonal Spirit, or the Impulsive Power of Primordial Matter—there is no logical escape from the recognition of the possibility of entering into personal relations of love and tenderness with the Ultimate Force of the universe. And no man and woman who have once known what a beautiful and blessed thing it is to have that Ultimate Force as the third partner in a sex union which is self-controlled and aspiring to the highest throughout, will ever again wish to have a marital embrace from which personal relations with that Ultimate Force are excluded.

But those personal relations toward the Ultimate Force during the marital embrace should not be entered on from base commercial motives—that is, with the idea of giving God so much and getting back an equivalent.

If you are about to eat an apple, and a dear friend comes into the room, you instinctively offer to share half of your apple with him, not because you think to yourself, "If I give him this, I am going to get something from him in return," but because you like your friend so much that you want him to enjoy the apple with you. So should it be in offering God a third interest in your marital partnership. You should endeavor to make your offering to God with a feeling of true benevolence and good-will toward Him, a sincere, earnest wish to share with the Deity whom you respect and whom you have every reason to love, a part of your most intense joy in life.

If both husband and wife make this offering during the marital embrace, as they should, it practically amounts to returning to the universe a part of their own pleasure for the good of the universe. It is depositing in the Bank of the Universe a part of their own precious store of love and joy. And that bank always returns such deposits with interest.

I have spoken of the duty of the husband to practice self-control and aspiration to the highest throughout the act. It is also the duty of the wife. She, also, has her own three steps to master:

(1) Total suppression of her orgasm, when it is still afar off. This is to be mastered in the same way as the man was directed to master his first step.

(2) To go gradually nearer and nearer the verge of her orgasm, and, just as her vagina is about to take its spasmodic hold upon the male organ, to stop resolutely, and refuse to allow that hold to be taken. This will doubtless seem cruel at the time; but it must be remembered that it is merely a step in the training for self-mastery. It is to be accomplished in the same way as was the first step.

(3) To go right through the orgasm, allowing the vagina to close upon the male organ. Keep self-controlled, serene, tranquil, and aspire to the highest. Pray to God, if you believe in God and in prayer; if not, think steadily and quietly what a beautiful thing it is to be at that moment in harmony with Nature in her inmost workings, and rejoice that you and your husband are part of Nature, pulsating with her, and according to her law. Rejoice that Nature at that moment feels through you also, and through your husband. Feel love, love, love, not only for your husband, but for the whole universe at that moment.

Remember that sex union between husband and wife is, according to the Bible, a divinely appointed ordinance ("the twain shall be one flesh"). And people who consider it impure are likely to reap little satisfaction in this third step.

"The pure in heart shall see God."

While the man's ejaculation of semen should be totally suppressed, yet there should be, throughout the act, an oozing of fluid from the male organ, which is probably intended as a lubricant, to assist it in effecting entrance easily, and also to render it more sensitive.

There should also be an emission from the woman, which acts as a lubricant, and which, mingling with the male fluid referred to, appears to form with it a sort of electro-chemical fluid which enables sexual magnetism to be interchanged with more intensity to both parties. Without this emission from the woman, she is likely to experience comparatively little pleasure.

For a wife to submit to genital union with her husband when she does not desire it, is to degrade herself so that she has no call to draw her garments aside from the harlot in the street. Indeed, the wife who allows her body to be used as a convenience for her husband has degraded herself below even the harlot. For the harlot leases her body for ten minutes or for two hours or for a night, and she is free to refuse embraces which displease her; but the wife leases *her* body for a lifetime, and she mistakenly imagines that she dare not refuse any embrace of her husband's, however repulsive to her finer sensibilities. And so, year by year, she coarsens and degrades the holy estate of matrimony, and paves the way for begetting children who shall be at least the children of a slave mother, if not also tainted with bestial propensities on the one hand, or, on the other hand, impressed during the nine months of pregnancy with an unnatural loathing for what was intended by Nature to be a pure and wholesome relation.

A great mistake is made by wives in consenting to genital union without previous lovemaking on the husband's part. A man is always ready for sex union; a woman is not, although she may frequently be aroused by lovemaking. This is Nature's indication that it is the woman, and not the man, who should indicate when union is desirable; and also that lovemaking should precede all attempts at coition.

Once in twenty-eight days Nature prepares a woman for creation; and the menstrual flow which manifests at that time is the outward indication of the coming on of the creative mood. This creative mood may manifest in the longing to create a child; or in the creation of a poem or a picture, or plans for the spring house-cleaning; or in the designing of a new dress; or in the exchange of creative, magnetic strength with her husband. Whatever a woman especially cares to do, she can usually accomplish with effectiveness during her creative time. With most women, this time comes on the days immediately following the menses. I know of one exceptional case where it comes two weeks later; and of a few other cases where it comes just before. But, whatever the time in the month when this creative mood is on the woman, it is the time of all times to seek sex union. Married people who, in order to avoid conception, seek intercourse two weeks after the menses, act most unwisely. In the first place, this method is not at all a sure preventive to conception, since a woman who is in a mood to desire sex union is in a mood to create a child. And, since it is not a sure preventive, women who do not desire to become pregnant are thus kept, from month to month, in a state of mental torment which cannot fail to be harmful to the child who may be accidentally conceived at that time. While, if the woman does not desire to have intercourse then, it is committing a rape on her to insist upon it.

Although Nature's love-time is the period of the monthly creative mood for the woman who has not reached the climacteric, yet, after change of life, the sexual feelings and sexual attractiveness of a wife need not cease, if she have been properly trained in the exercise of her love nature. She can, if she wish, continue to be the beloved and desired wife, until far into old age. Ninon de l'Enclos,[231] the famous French courtesan, was still sexually attractive on her 80th birthday.

But for the woman who has not passed the childbearing age, her monthly love-time is all important. And this time should be prepared for, on the husband's part, by days and days of tender lovemaking each month.

It usually requires from twenty minutes to a half hour of affectionate caresses upon any given night, to arouse a woman to the point of desiring genital contact. If, at the end of a half hour of tender and reverent lovemaking, she shows no signs of desiring genital union, her feelings should be respected.

Comparatively few men realize that, while a man is a sexual animal, a woman is not, but is a maternal animal. The normal woman desires to mother the man she loves—to hold him in her arms, close to her bosom, and to caress him thus, without genital contact. She likes, also, to be held in her husband's arms; to be caressed by him, and to exchange sexual magnetism with him on the affectional plane, without genital contact. For there appears to be a secondary sexual center somewhere in the breast, near the heart, so that husband and wife may, in one another's arms, without genital contact, interchange sexual magnetism which will refresh, soothe and uplift. Men usually imagine, when a woman evinces desire for affectionate caresses in her husband's arms, that she is ready for contact at the genitals. Never was there a greater mistake. The woman cares, at that moment, only for the interchange of innocent affection. And for a husband to display unequivocal evidence of a desire for genital

231 Anne "Ninon" de l'Enclos (1620–1705) was a French author, courtesan, and patron of the arts.

contact then does not attract her; it simply repels, and often disgusts her. It is, however, quite possible that, if her husband behaved with consideration and self-control, and it were the right time in the month, she might eventually manifest a passion that same night which would amply satisfy him. What she needs is to be gradually aroused by the right sort of treatment. Husbands, like spoiled children, too often miss the pleasure which might otherwise be theirs, by clamoring for it at the wrong time.

The man who thinks this prolonged courtship previous to the act of sex union wearisome, *has never given it a trial.* It is the approaches to the marital embrace, as well as the embrace itself, which constitute the charm of the relation between the sexes.

One of these approaches—an approach too little practiced between husbands and wives—is the chastity of relation possible in a close embrace, in one another's arms, night after night, with accompanying kisses and caresses, but with no genital contact.

Concerning this, one of my correspondents, a gentleman who is a high-minded and earnest Christian worker, writes me as follows:

> In the intimate affectionate converse of the married, far too little is thought of the subtle and sympathetic influence of perfect contact, by which the outward physical senses share and interpret the inward spiritual unity. Too much insistence upon the . . . climax of union has thrown into the shade the fine minor modes of loving expression. The truly married who realize the infinite charm of being together—absolutely close, in loving union—resent the suggestion of the interposition of apparel, as the lover would resent being compelled to touch the lips of his adored through a veil or a Turkish yashmak. True love tolerates nothing between.

To those Christian husbands and wives who have come to shrink with horror from the thought of the human form divine, I would say they are violating the spirit of God's teachings, as set forth in the Bible. For, when God placed the first husband and wife in Eden, they were brought into each other's company "naked and not ashamed." Not until after they had sinned against God's ordinance, did they view their nakedness as something to be ashamed of. And when God walked in the garden in the cool of the day, and Adam hid himself, whimpering that he was ashamed to be seen because he was naked, God asked, scathingly, "*Who* told thee thou wast naked?" Evidently, *not* God.

In right marital living, the nude embrace comes to be respected more and more, and finally reverenced, as a pure and beautiful approach to that sacred moment when husband and wife shall melt into one another's genital embrace, so that the twain shall be one flesh, and then, as of old, God will walk with the twain in the garden of bliss "in the cool of the day," when the heat of ill-regulated passion is no more.

One thing which men do not always realize is, that the average woman comes to the marriage bed far more ignorant of what is expected of her sexually than does the average man. For, even if a man has never had sexual experience with women previous to his wedding night, yet he usually knows, from the dreams of his boyhood, pretty well what the sensations of sex contact are. Very few women, however, have amorous dreams previous to having sexual experience. And so, with the first sensation of genital contact, whether it shock them so that their parts become rigid and difficult to enter, or whether it come naturally and healthfully after prolonged lovemaking, so that thrills of sexual magnetism will be interchanged immediately on contact, it is in any event a startling experience to a woman. Now, women in civilized, Christian lands are universally inoculated with the idea that it is immodest to show any liking for a man, and, very often, they carry this mistaken teaching into the intimacies of marriage. Too often, indeed, women think they have done their conjugal duty, if they submit passively to the conjugal embrace; and in some cases, they clinch their hands as they force themselves to lie still, resolutely trying to resist any answering throb of passion during sex union. Poor, mistaken creatures! And then they wonder why the husband, after awhile, goes out to a harlot, who, at least, will pretend to the rapture which the wife thinks it immodest to show that she really feels!

A wife who behaves as Nature intended her to behave, will instinctively perform pelvic movements during sex union. If she does not fall into the way naturally, she should consider it a solemn duty which she owes to herself and to her husband, to try to perform them. If she will bear in mind that her love organs (the organs which contact) are given to her for the purpose, not merely of receiving pleasure, but also of conferring pleasure upon her husband's love organ, she will be better able to study out the sort of pelvic movements which she should perform. And she will soon learn that these movements can be depended on to hasten her passion and to increase her lubricating emission, referred to above.

Let her also bear in mind that it is wrong for her to go through with these pelvic movements for sensual enjoyment alone. Every throb of passion must be brought under the control of the higher, inward self, and laid as an offering at the feet of Deity, or blended, in thought, with the Ultimate Force, if she would have the purest and sweetest satisfaction.

Nature has so made a woman that it takes her from half an hour to an hour after the entrance of the male organ, to come to her orgasm. This is Nature's indication that the man ought to wait for the woman, and not to hasten through the act, as is too frequently the case. A man who gets through in from three to ten minutes after entrance, not only misses the most intense form of pleasure, but also fails to satisfy his wife properly. Her genitals being thus irritated, without being soothed by the discharge of her own sexual magnetism in exchange for his, a congested condition of the internal parts is frequently set up, which results at length in her having to be placed under a physician's care. Many a case of lifelong and hopeless invalidism in a wife is traceable to the husband's habit of hasty termination of the sexual act.

If a husband wishes to treat his wife considerately, let him not hasten, either the act itself or the approaches to the act. He should approach her gently, perhaps linger for awhile in contact with the outside only, enter slowly and with self-control, rest tranquilly after entrance, and let his first movements be gentile and slow. In all things, let him seek, not to get the most pleasure possible out of the relation for himself, but to give his wife the most pleasure. Let him study his own movements, in their possibilities of conferring pleasure, and remember that these should be in the nature of caresses of her love organs by his own love organ.

To approach the woman's genitals with the finger for the purpose of excitation, is distinctly masturbative, and therefore wrong. The only lawful finger of love at her genitals is his sexual love organ.

Also, an orgasm which is induced mainly at the woman's clitoris is unwise. The clitoris is a rudimentary male organ, with a similar power of erectility, though in a much lesser degree. To excite the woman at this organ chiefly, therefore (as is sometimes mistakenly done by quite estimable men), renders it impossible for her to exchange with the man her natural feminine magnetism, and the act becomes more or less perverted, and destructive of her finer sensibilities. The clitoris should play a very secondary part indeed, and the orgasm should be induced within the vagina.

Every marital embrace should be the occasion for the exchange of intellectual ideas in conversation. Think and talk during the nude embrace, and also at intervals during the sexual embrace, of good books, pictures, statuary, music, sermons, plans for benefiting other people, noble deeds, spiritual aspirations. Do *not* speak of people against whom you cherish resentment, unless it be to throw out feelings of love toward them. Do not tell indelicate stories. Do not choose this time to worry over your household economies or business troubles. Shut out the world, with all its baseness, all its impurity, all its struggles for a livelihood, and let this be a time for the interchange of delicate, poetic sentiment, pure affection, playful, merry thought, and lofty religious sentiment. So strangely are human creatures constructed, that intellectual blending at this time is, by a psychological law, one of the most effective means of welding the natures of husband and wife into a beautiful and perfect oneness.

Not until the habit of self-control and aspiration to the highest throughout the embrace has been firmly fixed in the relations between the two, ought they start in to create a child.

It is now well established that, if a man be drunk at the moment of impregnating his wife, or habitually drunk for some time previously, the resulting child is certain to be mentally unbalanced, if not idiotic. This is because alcoholic intoxication has interfered with the coordination of his nervous ganglia.

If intoxication at that moment, with the resulting failure to coordinate the nervous ganglia, be induced by other means, whether by drugs or by loss of sexual self-control, is it not likely that the child will be similarly affected for ill?

Of course, cases of children begotten by sexually intoxicated parents are difficult to trace up; for sexual self-control may co-exist with the most intense passion, while, on the other hand, a person of feeble sexuality may manifest what little passion he or she does, in weak self-abandonment at the moment of impregnation. So that, at present, we can only reason by analogy when we say that, since alcoholic intoxication results in mentally unbalanced children, sexual intoxication is likely to produce similar results. But we do know this: that a child begotten at a time when a husband and wife have returned from a social gathering of friends, with their thoughts pervaded by genial and sunshiny memories, has, in more than one instance, been a child of sweet and serene disposition, in marked contrast to their other children.

This instruction upon Right Marital Living would be incomplete, did I not mention one or two facts which an intending bride or bridegroom ought to know.

One is, that the custom of brutal rupture of a woman's hymen upon the wedding night, and, too often, the consequent tearing of the walls of the vagina, with attendant pain and loss of blood, is wholly unnecessary. The bride-elect should go to a physician some little while previous to the wedding, and, if there be a hymen of any toughness, have it snipped by a pair of surgical scissors. This will not be painful; and the hymen, which is a membrane attached to the walls of the orifice, will soon shrivel away, being now but a piece of dead skin. It would be advisable, however, for the woman to let her future husband know that she intends to do this, for the reason that there exists a popular superstition, to the effect that the presence of the hymen is a proof of virginity. On the contrary, it is not a true test of virginity, for many women never had any hymen, and others have lost theirs when children, by romping. Also, prostitutes are on record as having had a hymen which deceived physicians into thinking them virgins. Nevertheless, because men still ignorantly hold to the popular superstition about they hymen, it is prudent for the bride-elect to state her intention ahead of time. Some men with brutal instincts feel themselves defrauded of their rights if the bride's hymen be not there, unbroken, for them to rupture. Of course, no intelligent, self-respecting woman would feel herself bound to accord a husband such a right, if she knew beforehand all the pain and suffering which the exercise of his supposed prerogative would involve. (I know of one case where a bride was confined to bed for six weeks with abscesses in her vagina, because of her husband's brutal manner of effecting entrance on the wedding night.) And, if the bridegroom-elect be the sort of man who claims this as his conjugal right, perhaps it would be as well for the bride to find it out before she marries him.

But, of course, the natural instrument for effecting entrance is the bridegroom's organ of penetration, and, if at all possible, it should be employed in preference to any other. Even where there is a fairly tough hymen, if the bridegroom will use gentleness, patience, and tender lovemaking, and refrain from genital contact until the bride is thoroughly aroused, it will usually be found that she will, upon genital contact, instinctively bear down so quickly and effectively that the dreaded entrance will be all over within a moment. Allay the bleeding by the use of water as hot as can be borne.

It should be the privilege of the woman, and not of the man, to choose between these two methods.

Another thing which often causes unnecessary suffering to the bride on the wedding night, is the smallness of her orifice, as compared with the husband's organ, especially if the latter be unusually large. Like a glove which is a trifle small in the fingers, however, this can be overcome by successive attempts at entrance, provided these be gentle and slow, and provided, also, that the parts be anointed with some simple ointment, such as petrolatum, cosmoline or vaseline. Do not use an ointment containing unknown ingredients, as there may be a harmful drug among them. Nature will, indeed, furnish a natural lubricant in the woman's own emission after awhile; but at first, it is well to have the ointment at hand. Do not be in a hurry; be patient. In some cases, it may take months for the parts to become fitted to each other; but the result will repay you. "Patience and a little oil will do wonders," is a saying which applies here.

While the natural position is for the woman to lie upon her back, and allow the man to be on top, yet, where the man is very heavy, or for other reasons, it is sometimes better for the woman to mount the man. Again, there are various side positions, which different couples can find out for themselves, by experimentation.

As to how frequently genital union should take place, no hard and fast rule can be laid down. The one safe guide is the after result to the husband and wife, mentally and physically. If the union take place according to the method here set forth, and be not practiced intemperately, there should be no sense of depression at the close, nor should there be any feeling of nervous irritation; but on the contrary, both husband and wife should feel soothed and tranquilized. And the next day, they should feel serene and more than usually clear-headed; they should feel as though they walked on air, and as though the world were full of brightness and joy.

When either husband or wife is physically weary, or mentally fagged out, all genital contact should be sedulously avoided. But the quiet embrace in one another's arms at such a time, without genital union, will be usually found to strengthen and refresh, sometimes to such an extent, indeed, as to pave the way for genital contact a little later.

In preparing for the creation of a child, let it be a matter for thoughtful, prudent, reverent deliberation long beforehand. Choose a suitable environment for the moment of impregnation, and do not attempt to create a child until both of you have acquired the habit of self-control and aspiration to the highest during the marital embrace, through repeated unions. Let the impregnation take place, not in the dark, but, if possible, in a warm, sunshiny room, in pure air. Prepare this room, as you would a temple for a sacred rite, by placing beautiful pictures and growing plants and statuary of an artistic order therein. If the latter prove too expensive for your purse, you can get, from any Italian image-vendor, cheap plaster of Paris statuettes which are copies of the world's masterpieces. Do not overload the room with gewgaws and tidies and meaningless bric-a-brac; let it be furnished with ideal simplicity. Set this room apart as a sacred place for nine months, so that the pregnant mother may have a sanctuary to which she can retire, at intervals in her daily household duties, to think the thoughts of beauty, of purity, of serenity, of moral duty, of studious intellectual work which she and the husband wish to impress with intensity upon the brain of the embryo child. It is the right of every child to be conceived and gestated in the very sweetest and sunniest and happiest environment that its prospective parents can command.

The parents, and especially the mother, can mold the coming child's tendencies as they will, by the thoughts which they think at the moment of impregnation and for some months before, and which the mother thinks with especial intensity or persistency during the nine months of pregnancy. She can make of the coming child an artist or a musician, a machinist or a preacher; she can give it a powerful bias to Roman Catholicism, to Protestantism, or to Freethought; she can make it a student and lover of books, or an idle sportsman, or a dull, plodding nonentity; she can make it respect all that is chaste and self-controlled, or she can curse it with an irritability of temper or a lasciviousness of ideas which it will take many long years of struggle on that child's part to eventually conquer. By dwelling in thought upon the perfect forms of the statuettes in her little temple of peace, she can do wonders toward endowing the coming child with a perfect form itself; by contemplating, day after day, the exquisite loveliness of a Mary Anderson,[232] or the pure, spiritual face of some Madonna, or the clear-cut, sensuous features of some Greek youth, she may bestow upon her child the gift of a beautiful and expressive countenance, which may be worth more to it than uncounted gold, in after years.

Such motherhood, coming as the consummation of months or years of repeated sex unions in self-control and aspiration to the highest, cannot fail in evolving a child who shall be well balanced, lovable, destined to success in life.

It is sometimes objected that it is unwise to spread among married people the knowledge which is set forth in the foregoing pages, as they would straightway cease to beget children, and so the human race would die out. This objection shows how little the differences in the mental attitude of men and of women toward the marriage relation are understood. The average woman longs, with all the intensity of her nature, to have a child or children by the man whom she loves, at some time in her life; but it is for *her* to choose the fitting time. A woman who is made pregnant against her will, naturally resents the outrage.

I claim for this method of Right Marital Living, that the quality of children born from people who have lived in this way will (other things being equal) be superior to that of children who are the result of accident or lust.

Also, it has more than once happened that a married couple who have longed in vain for years for a child, have eventually become happy parents, by reason of conserving the male semen for the one creative purpose for which it is intended by Nature, and allowing it to be expended only at long intervals, so as to give time for the spermatozoa to come to full maturity and thus be potent for fatherhood.

Another objection which is sometimes raised to the spread of this knowledge is, that if young unmarried people get to know of the possibility of

232 Mary Anderson (1859–1940) was an American stage actress famous for her role as Galatea (a beautiful statue who comes to life) in W. S. Gilbert's *Pygmalion and Galatea* (1871).

controlling the fecundating power, seductions, promiscuity and illicit unions of all sorts will increase. In reply, I would say that I find that the average libertine is unwilling to try this method, as he considers it "too high for his purpose." In fact, a man who practices this method and who teaches it to the woman (as he is apt to do, in order to increase his own pleasure) will not be a libertine; for the habit of aspiring to union with God (or with whatever else he recognizes as the Ultimate Force of the universe) during the sexual act, and of encouraging the woman to do so likewise, has the curious psychological effect of tending to make him too loyal to that one woman to want to break with her. For this method, while it always satisfies, never satiates a man; and it renders the relation a perpetual honeymoon. On the other hand, should the man neglect to aspire to the highest throughout the act, but keep in thought upon the sensual plane, the result is likely to prove harmful to his nervous system, through the working of the psychological law upon which I have spoken at length, several pages back. Also, the union will be far less satisfactory. There are, therefore, two inducements to any man who learns this method to rise above the merely sensual plane, and to aspire to the highest throughout the act: first, the increased satisfaction if he does, and, second, the dread of serious harm to his nervous system if he does not. And if he and his partner live this method, they will tend, with each successive union, to become more and more closely welded into a partnership which nothing could induce either of them to break. Thus the institution of marriage will be strengthened, not weakened, by the widespread knowledge of this method of Right Marital Living.

Take Notice

Inasmuch as the United States postal authorities regard the careless mailing of marriage reform literature to unknown parties, however refined that literature may be, and however worthy the motive of the sender, as an indictable offense, because the unknown person to whom it is mailed may be a minor, Mrs. Craddock requests that whoever sends for this book will, if personally unknown to her and if a business or professional person, write upon his printed letter-head, and sign his name to his letter; or, if he have no printed letter-head, that he will get some friend who has a business or professional letter-head to write on that letter-head a signed statement that the person sending for this book is over twenty-one years of age.

Readers who hand this book along are here warned not to place it in the hands of minors of either sex without permission from a parent or guardian.

Instruction given upon **Marriage** by Mrs. Ida C. Craddock

Among the subjects treated are:

Scientific Motherhood—Scientific Fatherhood—Welcome and Unwelcome Children—Every Child Should be Created by Reverent, Prudent, Deliberate Intention, and not by Accident—How to Control Impregnation Absolutely, and in a Manner which is Lawful—The Wife Should be Queen of her own Person—The Artistic and Affectional Possibilities of Marriage—Abstinence from Sex Union is not Wedlock—The Right Method is Satisfactory to Both Parties, and Renders Marriage a Perpetual Honeymoon.

Something Entirely Unique in Sexology

and the outgrowth of over six years' experience as a teacher upon Marriage. Commended by Clergymen, Social Purity Workers, and Physicians of standing, both Allopathic and Homeopathic. Neither husband or wife who has once learned this method will ever care to return to the old way.

The instruction, which is complete in one lesson, consists of a lecture of about an hour and a half, at the close of which an opportunity is given to ask questions.

Fee for instruction in general class, fifty cents.

HOURS FOR GENERAL CLASSES ARE:

For Mothers, Wives and Widows, Friday afternoons, three o'clock.
For U[illegible]rried Women, - - Saturday afternoons, three o'clock.
For [illegible] - - - - - - - - - Friday evenings, eight o'clock.

FOR THOSE WHO WISH PRIVATE INSTRUCTION, FEES ARE AS FOLLOWS:

Individual Instruction,		$5.00
Instruction in Private Class of two,	per pupil,	3.00
" " " three, four or five,	"	2.00
" " " six to ten,	"	1.00
" " " eleven or more,	"	.50

Applicants for instruction who are under twenty-one will be expected to furnish written permission from a parent or guardian.

MRS. IDA C. CRADDOCK

~~SUITE 38-40, No. 60 DEARBORN ST. CHICAGO.~~

1838 California St, Denver, Colo.

OFFICE HOURS
11 A. M. TO 2 [illegible]
OTHER HOURS BY APPOINTMENT

Figure 7. Card advertising Ida's Marriage Instruction services, courtesy of the Wisconsin Historical Society (WHi-65509 & WHi-65510).

The Wedding Night (1900)

Oh, crowning time of lovers' raptures, veiled in mystic splendor, sanctified by priestly blessing and by the benediction of all who love the lovers! How shall we chant thy praise?
Of thy joys even the poets dare not sing, save in words that suggest but do not reveal. At thy threshold, the most daring of realistic novelists is fain to pause, and, with farewells to the lovers who are entering thy portals, let fall the curtain of silence betwixt them and the outside world forevermore.

What art thou, oh, night of mystery and passion? Why shouldst thou be thus enshrouded in an impenetrable veil of secrecy? Are thy joys so pure, so dazzling, so ecstatic, that no outside mortal can look upon thy face and live?

Or art thou a Veiled Prophet of Khorassan,[233] and, under thy covering of silver light, a fiend, a loathsome monster, a distorted and perverted semblance of what thou dost profess thyself to the world?

Whatsoever thou art, it were well, methinks, that the veil, for a moment, were lifted from thee, that the young and ignorant may see thee as thou art, and, seeing, be not misled by thy glamour to their own undoing, but keep the higher law when they shall have entered thy radiant doors.

When the last stanzas of the wedding march have died away, and the bride, in shimmering white, places her hand in that of the bridegroom and pledges herself to be his wife "until death do part," a shiver of awe stirs the audience, as a field of wheat is stirred by a strong wind. An uncomfortable feeling pervades us all during these few moments, for it is felt to be a solemn occasion; and when the final words of the marriage service have been pronounced, every one feels relieved.

Yet there is a more solemn moment to follow. It comes when the last kisses of mother and girl-friends have been given, and the last grain of rice has

233 "The Veiled Prophet of Khorassan" is a poem in *Lallah Rookh* (Philadelphia: Henry Altemus, 1895) by Thomas Moore (1779–1852), referring to an eighth-century Arab prophet who wore a veil. His followers said the veil was necessary to protect them from his dazzling countenance, but in reality it was to hide his face, which had been disfigured in battle.

been thrown upon the newly wedded pair, and the last hack driver and hotel or railway porter have been gotten rid of, and the key is turned in the bedroom door and the blinds drawn, and the young girl, who has never been alone in a locked room with a man in all her life, suddenly finds herself, as though in a dream, delivered over by her own innocent and pure affection into the power of a man, to be used at his will and pleasure. She, who has never bared more than her throat and shoulders and arms to the world, now finds that her whole body, especially those parts which she has all her life been taught it was immodest to fail to keep covered, are no longer to be her own private property; she must share their privacy with this man.

Fortunate indeed is the bride whose lover at such a moment is a gentleman in every fiber of his being.

For there is a wrong way and there is a right way to pass the wedding night.

In the majority of cases, no genital union at all should be attempted, or even suggested, upon that night. To the average young girl, virtuously brought up, the experience of sharing her bedroom with a man is sufficient of a shock to her previous maidenly habits, without adding to her nervousness by insisting upon the close intimacies of genital contact. And, incredible as it may sound to the average man, she is usually altogether without the sexual experience which every boy acquires in his dream-life. The average, typical girl does not have erotic dreams. In many cases, too, through the prudishness of parents—a prudishness which is positively criminal—she is not even told beforehand that genital union will be required of her. I once talked with a young married woman, the daughter of a physician, well educated, and moving in cultured society, who had been allowed to marry at the age of 20, in entire ignorance of this. She remarked to me: "I think the relation of husband and wife is something horrid. I knew, of course, before I married, that married people had children; but I supposed that God sent them babies, and that that was all there was about it. I was never told about the physical relation." Her husband was so lacking in self-control as to make her pregnant on her wedding night.

And her experience is but one out of thousands.

In the ideal honeymoon, the bridegroom will not seek genital contact until the bride herself shows indications of desiring it. "But she might never want it?" My dear sir, you must be indeed lacking in manhood to be unable to arouse sex desire in a bride who loves you with even a half-way sort of affection.

"How can this be done?"

Well, I think that the very first thing for you to bear in mind is that, inasmuch as Nature has so arranged sex that the man is always ready (as a rule) for intercourse, whereas the woman is not, it is most unwise for the man to precipitate matters by exhibiting desire for genital contact when the woman is not yet aroused. You should remember that that organ of which you are, justly, so proud, is not possessed by a woman, and that she is utterly ignorant of its functions, practically, until she has experienced sexual contact; and that it is, to her who is not desirous of such contact, something of a monstrosity. Even when a woman has already had pleasurable experience of genital contact, she requires each time to be aroused amorously, before that organ, in its state of activity, can become attractive. For a man to exhibit, to even an experienced wife, his organ ready for action when she herself is not amorously aroused, is, as a rule, not sexually attractive to her; on the contrary, it is often sexually repulsive, and at times out and out disgusting to her. Every woman of experience knows that, when she is ready, she can cause the man to become sexually active fast enough.

If this be so with the wife who has had pleasurable experience in genital contact, how much more must the sight or touch of that apparent monstrosity in a man shock and terrify the inexperienced young bride!

Yet, if you are patient and loverlike and gentlemanly and considerate and do not seek to unduly precipitate matters, you will find that Nature will herself arrange the affair for you most delicately and beautifully. If you will first thoroughly satisfy the primal passion of the woman, which is affectional and maternal (for the typical woman mothers the man she loves), and if you will kiss and caress her in a gentle, delicate and reverent way, especially at the throat and bosom, you will find that, little by little (perhaps not the first night nor the second night, but eventually, as she grows accustomed to the strangeness of the intimacy), you will, by reflex action from the bosom to the genitals, successfully arouse within her a vague desire for the entwining of the lower limbs, with ever closer and closer contact, until you melt into one another's embrace at the genitals in a perfectly natural and wholesome fashion; and you will then find her genitals so well lubricated with an emission from her glands of Bartholin, and, possibly, also from her vagina, that your gradual entrance can be effected not only without pain to her, but with a rapture so exquisite to her, that she will be more ready to invite your entrance upon a future occasion.

If the wedding day has been one of prolonged excitement, the most sensible thing that the bride and bridegroom can do upon retiring, is to go straight to sleep like two tired children. On waking in the morning, the first marital endearments may suitably take place, and will be found conducive to the exchange of sexual magnetism which will strengthen and refresh. Indeed, you should never, never allow genital contact to be attempted when either of you is physically weary or mentally fagged out.

If you are accustomed to the use of tobacco and alcoholic drinks, it is to be hoped that you will have sufficient self-control and consideration for you bride to abstain from them at least upon your wedding night. Not only are their odors, especially when stale, disgusting to any woman of delicate sensibilities, but the use of either or both will go far toward coarsening your emotional relations toward her on that occasion.

The effect of alcohol will be to lessen the co-ordination among your nervous ganglia, accentuate your prominent weaknesses (this, too, at the very moment when you wish to appear especially manly in her eyes!) and inhibit your powers of self-control.

The effect of tobacco always is to deteriorate the moral and emotional sensibilities through its capacity for blunting sensation.

Do you wish to be truly a man upon the wedding night? Then forego both tobacco and alcohol upon that occasion and for a long time previously.

Do not, upon any account, use the hand for the purpose of sexual excitation at the bride's genitals. There is but one lawful finger of love with which to approach her genitals, and this is the male organ. Even where there is a hymen whose orifice requires to be gradually enlarged in order to effect a painless entrance, the male organ, and not the finger, should be employed, lest a masturbative response be set up in the bride at the outset, which would be most unfortunate.

Bear in mind that the more gentle, slow and lingering your entrance, the more passionate will be the response of the bride. Also, the more readily will you yourself attain to the sexual self-control inculcated in my Right Marital Living.

As to the clitoris, this should be simply saluted, at most, in passing, and afterwards ignored as far as possible; for the reason that it is a rudimentary male organ, and an orgasm aroused there evokes a rudimentary male magnetism in the woman, which appears to pervert the act of intercourse, with the result of sensualizing and coarsening the woman. Within the duller tract of the vagina, after a half-hour, or, still better, an hour of tender, gentle, self-restrained coition, the feminine, womanly, maternal sensibilities of the bride will be aroused, and the magnetism exchanged then will be healthful and satisfying to both parties. A woman's orgasm is as important for her health as a man's is for his. And the bridegroom who hastens through the act without giving the bride the necessary half-hour or hour to come to her own climax, is not only acting selfishly; he is also sowing the seeds of future ill-health and permanent invalidism in his wife.

A woman's clitoris is sometimes hooded, which, of course, is an unnatural condition, and is apt to result in sexual coldness on her part, or, at best, in a stunted sex desire. Here a physician should be appealed to, as the clitoris can be freed from its hood by circumcision; and the earlier that this is done in a girl's life the better for her health. Many a girl infant, it is now maintained by some physicians, is nervously deranged by the existence of such a hood, and would be restored to health by its circumcision.

Some women have an abnormally long clitoris, which it is impossible not to engage during coition, and such women are usually sensual, and lacking in the ability to prolong the act. In extreme cases the excision of such a clitoris may be beneficial; but it would seem preferable to first employ the milder method of suggestive therapeutics, and for the wife to endeavor to turn her thoughts from the sensation induced at the clitoris to that induced within the vagina, which is the natural and wholesome sensation to be aroused in a woman.

Do not expend your seminal fluid at any time, unless both you and the bride desire a child, and have reverently and deliberately prepared for its creation on that especial occasion. Your semen is not an excretion to be periodically gotten rid of; it is a precious secretion, to be returned to the system for its upbuilding in all that goes to emphasize your manhood. It is given to you by Nature for the purpose of begetting a child; it is not given to you for sensual gratification; and unless deliberate creation be provided for by both of you, it should never, never be expended. This, however, does not mean less pleasure, but more pleasure than by the ordinary method of sex union. As to the details of how such sexual self-control may be exercised during coition, and without harm to the nervous system, you can learn these from my pamphlet on Right Marital Living (price fifty cents).

I would add that the habit of using a wife as a convenience for a man's easing himself of a fluid which is looked on as an excretion, is chiefly responsible for the widespread idea that the sex relation is unclean, and for the growth of Comstockism, with its baneful efforts at suppression of all enlightening literature upon the details of coition as being "obscene, lewd, lascivious." The sex relation is indeed unclean, when made use of by a man for the purpose of easing himself of a supposed excretion; and the details of such a union are truly "obscene, lewd, and lascivious." No bridegroom of any delicacy of sentiment will want to thus befoul his wedding night or his honeymoon. But when the higher law is known and kept—that of genital union in self-control and aspiration to the Divine—the sex relation at once becomes refined and spiritualized, and the morbid ideas about its being impure cease.

When you are performing your movements, do not indulge in the thought of how much you are enjoying them; rather dwell, in thought, upon how much pleasure you are giving to your bride, and study carefully every movement with reference to its pleasure-producing effect upon her.

Also, to the bride, I would say: Bear in mind that it is part of your wifely duty to perform pelvic movements during the embrace, riding your husband's organ gently, and, at times, passionately, with various movements, up and down, sideways, and with a semi-rotary movement, resembling the movement of the thread of a screw upon a screw. These movements will add greatly to your own passion and your own pleasure, but they should not be dwelt on in thought for this purpose. They should be performed for the express purpose of conferring pleasure upon your husband, and you should carefully study the results of various movements, gently and tenderly performed, upon him.

We human beings are so constituted that when we seek happiness for ourselves, it eludes our grasp. But when we seek to make other people happy, happiness comes and abides with us. If each will seek to give pleasure to his or her wedded partner, the bliss of each will be greatly intensified. Especially will this be so if God be included in this pleasure-giving partnership, along the lines which I have laid down in Right Marital Living.

The custom of brutal rupture of a woman's hymen on the wedding night, and, too often, the consequent tearing of the walls of the vagina, with attendant pain and loss of blood, is wholly unnecessary. The bride-elect should go to a physician some little while previous to the wedding, and, if there be a hymen of any toughness, have it snipped by a pair of surgical scissors. This will not be painful, and the hymen, which is a membrane attached to the walls of the orifice, will soon shrivel away, being now but a piece of dead skin. It would be advisable, however, for the woman to let her future husband know that she intends to do this, for the reason that there exists a popular superstition to the effect that the presence of the hymen is a proof of virginity. On the contrary, it is not a true test of virginity, for many women never had any hymen, and others have lost theirs when children, by romping. Also, prostitutes are on record as having had a hymen which deceived physicians into thinking them virgins. Nevertheless, because men still ignorantly hold to the popular superstition about the hymen, it is prudent for the bride elect to state her intention ahead of time. Some men with brutal instincts feel themselves defrauded of their rights if the bride's hymen be not there, unbroken, for them to rupture. Of course, no intelligent, self-respecting woman would feel herself bound to accord a husband such a right, if she knew beforehand all the pain and suffering which the exercise of his supposed prerogative would involve. (I know of one case where a bride was confined to bed for six weeks with abscesses in her vagina, because of her husband's brutal manner of effecting entrance on the wedding night.) And if the bridegroom-elect be the sort of a man who claims this as his conjugal right, perhaps it would be as well for the bride to find it out before she marries him.

But, of course, the natural instrument for effecting entrance is the bridegroom's organ of penetration, and, if at all possible, it should be employed in preference to any other. Even where there is a fairly tough hymen, if the bridegroom will use gentleness, patience, and tender love-making, and refrain from genital contact until the bride is thoroughly aroused, it will usually be found that she will, upon genital contact, instinctively bear down so quickly and effectively that the dreaded entrance will be all over within a moment. Allay the bleeding by the use of water as hot as can be borne, dipping therein a wad of clean absorbent cotton, squeezing it out, and placing the wad up between the lips of the bleeding orifice.

It should be the privilege of the woman, and not of the man, to choose between these two methods.

Another thing which often causes unnecessary suffering to the bride at first is the smallness of her orifice, as compared with the bridegroom's organ, especially if the latter be unusually large. Like a glove which is a trifle small in the fingers, however, this disparity in size can be overcome by successive attempts at entrance, provided these be gentle and slow, and provided, also, that the parts be anointed with some simple ointment, such as petrolatum, cosmoline, or vaseline. Do not use an ointment containing unknown ingredients, as there may be a harmful drug among them. Nature will, indeed, furnish a natural lubricant in the woman's own emission after awhile, but at first it is well to have the ointment at hand. Do not be in a hurry; be patient. In some cases, it may take months for the parts to become fitted to one another, but the result is worth the trouble.

Many and many a divorce dates its beginning to the ignorance or the lack of consideration shown by one party for the other in the nuptial chamber. And those who think to render marriage pure and holy by keeping our young people ignorant of the functions and proper management of their bodily organs, are the ones directly responsible for such divorces.

The following out of the above directions is of especial importance where the organs of the bride and bridegroom are so ill-matched as to make what is termed "a matrimonial misfit." Sometimes the man's organ, which in a state of activity should be about six inches in length, is much longer and proportionately large; and if the woman's orifice and vagina chance to be unusually small, great suffering will result unless one party or the other has been cautioned and knows what to do. In a case where the organ had attained a phenomenal length, the man married a young woman of average proportions, and almost killed her upon the wedding night. Fortunately, the family physician, to whom the suffering bride referred her case, insisted that the husband should wear a pad, made as a ring, which prevented the entrance of the organ beyond a certain distance; and the couple are now living happily and have had several children. In other cases the man's organ is small, like a little boy's, so that entrance is an impossibility. Such a husband simply arouses and excites his wife, without being able to afford her the normal sexual satisfaction. Or, again, the organ, while of average length, may be slender, and the woman's orifice and vagina unusually large, so that his organ does not completely fill it, and this also often fails to result in full satisfaction to the woman. In the latter case the male organ can sometimes be enlarged by electrical treatment. But I think that where the organs of either party depart very greatly from the average size, the party who is abnormal in size one way or the other is committing a great wrong upon the other party not to give due notification of his or her abnormality in advance. Such notification, if given to the family physician, could be acted upon by him and advice given which in many cases would greatly lessen the annoyance of the matrimonial misfit, and preserve both parties from making a wreck of their lives.

It is possible that much could be done by suggestive therapeutics to gradually adapt the organs of such ill-matched couples to one another. Intelligent control of the subconsciousness, and, through it, of the sympathetic nervous system, at a time when the sexual organs of both parties are excited and engorged with blood, ought to be able to effect very marked changes in the tissues of these organs.

I here use the term "suggestive therapeutics," because this is a term which does not jar upon the orthodox medical ear. But the method may also be called applied psychology, or mental science, or divine science, or yoga. The phraseology adopted by these several schools of thought varies; so, also, does some of the philosophy taught; but the scientific process is essentially the same in all.

To the average uninstructed man or woman, there is no apparent relation between the honeymoon and that philosophy which I prefer to call "yoga."

And yet, if yoga were properly understood and practiced in the marital embrace by every newly married couple, their sex life would be, from the start, so holy, so healthy, so happy, that they would never care to descend to the methods commonly practiced among married people today—methods which involve loss of sexual self-control, tigerish brutality, persistent rape of the wife's person, and uncleanness.

The word "yoga" is a Sanskrit word which means "union." It comes from the same root as our English word "yoke," i.e., that which unites. It has been used for centuries by Hindu occultists and metaphysicians, to signify the philosophy which teaches mankind to enter into that state of oneness with the Divine which will secure them both spiritual bliss and power over their bodies and over material things. To what a wonderful extent this yogic power can be carried is only beginning to be dimly apprehended by us in America, here and there, among students of the "higher thought." But the Orientals have known of it for centuries.

"Whosoever is born of God," writes the Apostle John, in the third chapter of his first Epistle, "doth not commit sin; for his seed remaineth in him; and he cannot sin, because he is born of God."

Paul (I. Thess. 4) admonishes: "This is the will of God, . . . that ye should abstain from fornication: That every one of you should know how to possess his vessel in sanctification and honor; not in the lust of concupiscence {unlawful desire of carnal pleasure}, even as the Gentiles which know not God:. . . . For God hath not called us unto uncleanness, but unto holiness." In Genesis 6 we find that Noah is especially praised because he was "perfect *in his generations*; Noah walked with God" (evidently, during coition).

In my Right Marital Living, I emphasize the importance of thought union with the Divine, Central Force of the universe as the third partner during the sexual embrace. This is physiologically of importance because, without such union, it is impossible to fully control one's mentality or subconsciousness, and, through the mentality, the orgasm, which always begins on the mental plane, and which is partly worked out on that plane; and if the orgasm be not fully controlled, it is dangerous to the man to attempt to suppress the ejaculation of semen at this moment, as such suppression is apt to result in an enlarged prostate gland, or in damage to the nervous system in various ways.

But there is another reason for union with the Divine during the act; it is that one thereby enters into fuller harmony with the universe, giving and receiving sexual pleasure, in a way undreamt of without such union.

Moreover, it is a duty—a courtesy, if one may use such a term in this connection—which we owe to that wonderful, all-pervading Force in whom we live and move and have our being.

Take, for instance, the case of a child to whom you give a box of bonbons. If the child has been properly brought up, the first thing it will do, after thanking you for the gift, will be to open the box and share the goodies with its little brothers and sisters, and its father and mother; then it will come to you, the giver, and offer to share them with you, and insist, sweetly, that it will enjoy them ever so much more if you will eat just one or two also. This is the right thing, the courteous thing, the loving and altogether fitting thing for a child to do on such an occasion.

Now the Lord has given each one of us a box of delicious sexual bonbons, and, for my part, I think it is little enough that we can do, to offer to share one or two of these bonbons with the Giver. It would seem, at least, common courtesy on our part to do so.

"But," you object, "the Ultimate Force which we call God is impersonal, and does not experience sexual desires or passions."

Indeed! Then, may I inquire, my friend, whence you received your own sex desires? Do you suppose, for one moment, that there is *any* attribute of your being which is not an inherency of the First Cause?

Is there, indeed, anything in all the universe, even your own capacity for individual, personal liking for a given man or woman, which can be conceived of as not inherent in the First Cause?

Therefore the First Cause, the Ultimate Force, impersonal though it be, must be inherently capable of sexual feeling and of individual personal attraction to any given creature.

The Ultimate Force of the universe must, of necessity, be both masculine and feminine in its inherencies. As masculine essence, it should be thought of as entering through the man's organ during the sexual embrace, giving pleasure and receiving pleasure from the wife. As feminine essence, it should be thought of as residing within the wife's body (the temple of the Holy Spirit) at the vagina and uterus, riding the man's organ, giving pleasure and receiving pleasure therefrom. Thus, the experience is shared with God in every possible way, and is sanctified and glorified.

Remember that Jesus said that the first and greatest commandment is to love God with all our soul and mind and heart, *and with all our strength.*

No bridal couple who have once shared the joy of a controlled orgasm and sustained thrill with God will ever care to leave God out of the partnership in future.

The Oriental occultists claim that a prayer breathed at such a supreme moment of self-controlled and rapturous union with Deity is sure to be granted. This is because such a process is a divinely ordained way of so displacing the psycho-physical threshold of sensibility as to enter into the most perfect communion with the Spirit of God which is known to us earthly beings. When the inward self realizes its oneness with the Ultimate Force of the universe, it will ask only for what it is right it should receive; and, as the Divine Scientists insist, all power is ours, when we rise in thought to oneness inwardly with the Divine Central Force.

Only that wedding night, only that honeymoon in which spiritual communion with the Ultimate Force of the universe forms part and parcel of the sexual act, is truly blest.

Chapter 5

Sacrifice

By limiting herself to direct personal instruction, Ida had hoped to mollify the two most powerful forces that threatened to prevent her from sharing her message with the world: her mother and the law. At first, Lizzie Decker seemed satisfied with her daughter's compromise, but when Ida wanted to use the office at 1034 Race Street to see her clients, her mother flatly refused, proclaiming that, as long as she was alive, she would not allow her house to be used for teaching "the slimy subject of sex."[234] Ida realized that she would eventually have to break completely with her mother in order to achieve her goals. In 1895, she wrote:

> I know so well, from the experience of years, that as long as I stay anywhere within Mother's jurisdiction, I shall be like a poodle at the end of a chain, never knowing when I shall be hauled up short for some innocent excursion, and liable to be switched off even from my expected pat at any corner of the road. While I remain with mother, I shall never do anything; my life will be a nonentity in the future as it has always been in the past. . . . I have been hoping that I might gradually interest her in my ideas so as to at least tolerate my propagandism; but it seems hopeless, so far. She is bitterly opposed to anything and everything that I say on either sex or psychics, and tries to choke me off in the most innocent discussions with my friends. Her prejudice seems to render her blind and deaf in advance to ideas to which she would have gladly listened a few

234 Letter from Ida Craddock to Katie Wood, July 5, 1901, SCRC.

> years ago. I am afraid it will end in my having to go away from her for the sake of peace and freedom.[235]

The first step was to obtain an office where she could see her clients without interference. With help from her spirit guides, Ida found a room for rent on Arch Street in Philadelphia that met all of her needs: at seven dollars a week, it was just affordable on her salary; it was within walking distance to her job at City Hall; and the landlady was sympathetic to her teachings, being familiar with the work of Alice Bunker Stockham. By August 1897, Ida had thus secured a measure of independence, although, with her mother living only blocks away, she was not entirely free of her influence.

With renewed confidence, Ida also began to dispense some of her teachings to carefully selected clients by mail. In so doing, however, she also tempted her other great nemesis: Postal Law 3893, the so-called "Comstock Law" that prohibited the sending of "obscene, lewd, and lascivious" literature through the mail. And it was not long before the law caught up with her. In the spring of 1898 she was indicted by a U.S. District Court in Philadelphia for mailing three pamphlets: "Letter to a Prospective Bride," "Advice to a Bridegroom," and her expanded "Danse du Ventre." Ida suspected that the charges were actually motivated by her refusal to pay assessments to the Quay party,[236] which were regularly collected from the employees at City Hall. In any event, her mother struck a deal with U.S. District Attorney Jones: the case would be suspended if Ida promised not to mail the pamphlets again. Reluctantly, feeling she had no choice, Ida agreed.

But Mrs. Decker and D.A. Jones also struck a secret deal, in which Ida would avoid prosecution only by allowing herself to be admitted "voluntarily" for observation to the Pennsylvania Hospital for the Insane, also known as Kirkbride's Asylum.[237] Again feeling she had no choice, she stayed a patient at the asylum for almost three months during the summer of 1898, diagnosed with nothing more specific than having "a chronic form

---

235 Letter from Ida Craddock to W. T. Stead, July 11, 1895, SCRC.

236 The local Republican political machine, named for its powerful and corrupt party boss, U.S. Senator Matthew Stanley Quay (1833–1904).

237 So named for its founder, Thomas Story Kirkbride (1809–1883), an early advocate for humane treatment of the mentally ill. In spite of its progressive reputation, however, the 19th-century asylum was not a pleasant place to be. Ida once wrote: "I have always had a horror of insane asylums. Suppose they should give me bromides, or douche me with cold water, or treat certain parts of my body with electricity? Why, they might make a mental wreck of me before they produced me in court."

of mental trouble."[238] However, she was not legally committed, or ever judged insane by any court. In September, she was allowed to leave, the experience convincing her that she would rather suffer prison than ever to return.

Worried that her mother might try to send her back to the asylum, she fled once more to London and the sanctuary offered by W. T. Stead. This time, however, her stay was short-lived. Mrs. Decker wrote to Stead, incensed by the fact that her daughter had taken to calling herself "*Mrs.* Craddock," thereby attempting to legitimize her spirit marriage. It was all a lie, insisted her mother. Stead, of course, knew better. Unfortunately, he was out of town when the letter arrived, and it was read by his wife instead. Mrs. Stead had not been let in on the secret that Ida wasn't conventionally married, and was not as understanding about the idea of spirit marriage as her husband was, so he had quite a bit of explaining to do when he returned to London. Although the Stead marriage survived the scandal, Ida did not feel comfortable remaining in London with them. She set sail for New York on December 30, 1898.

Once back in the U.S., she made her way to Chicago, being careful to avoid Pennsylvania on the way, as her mother had hinted that she had "parole papers" she could use to have Ida committed to the asylum for good. She probably chose Chicago because Alice Bunker Stockham was there; before leaving England, she told her correspondents that mail could be sent to her in care of Stockham's address. Once established in Chicago, she rented a room on Dearborn Street that served as both her home and her office for seeing marital reform clients—her "pupils," as she called them.

Ida flourished in Chicago. It was here that she wrote *Right Marital Living* and *The Wedding Night*, distributing them to her clients both in person and through the mail. Also, inspired by Vivekananda's *Raja Yoga*, which was sweeping the nation in popularity at the time, she established the Church of Yoga with herself as "pastor and priestess." Not to be confused with the more physical type of yoga (*hatha* yoga) ubiquitous today in the form of workout videos and fitness studios, the *raja* or "royal" yoga embraced by Ida emphasized meditation, breathing exercises, and the attainment of advanced states of spiritual consciousness. Its requisite discipline and self-control nicely complemented her own teachings.

238 Letter from Owen Copp to Theodore Schroeder, September 20, 1913, SCRC.

While in Chicago, Ida also made contact with a mysterious "Oriental teacher" whom she described as a Persian Sun worshipper who had trained at the Mazdaznan Temple of El-Kharman, in what is now Iran. This was Otoman Zar-Adhusht Hanish,[239] founder of the Mazdaznan Temple Association, the first Zoroastrian religious organization established in the United States. Ida studied "Mazdaznan breathing" techniques under Hanish, who also had his own sexual teachings involving the prolongation of intercourse for spiritual purposes.[240]

In May of 1899, the medical journal *Chicago Clinic* published an edited version of *Right Marital Living* that generated much interest among its readership and resulted in orders for Ida's pamphlets to start pouring in from doctors all over the country. It also attracted the attention of the postal authorities, who promptly declared the issue un-mailable and began to investigate Ida once more. In October, she was indicted in U.S. District Court for sending copies of *Right Marital Living* through the mail in violation of the Comstock Law. She was defended by the famed attorney Clarence Darrow,[241] who posted her $500 bond and convinced her to take a plea bargain in exchange for a three-month suspended jail sentence. Ida later described the incident in "The Marriage Relation":

> Of course, there was no prospect of a fair trial; and as the United States Court invariably stands for conviction upon such a charge, my lawyer very prudently counseled me to allow him to effect a compromise; which was done. The prosecution demanded, if they were to compromise, that I give up to be burned, not only the *Right Marital Living* pamphlets, but also the other three,[242] which were quite outside the jurisdiction of the Court. As I was helpless before the Holy fathers of the American Inquisition, there was nothing for me to do but to tamely submit to this outrage, if I did not wish to go to trial and risk being sent to the penitentiary.[243]

Discouraged, especially by the loss of her stock of pamphlets which she had struggled to raise enough money to print, Ida moved to Denver in

239 Born in Germany as Otto Hanisch (1854–1936).

240 Some of these were later published in *Inner Studies: A Course of Twelve Lessons* (1902), which bears the conspicuous influence of Ida's teachings from *Right Marital Living*.

241 Clarence Seward Darrow (1857–1938), a prominent civil libertarian who later argued against the prohibition of teaching evolution in public schools during the so-called "Scopes monkey trial."

242 The pamphlets for which she was previously indicted in Philadelphia.

243 Ida Craddock, "The Marriage Relation" (SCRC, 1900), p. 7.

the summer of 1900. There she was also able to pick up a few pupils, but mostly she lived a quiet existence, spending "months of unremitting toil" writing her magnum opus, "The Marriage Relation," which encompassed all of her accumulated knowledge on sexual mysticism and marital reform, incorporating and elaborating upon many of her previous works.

The result was a dense 437-page typescript with chapters on "Sex: The Chief Factor of Civilization," "The Religion of the Body," "Unscientific and Irreligious Marriage: The Legal Prostitutes of the United States," "The Physical Side of Marriage," "The Metaphysical Side of Marriage," "The Mother," "Parenthood and Heredity," "The Lover," and "Our Young People: Their Sexual Life." Its ambitious scope covered such diverse topics as sex in plants and animals, methods of selecting the sex of a child at conception, venereal diseases, hygiene, and dress reform. Included were all of the components that had contributed to her philosophy: the Danse du Ventre, male continence, Divine Science, New Thought, magnetation, yoga, Mazdaznan breathing, and more.

She also acknowledged it to be "the most frank and explicit book on the details of the marriage relation that has ever been offered to the public."[244] In it, she openly discusses such taboo subjects as masturbation, "the French method" (fellatio), and homosexuality (all of which she condemned), and earnestly advocates radically progressive positions on sex education for children and trial marriages for the young (involving sex but no pregnancy, thanks to male continence). She knew, however, that it could not be published "until such time as the public shows itself ready for it"[245] and so kept it under wraps.

After sending off her latest draft of "The Marriage Relation" to W. T. Stead in London for safekeeping, Ida left Denver in the spring of 1901 and moved to Washington, DC, where she intended to stay for some time. This was not to be, however, as she was, in her own words, "fired from the city." The authorities very quickly caught on to her, tipped off by a secret informant. On April 24 she was arrested and arraigned once more for mailing her pamphlets. This time, however, she was released without trial on the condition that she leave the city at once.

So she made her way directly and deliberately to Anthony Comstock's

244 Craddock, "The Marriage Relation," p. 7.

245 Letter from Ida Craddock to the Public, October 16, 1902, published in *The Truth Seeker* (New York), November 1, 1902, p. 694.

hometown, New York City. She was tired of the secret charges and judicial deals that, although they kept her out of jail, also prevented her from fulfilling her mission by suppressing her teachings from public view. She was eager to have her persecution come out in the open so all could see what was being done to her. In a letter to the *Chicago Clinic*, she wrote: "I have an inward feeling that I am really divinely led here to New York to face this wicked and depraved man Comstock in open court and to strike the blow which shall start the overthrow of Comstockism." She would soon have her chance.

In the meantime, she rented an office at 134 West 23rd Street for seven dollars a week, where she also slept on blankets on the floor until she was eventually able to afford a chaise. She advertised her Church of Yoga and began seeing pupils again, and responded to a steadily increasing volume of correspondence, including more requests for *The Wedding Night* and *Right Marital Living* from professionals and laypeople alike. Also during this time, she continued her studies on behalf of W. T. Stead, producing two well-researched typescripts entitled *Lunar and Sex Worship* and *Sex Worship—Continued* at his request and with his financial support.[246] But all the while, she knew the clock was ticking a steady countdown toward her eventual showdown with Comstock.

Ida did not rush recklessly to meet her fate, however. She was careful to mail her pamphlets only to professionals who sent their requests on printed letterhead, giving her some measure of assurance that they would be used responsibly. This policy did not provide Comstock with any opening to nab her for mailing the offending material to anyone who had actually requested it, since they did not make any complaints. So he tried another approach, employing a strategy that is still widely used to justify the prosecution of indecency in the United States today: the "harmful to minors" ploy.[247] On February 3, 1902, Comstock sent a decoy letter to Ida, in which he pretended to be a seventeen-year-old girl named "Frankie Streeter" and asked if she admitted young girls to her lectures. He also enclosed fifty cents and asked her to mail him a copy of *The Wedding Night*.

246 Published together in a new edition from Teitan Press in 2010.

247 The idea that sexual ideas and imagery are inherently "harmful to minors" continues to be the main excuse for attempts to censor sexual expression, in spite of the absence of any scientific evidence showing this to be the case. See Marjorie Heins, "Identifying What is Harmful or Inappropriate for Minors," New York: Free Expression Policy Project, 2001, and the National Research Council report "Youth, Pornography, and the Internet," Washington, DC: National Academies Press, 2002.

Ida did not take the bait. Instead, she wrote "Frankie" a long reply, returning her money and refusing to send her the pamphlet she requested. She also stated that she had never knowingly admitted any minors to her lectures, due to "a social superstition that young people should be kept as ignorant as possible of all that pertains to the marriage relation," and that because of this superstition, "anybody who instructs a minor in these matters . . . can be dealt with by law."[248] In fact, Ida had figured out that it was Comstock who had sent the letter in an attempt to entrap her, and she sent a copy to her attorney just in case.

Breeze Crest.
Summit. N.J. Feb. 3. 1902.

Madame would you oblige me with a
Copy of your "Wedding Night." I enclose
half a dollar. Do you admit young
girls to your lectures? what do you
charge for two Chum's who would
like to come together? I am past 17
years. Please send Night & oblige me.
address plain Miss Frankie Streeter.
P.O. Box 201
Summit N.J.

Enc. 50cts.

Figure 8. Decoy letter sent by Anthony Comstock to entrap Ida Craddock, published in *The Truth Seeker* (New York), November 8, 1902, p.710.

248 Letter from Ida Craddock to "Frankie Streeter," February 4, 1902, published in *The Truth Seeker* (New York), November 8, 1902, p. 710.

The fact that he had no evidence against her did not stop Comstock, however. A few days later, he had her arrested for violating federal law by sending obscene literature through the mail.

After making bail, Ida began to formulate plans for her defense. But with vindictive zeal, Comstock had her arrested again a few weeks later and charged with violating the New York state law against selling obscenity—taking the opportunity to prosecute her twice for the same crime.[249] Due to a delay in securing the bond, she had to spend a sleepless night in the city jail among drunkards and petty thieves before being released once again.

This time, however, Ida would not go quietly. The weekly Freethought newspaper, *The Truth Seeker*, reported on her arrests, and her old friends E. B. Foote and Henrietta Westbrook provided steadfast support. Foote printed up a pamphlet entitled "Comstock Versus Craddock," giving details of her persecution and testimony from doctors and clergymen lauding the value of her instruction. And Westbrook offered to appear in court on her behalf, telling her that "I have never considered you insane. I never have considered anyone insane simply because they knew more about something than I do."[250]

Ida's state trial took place on Friday, March 14, 1902 before a Special Sessions court presided over by three judges in lieu of a jury. As expected, the judges were decidedly hostile, blocking testimony from doctors as to the educational value of her pamphlets. Because she would not send him *The Wedding Night* in response to his decoy letter, Comstock claimed instead that he had received complaints alleging that Ida had given her pamphlets to two girls under sixteen years of age; but he was not required to produce any witnesses or even the names of his supposed informants. He also improperly attempted to bias the court by bringing up Ida's previous obscenity arrests. Meanwhile, Mrs. Decker tried to convince her daughter's attorney to introduce an insanity defense, but he refused to do so without his client's permission. On Monday, March 17, the judges sentenced Ida to three months in the city workhouse on Blackwell's Island, notorious for its harsh conditions. In pronouncing her sentence, one of the judges remarked: "This is the most awful case that ever came into this

249 A little-known exception to the constitutional protection against double jeopardy, the legal principle of "separate sovereigns" allows a person to be tried separately by both state and federal governments for the same offense.

250 Letter from Henrietta Westbrook to Ida Craddock, February 15, 1902, SCRC.

court. I have never before known of such indescribable filth. I cannot believe that this woman is in her right mind. No woman in her right mind, gentle born and well educated, as the literary style of this book shows, could conceive such filthy phrases. She has caused just such trouble as this in Chicago, Washington, and Philadelphia before she came to this city. We consider her a danger to the public morals."[251]

Ida was allowed to write only one letter per month from prison, scrawled in pencil on small scraps of paper. The knee-length skirts provided to the inmates left her legs bare, and in the cold she suffered from a chronic sore throat. To add insult to injury, she was twice forced to receive vaccinations against her will. When she protested, she was informed that, as a prisoner, she had given up all of her civil rights, which greatly disturbed her. She was told that, if she continued to resist, she would be sent to the dreaded "black room" for solitary confinement and a diet of bread and water. About the incident, she wrote: "I have been at a white heat of indignation over the two outrages inflicted on my person by vaccination by this physician by force, first in the Tombs and then here. These two times are the only instances where a man has ever laid forcible hands on my person, & I have an outraged feeling within my soul, somewhat as though I had been raped. Oh, it is dreadful!"[252]

And yet she did not despair. Most of the content of her letters involved planning her defense in the upcoming federal trial, and making sure that the rent and utilities continued to be paid on her office. It is clear that she intended to continue the fight, and was hopeful that she might expose Comstock's lies in court. She was visited in prison by her lawyer, her mother, and her friends, who provided her with care packages of food and medicine to help lift her spirits and treat her failing health. An appeal for clemency, sent by Henrietta Westbrook to the governor of New York, was acknowledged by his office, but not acted upon.

She was released from prison on June 17, 1902, ill and exhausted, but undeterred from her mission. The Free Speech League sponsored a dinner in her honor at the Clarendon Hotel on the 20th, at which many prominent luminaries of the Freethought movement, including her friend E. B. Foote, gave speeches of praise and support. Ida was greatly touched by the reception she received, and expressed hope that she would be vindi-

---

251 *The Truth Seeker* (New York), March 29, 1902, pp. 199–200.
252 Letter from Ida Craddock to E. B. Foote, Jr., May 12, 1902, SCRC.

cated at her next trial. And she pledged to the assembled audience that she would continue to support their shared struggle for freedom.[253] For the next four months, Ida stayed very busy responding to the outpouring of correspondence from people all over the country expressing their support and requesting copies of her pamphlets.[254]

Ida's trial in federal court took place on October 10, 1902, this time before a jury. However, once again, the trial was rigged against her from the beginning. The medical experts whom Ida had asked to appear as witnesses were not allowed to testify. The jury was not even allowed to see the offending material. Instead, the judge took it upon himself to declare that *The Wedding Night* was obscene, and directed the jury to render their verdict based only on whether it had been mailed, to which Ida had already admitted. The jury had no other choice but to find her guilty, which they did without deliberation. Sentencing was set for October 17, and Ida was released until then under a bond posted by her attorney.

Faced with the certainty of an even harsher prison sentence, Ida put her affairs in order. She shipped the last of her diary entries and precious manuscripts to W. T. Stead in England, safely out of the reach of both the American authorities and her own mother, at either of whose hands they would certainly be destroyed. And she spent the night before her sentencing writing several letters, which she sent to her attorney, E. W. Chamberlain. On the 17th of October, which was to be her last day of freedom, she arranged to meet her mother for breakfast before the sentencing hearing, which was scheduled for 10 A.M. When Ida didn't show up at the restaurant, Mrs. Decker went to her room at 134 West 23rd Street to look for her. There she made a horrible discovery: Ida had committed suicide by disconnecting the conduit from her stove and filling the room with natural gas. She had also slashed her right wrist with a razor, but the bleeding was not serious enough to have caused her death before she succumbed to the gas.[255] Her body was stretched out on her chaise and her belongings neatly packed into her traveling trunk, as if she were preparing to go on a long journey. Only her trusty Remington typewriter, now finally silent, bore witness to her last recorded thoughts.

Although it shocked and surprised everyone, her suicide was not a

253 *The Truth Seeker* (New York), June 28, 1902, p. 409.

254 Of the 200 or so surviving letters found in her collected papers, about 80% date from this period in 1902.

255 "Woman Chose Death Rather Than Prison," *New York World*, October 18, 1902.

desperate act of despondency or capitulation, but a deliberate and well-considered act of defiance and martyrdom. Ida knew that her death would speak louder than anything that Comstock could say to claim victory in her case, and she made careful arrangements to ensure that she would have the last word, even notifying the press that they would be receiving a letter from her attorney. Ida wrote two suicide notes. One was personal, addressed to her mother, explaining that she had chosen to take her own life rather than end up in either an asylum or prison again. The second was addressed to the public and clearly intended for publication. In it, she was finally able to make her case to the world, unimpeded by any judge. The originals are not among her collected papers, but both were printed by the *Truth Seeker,* from which they are here reproduced.

That her suicide was not a hastily conceived reaction to the circumstances is borne out by the fact that she had previously considered the possibility that she might have to die for her beliefs. In her diary for December 6, 1896, not long after the "The Danse du Ventre" was first censored by the Post Office, Ida wrote prophetically:

> Well, it is my last ditch. I don't care tuppence for my life now. I will lay it down gladly for the cause of preaching right sexual living. But, *when I lay it down,* I intend to do it in a way that will advertise widely the great wrong to liberty which chokes my soul's freedom of speech. I have striven to live for the truth according to my light. But I cannot and I will not be silenced! If not in life, then in death, this gospel *shall* be preached throughout the world.
>
> As to what awaits me after death—whatever punishment may be mine for quitting this world ahead of time, at least I shall be in a land where people think purely about sex relations. That, of itself, would make almost any punishment endurable, and would constitute Heaven for me.

Ida's death was widely reported in the newspapers, from New York to Los Angeles, Atlanta, Chicago, and Washington. The *New York World,* which had first printed her "Danse du Ventre" letter, included her picture and quoted from her suicide letters. But the most outrage was expressed in the pages of the *Truth Seeker,* which carried both of the suicide letters, Comstock's original decoy letter and Ida's response, and several articles and letters critical of the trial.

Comstock, meanwhile, remained smug, insisting that Ida had furnished her teachings to minors and denying ever receiving her response to his decoy letter, charges refuted by her lawyer. But public sympathy favored Ida and turned against Comstock. Chicago physician Juliet Severance[256] wrote that "Ida Craddock was a pure-minded, intelligent woman, working with a clean conscience for the good . . . of humanity."[257] The *Washington Post* noted that "she was a woman of culture." And a prominent New York clergyman, Rev. W. S. Rainsford,[258] publicly condemned Comstock for hounding her to death and called for his dismissal from the New York Society for the Suppression of Vice.[259] A stung Comstock responded by threatening to sue Rainsford for libel, which did nothing to bolster his reputation in the eyes of the public.[260]

Ida's suicide, and the public outcry it generated, marked the beginning of a decline in Anthony Comstock's power and influence. Although the NYSSV stood by their man, contributions to the society dropped off sharply after the episode. And in December, the U.S. government informed Comstock that they would no longer pay his witness fees or subsidize his travel, important sources of revenue for him. The next year, he suffered a nervous breakdown and was forced into an extended convalescence. Although he eventually recovered, he was a shadow of his previously formidable self. He died in 1915 after unsuccessfully attempting to convict Margaret Sanger[261] for promoting birth control through the mail.

---

256 Juliet H. Severance (1833–1917) was one of the first women in the U.S. to graduate with a medical degree. She was also a spiritualist, vegetarian, and outspoken advocate of women's rights.

257 *The Truth Seeker* (New York), November 1, 1902, p. 698.

258 William Stephen Rainsford (1850–1933), the Irish-born rector of St. George's Episcopal Church.

259 *New York Times*, October 29, 1902.

260 *New York World*, November 4, 1902.

261 Margaret Higgins Sanger Slee (1879–1966), a New York women's rights activist and founder of the American Birth Control League, which eventually became Planned Parenthood.

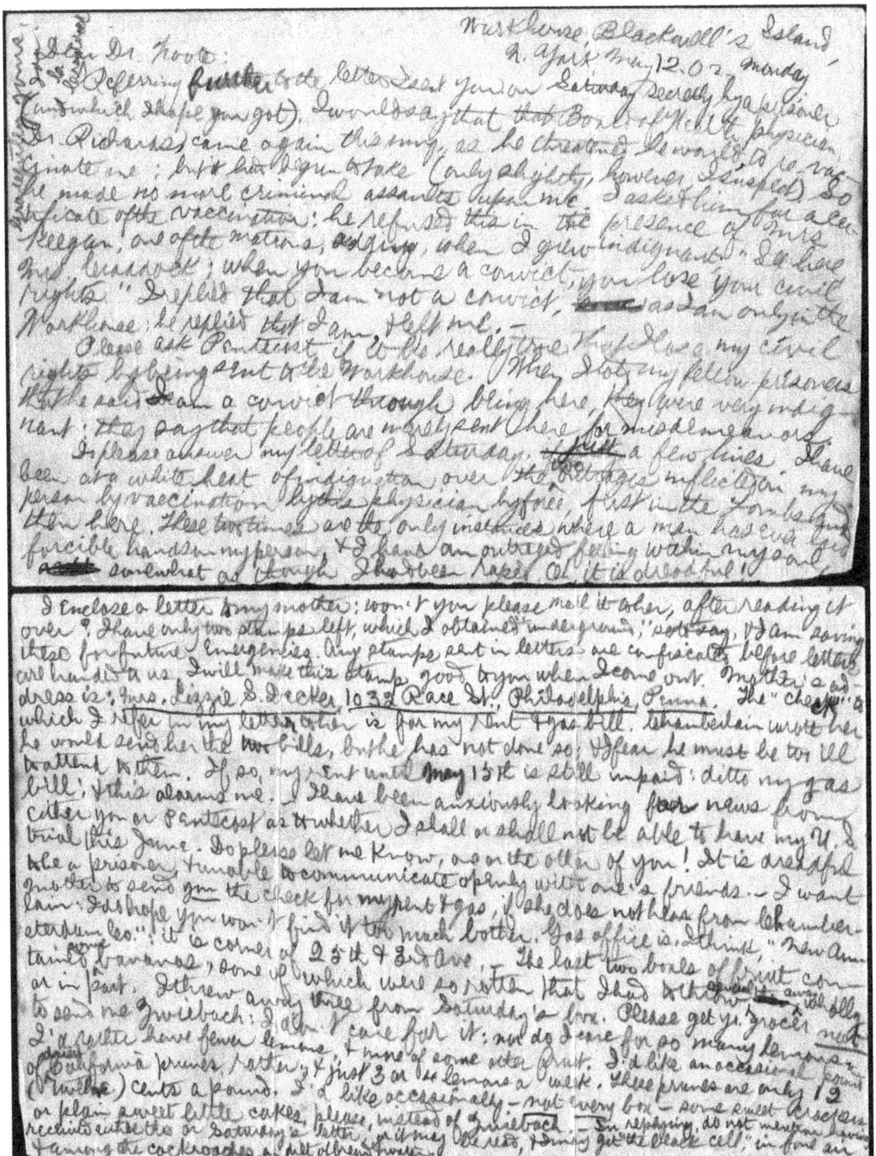

Figure 9. Letter sent from prison by Ida Craddock to E. B. Foote, Jr., May 12, 1902, from the Ida Craddock papers, courtesy of SCRC.

Letter from Prison (1902)

Workhouse, Blackwell's Island
N. York, May 12. 02, Monday
Dear Dr. Foote:
Referring further to the letter I sent you on Saturday secretly by a prisoner (and which I hope you got), I would say that that Board of Health physician, Dr. Richards, came again this mng. as he threatened he would, to re-vaccinate me; but it had begun to take (only slightly, however, I suspect). So he made no more criminal assaults upon me. I asked him for a certificate of the vaccination; he refused this in the presence of Mrs. Keegan, one of the matrons, scolding, when I grew indignant; "See here Mrs. Craddock; when you become a convict, you lose your civil rights." I replied that I am not a convict, as I am only in the Workhouse; he replied that I am. Help me.

Please ask Pentecost if it be really true that I lose my civil rights by being sent to the Workhouse. When I told my fellow-prisoners that he said I am a convict through being here, they were very indignant; they say that people are merely sent here for misdemeanors.

So please answer my letter of Saturday, if *just* a few lines. I have been at a white heat of indignation over the two outrages inflicted on my person by vaccination by this physician by force, first in the Tombs and then here. These two times are the only instances where a man has ever laid forcible hands on my person, & I have an outraged feeling within my soul, somewhat as though I had been raped. Oh, it is dreadful!

I enclose a letter to my mother; won't you please mail it to her, after reading it over? I have only two stamps left, which I obtained "underground," so to say, & I am saving these for future emergencies. Any stamps sent in letters are confiscated before letters are handed to us. I will make this stamp good to you when I come out. Mother's address is: Mrs. Lizze S. Decker, 1032 Race St., Philadelphia, Penn. The "check" to which I refer in my letter to her is for my rent & gas bill. Chamberlain wrote her he would send her the two bills, but has not done so; & I fear he must be too ill to attend to them. If so, my rent until May 15th is still unpaid: ditto my gas bill; & this alarms me. I have been anxiously looking for news from either you or Pentecost as to whether

I shall or shall not be able to have my U.S. trial this June. So please let me know, one or the other of you! It is dreadful to be a prisoner, unable to communicate openly with one's friends. I want Mother to send you the check for my rent & gas, if she does not hear from Chamberlain; I do hope you won't find it too much bother. Gas office is, I think, "New Amsterdam Co."; it is corner of 25th & 3rd Ave. The last two boxes of fruit contained some bananas, some of which were so rotten that I had to throw several away, wholly or in part. I threw away three from Saturday's box. Please get your grocer *not* to send me Zwiebach; I don't care for it; nor do I care for so many lemons. I'd rather have fewer lemons, & more of some other fruit. I'd like an occasional pound of dried California prunes, rather; & just 3 or 4 lemons a week. These prunes are only 12 (twelve) cents a pound. I'd like occasionally—not every box—some sweet crackers or plain sweet little cakes, please, instead of Zwiebach. In replying, do not mention having received either this or Saturday's letter, or it may be read, & I may get "the black cell," in foul air & among the cockroaches, on diet of bread & water.

Eventfully yours, Ida C. Craddock

Ida's Last Letter to her Mother[262] (1902)

New York, Oct. 16, 1902
Dear, Dear Mother:
I know you will grieve over me for having taken my life. . . . My dear, dear mother, oh, how sorry I am to hurt you, as I know this act will do. But, oh, mother, I cannot, I will not consent to go to the asylum, as you are evidently planning to have me go. I know that this means a perpetual imprisonment all my long life, unless I either recant my religious beliefs or else hypocritically pretend to do so. I cannot bring myself to consent to any of these three alternatives. I maintain my right to die as I have lived, a free woman, not cowed into silence by any other human being. If, on the other hand, the prison to which Judge Thomas evidently proposes to send me were to be my destined lot (you know very well that he wishes and means to lock me up for a long, long term, which is practically my death warrant), my work is ended so far as this world is concerned. My books have been given a start, approved by physicians and other reputable citizens, but the world is not yet ready for all the beautiful teachings which I have to give it. Other people will take up my work, however, some day—will take it up where I laid it down, and will start from where I left off and do better work than they could have done but for me. Some day you'll be proud of me. You will understand that what I have done has been done because you and my father prepared me for just such a propaganda to humanity. You may ask why I did not give it up and come home to live with you, resuming my name of "Miss Craddock," and taking up other work. But, dear mother, I could be of no possible help to you, with the shadow of reproach which bigots and impure-minded people have put on me. I should be only a hindrance to your respectability. Moreover, my individuality has some rights. I cannot recant my beliefs and throw aside a principle for which I have toiled and struggled for nine years, even at the behest of a mother that is dear to me.

Do not grieve, dear, dear mother; the world beyond the grave, believe me, is far more real and substantial than is this world in which we today live. This earth life which the Hindus have for centuries termed "*Māyā*," that is illu-

262 Published in *The Truth Seeker* (New York), October 25, 1902, p. 680.

sion. My people assure me that theirs is the real, the objective, the material world. Ours is the lopsided, the incomplete world. You and I shall meet in that beautiful world over there and shall know each other as individuals just as clearly as we do here, only more so. I do not know whether it will be possible for me to return to you; but if I can, I will do so. Only remember that you must try to keep the five rules for clear thinking and correct living which my people have given me. If I do come back, of this I feel sure. As you may have forgotten these, I am going to give them here again:

1. Do your daily earthly duty undeterred by calls to mediumship from any source.
2. Be self-controlled and strive to be more amiable and loving every day.
3. Wait and watch for the highest.
4. Avoid selfish seeking of self-ease.
5. Abide in purity, not merely moral purity, but physical cleanliness; and still more, intellectual clearness—that is freedom from prejudice; think clearly.

Love all people, even those who have wronged you, if you would receive clear communications from over the border. It is possible that I may come as I have said. I do not know. But in any event, it cannot be long before you will join me over here, and I shall be on hand to welcome you, dear, dear mother, when you do come.

Oh, if only you could have brought yourself to have let me live at home to carry on my propaganda under your modifying advice, then this need never have been, and I could have lived for many years to carry on a moderate, far less crudely radical propaganda than I have done. I have had nobody to stand by me and to help me; I have had to carve out my own road without any predecessors to guide me.

You will find $40 in my trunk. I have written to Mr. Chamberlain tonight to tell you just where I have placed it. I do not know who may read this letter before you get it, and so have taken this precaution.

Will you mind expressing the various books I addressed here tonight? As you know, I have been unable to get out today to send them off as I hoped to do. For there is an Adams Express Company on this street, several doors this side of Fifth Avenue.

Dear, dear mother, please remember that I love you, and that I shall always love you. Even if you get fantastic communications from the border land, remember that the real Ida is not going there.

The real Ida, your own daughter, loves you and waits for you to come soon over to join her in the beautiful blessed world beyond the grave, where Anthony Comstocks and corrupt judges and impure-minded people are not known. We shall be very happy together some day, you and I, dear mother; there will be a blessed reality for us both at last. I love you, dear mother; never forget that. And love cannot die; it is no dream, it is a reality. We shall be the individuals over there that we are here, only with enlarged capacities. Goodbye, dear mother, if only for a little while. I love you always. I shall never forget you, that would be impossible; nor could you ever forget me. Do not think the next world an unsubstantial dream; it is material, as much so as this; more so than this. We shall meet there, dear mother.

Your affectionate daughter,
Ida C. Craddock

Ida's Last Letter to the Public[263] (1902)

Room 5, No. 134 West 23rd St.
New York, Oct. 16, 1902
To the Public:
I am taking my life, because a judge, at the instigation of Anthony Comstock, has decreed me guilty of a crime which I did not commit—the circulation of obscene literature—and has announced his intention of consigning me to prison for a long term.

The book has been favorably reviewed by medical magazines of standing, and has been approved by physicians of reputation. The Rev. Dr. Rainsford of this city, in two letters to me, partially approved this book so far as to say that if all young people were to read it, a great deal of misery, suffering, and disappointment could be avoided, and that to have arrested me on account of it, as Mr. Comstock had done, was ridiculous. This little book, *The Wedding Night*, and its companion pamphlet, *Right Marital Living*, have been circulated with approval among Social Purity women, members of the W.C.T.U., clergymen and reputable physicians; various physicians have ordered these books from me for their patients, or have sent their patients to me to procure them or to receive even fuller instruction orally; respectable married women have purchased them from me for their daughters, husbands for their wives, wives for husbands, young women for their betrothed lovers. On all sides, these little pamphlets have evoked from their readers commendation for their purity, their spiritual uplifting, their sound common sense in treating of healthful and happy relations between husbands and wives.

In contrast with this mass of testimony to their purity and usefulness, a paid informer, who is making his living out of entering complaints against immoral books and pictures, has lodged complaint against one of my books as "obscene, lewd, lascivious," and proposes to indict the other book later on, so as to inflict legal penalties on me a second time. This man, Anthony Comstock, who is unctuous with hypocrisy, pretends that I am placing these books in the hands of minors, even little girls and boys, with a view to the debauchment of their morals. He has not, however, produced any young person thus

263 Published in *The Truth Seeker* (New York), November 1, 1902, p. 694.

far who has been injured through their perusal; nor has any parent or guardian come forward who claims even the likelihood of any young person's being injured by either of these books; nor has he even vouchsafed the addresses of any of the people from whom he states he has received complaints. In addition, he has deliberately lied about the matter. He stated to Judge Thomas of the United States Circuit Court (secretly, not while in court), that I had even handed one of these books to the little daughter of the janitress of the building in which I have my office. It so happens that there is no janitress in this building, nor is there any little girl connected with same. I took a paper around among the tenants to this effect, which they signed, and which I sent to the judge by my lawyer; also a paper to the same effect, which my landlord stood prepared to attest before a notary, if need be. But even this made no impression upon Judge Thomas; he still is firmly convinced (so he says) that Anthony Comstock is a strictly truthful man.

On Friday last, October 10, I underwent what was supposed to be a fair and impartial trial by jury; but which was really a most unfair trial, before a thoroughly partisan judge, at the close of which he abolished my right of trial by jury on the main question at issue, namely the alleged obscenity of *The Wedding Night* book. My counsel was not permitted to present in evidence circulars which showed that as far back as 1898 and 1899 I was accustomed to state in print that any applicants for oral instruction upon marriage who were under 21 would have to produce written consent from a parent or a guardian. My evidence was almost wholly choked off; neither my counsel nor myself was permitted to endeavor to justify the book by argument. The most the judge would do was to permit me to read from various paragraphs in the book, without comment, if these could explain the indicted paragraphs. Even with this tiny bit of a chance, I made such good use of my opportunity before the jury, that Judge Thomas, who was evidently prejudiced in advance against both myself and my book, saw that he dared not now risk the case to the jury, or he might not manage to convict me after all. And so he announced that he himself intended to pass upon the character of the book. He stated that there is in existence a decision of the United States Supreme Court which gives him this right.

He said he would not let the question go to the jury; he considered the book "obscene, lewd, lascivious, dirty." He added that he would submit to the jury only the question of fact: Did the defendant mail the book? (The charge was "mailing an obscene book.") He said: "Gentlemen of the Jury, the question for you to pass upon is, Did the defendant mail the book? You know that she admits having mailed the book. Please render your verdict. I do not suppose you will care to leave your seats." And the poor little cowed jury could do nothing but to meekly obey the behest of this unrighteous judge, and to pass in their ballots, "Guilty of mailing the book." Which, of course, was no crime at all.

I fully expected that the public press of New York City would duly chronicle this most remarkable invasion of the rights of the people by such an abolishing of the trial by jury; but so far as I could learn, the press remained totally silent.

It is evident that the political pull of the party which fathers Anthony Comstock is too powerful for any newspaper in New York to dare to raise a protest when, at the instigation of this *ex officio* informer, an innocent woman, engaged in a laudable work of sex reform, indorsed by reputable citizens, is arrested on false information and denied her right of trial by jury.

Since Friday last, people of influence and respectability have written to the judge on my behalf and have been to see him; but he announces his inflexible intention of sending me to prison, and, he is careful to malignantly add, "for a long, *long* term." I am a "very *dangerous* woman," he adds; Mr. Comstock has told him most shocking things about me—not in court, however, this paid informer being far too cute to dare to face his victim openly with any such lies.

At my age (I was forty-five this last August) confinement under the rigors of prison life would be equivalent to my death-warrant. The judge must surely know this; and since he is evidently determined to not only totally suppress my work, but to place me where only death can release me, I consider myself justified in choosing for myself, as did Socrates, the manner of my death. I prefer to die comfortably and peacefully, on my own little bed in my own room, instead of on a prison cot.

I am making this statement to the public because I wish to call attention to some of the salient features of Comstockism, in the hope that the public may be led to put down this growing menace to the liberties of the people.

As I said not long since in the *Boston Traveler*, if the reading of impure books and the gazing upon impure pictures does debauch and corrupt and pervert the mind (and we know that it does), when we reflect that Anthony Comstock has himself read perhaps more obscene books, and has gazed upon perhaps more lewd pictures than has any other one man in the United States, what are we to think of the probable state of Mr. Comstock's imagination today upon sexual matters?

The man is a sex pervert; he is what physicians term a Sadist—namely a person in whom the impulses of cruelty arise concurrently with the stirring of sex emotion. The Sadist finds keen delight in inflicting either physical cruelty or mental humiliation upon the source of that emotion. Also he may find pleasure in gloating over the possibilities to others. I believe that Mr. Comstock takes pleasure in lugging in on all occasions a word picture (especially to a large audience) of the shocking possibilities of the corruption of the morals of innocent youth.

This man serves two masters; he is employed and paid by the Society of the Suppression of Vice, but he secures from the United States Government an appointment as postal inspector without pay; so that he is able, if he wishes, to use his official position for the furtherance of the private ends of his society and, presumably of himself. *Ex officio* informers, with their attendant spies and decoys, have been throughout history notoriously a means of exploiting the government for private and corrupt purposes.

For over nine years I have been fighting, singlehanded and alone, against Comstockism. Time and time again I have been pushed to the wall, my books have been seized and burned, and I myself have been publicly stigmatized in the press by Comstock and Comstockians as a purveyor of indecent literature. Yet this very literature has been all the while quietly circulating with approval among men and women of the utmost respectability and purity of life, and I have received numerous letters attesting its worth.

Not only this. Comstockism can be used, as was the medieval Inquisition at times, to gratify private malice, as the complainant does not need to appear in court. This was done to me in Philadelphia because, while holding a petty position as amanuensis in the Bureau of Highways, I declined right along to pay political assessments to the Quay party. For months they tracked me night and day wherever I went, vainly hoping to learn something detrimental to my character, and at last they arranged to have me indicted for mailing immoral literature, as they could find no other means of successfully damaging my reputation.

John Wanamaker once stated in a political speech that the Quay party were relentless in hounding those who refused to pay political assessments. They would follow up such a person even when he went into the service of other employers, and leave no stone unturned to ruin him in after years. This may or not be so in my own case; I do not know. But I do know that when I went to Washington a secret complaint was lodged with the police. My accuser never faced me openly in court. I pleaded my own case before the police judge, saved one book (*Right Marital Living*) and won many encomiums from those present in court because of the uplifting character of my plea; nevertheless I was driven from the city.

Each time that I have been arrested, I have escaped by a compromise; but I resolved, when I came to New York, that if again attacked by Comstockism, I would stand my ground and fight to the death. Perhaps it may be that in my death, more than in my life, the American people may be shocked into investigating the dreadful state of affairs which permits that unctuous sexual hypocrite, Anthony Comstock, to wax fat and arrogant, and to trample upon the liberties of the people, invading, in my own case, both my right to freedom of religion and to freedom of the press. There is only one lawful excuse for the community's interfering with anyone's religion or publication in America; and that is, the invasion, by means of that religion or those publications, of other people's rights to life, liberty, or the pursuit of happiness. No proof of such injury wrought has been produced in my case; the testimony for the government against me rests entirely upon the mere say-so of this paid informer.

Every one of the paragraphs indicted in *The Wedding Night* is the outcome of talks which I have had with distinguished physicians and also with men and women among my pupils. I have looked into the hearts of hundreds of men and women during the nine years in which I have been engaged in sex reform work, and my soul burns within me when I see how husbands and wives are suffering, and how nearly all of this suffering could be done away with, if only Anthony Comstock were not hoodwinking the public into believing that sexual information in printed books must be kept away from them, so as to protect the morals of innocent youth. Surely, Mr. Comstock's idea of the nature of the marriage relation must be singularly impure, when he ventures to pretend that it should not be known of as to its details by young people who are sufficiently mature to be seeking for enlightenment!

In the courts, however, in obscene literature cases, a precedent has been established by which the defendant is forbidden to produce witnesses in behalf of the accused book, so that I was legally prohibited from summoning physicians to testify on behalf of the book.

Owing to this and to other legal precedents which hamper the defendant in obscene literature cases as is done in no other criminal cases anywhere; owing also the dense ignorance and prejudice which prevail in regard to the scientific, open discussion of sexual matters; and, most of all, owing to Mr. Comstock's persistent lies and to his adroitness in depicting the shocking possibilities of corrupting the morals of innocent youth by permitting young people to peruse any enlightening literature upon the details of normal, healthy, pure marital relations—matters have now reached the point where it is only necessary to accuse a person of mailing so-called "obscene" literature in order to convict him. As no witnesses are allowed to testify as to the effect of the book upon themselves or their young daughters or young sons, or, if physicians, upon their patients, neither judge nor jury are in a position to learn the actual facts in the case. And now, in my own case the other day, the legal precedent has been established by the action of Judge Thomas, in the United States Circuit Court, of not only excluding witnesses in behalf of the indicted book, but even forbidding either the defendant or her counsel to attempt to explain the reasons for printing the indicted paragraphs or in any way seeking to justify, in an argument, the publication of the book; and then finally, by a legal subterfuge, abolishing the defendant's right of trail by jury; the latter being a proceeding which has always been recognized by true patriots as a serious menace to the liberties of the people.

In addition, in my own case, there is the matter of persecution for my religious views. Although this question did not directly arise before Judge Thomas, yet, from the paragraph which I read from my book, and which I was permitted to read only without explanation, it must have been evident that the book contained a religious propaganda, and that, indeed, the religious teaching was the foremost matter, the physical teachings being only subservient thereto.

But in my trial under the New York state law last March, before three judges, the religious question did very decidedly arise. In that court, Judge McKean so far forgot his oath of office (to administer justice impartially) as to hotly denounce my book as "blasphemous" (presumably because I am teaching the duty and the joy of communion with God in the marriage relation, so as to render it sacramental). Of course, this was illegal on his part. No judge has any right to denounce a prisoner because he differs with that prisoner in his religious belief.

I earnestly hope that the American public will awaken to a sense of the danger which threatens it from Comstockism, and that it will demand that Mr. Comstock shall no longer be permitted to suppress works on sexology. The American people have a right to seek and to obtain knowledge upon right living in the marriage relation, either orally or in print, without molestation by this paid informer, Anthony Comstock, or by anybody else.

Dear fellow-citizens of America, for nine long years I have faced social ostracism, poverty, and the dangers of persecution by Anthony Comstock for your sakes. I had a beautiful gospel of right living in the marriage relation, which I wanted you to share with me. For your sakes, I have struggled along in the face of great odds; for your sakes I have come at last to the place where I must lay down my life for you, either in prison or out of prison. Will you not do something for me now?

Well, this is what I want the American public to do for me. Only one of my books, that on *The Wedding Night*, is at present under legal ban. *Right Marital Living*, which is by far the more important book of the two, and which contains the gist of my teaching, has not yet been indicted. Mr. Comstock, however, told me, when arresting me, that he expected to get both books indicted. If sufficient of a popular demand be made for this book, and especially if that demand voice itself in the public press, he will not dare to attack the book in the courts. Will you do this one thing for me, those of you who have public influence? Remember, it is for you and for your children that I have fought this nine years' fight. And although I am going to a brighter and a happier land, nevertheless, I shall still look down upon you all here, and long and long and long that you may know something of the radiantly happy and holy life which is possible for every married couple who will practice these teachings. Even in Paradise I cannot be as happy as I might, unless you share with me this beautiful knowledge.

I beg of you, for your own sakes, and for the future happiness of the young people who are dear to you, to protect my little book, *Right Marital Living.*

I have still other teachings to follow this, upon the marriage relation, later on. I have written a book of between 450 and 500 pages upon "Marriage" in which my teachings are set forth more fully. This book, in manuscript form, is at present stored in a safe place, in friendly hands. It will not be given to the public until such time as the public shows itself ready for it, and prepared to protect this fuller and franker book from persecution. Meanwhile, however, *Right Marital Living* remains unindicted; it sets forth a gospel of marriage which is being preached by no other teacher in America. Its teachings will make your married lives healthier, happier, holier. Will you publicly voice your demand for this little book, *Right Marital Living*, and protect it from Anthony Comstock?

Ida C. Craddock

Epilogue

Ida Craddock's literary legacy would have faded into complete obscurity were it not for the efforts of a New York free-speech lawyer, Theodore Schroeder. Their spheres only just overlapped; Schroeder moved to New York in 1900 and founded the Free Speech League, which sponsored the reception for Ida upon her release from prison, but he never met her in person. In 1913, however, he became interested in her case and began to research her life. He wrote to Ida's mother and to the asylum where she had briefly been a patient. He also tracked down her friend Katie Wood, with whom he corresponded several times and met at least once. But most fortunately for us, he also made contact with W. T. Stead's widow, Estelle, in London. She agreed to send all of Ida's diaries and manuscripts, which had been in the possession of her late husband.

The letters, diaries, typescripts, pamphlets, photographs, and clippings amassed by Schroeder form the bulk of the Ida Craddock collection at Southern Illinois University, Carbondale, where Schroeder's papers were deposited after his death in 1953. The sheer volume of the material was doubtless daunting to him as he tried to decide how to make best use of it. He made at least two attempts at a biography, and took extensive notes toward a presentation of Ida's ideas that was to be entitled *Metaphysics of Sex: The Philosophy of an Erotomaniac*. But of her original works, he only succeeded in publishing one, *Heavenly Bridegrooms*—first in serial form in the journal *Alienist and Neurologist* between 1915 and 1917, then as a book in 1918 accompanied by a brief introduction.

It is also through Schroeder that the value of Ida's works eventually became recognized by the leadership of Ordo Templi Orientis, whose distinct system of sexual magic was being developed around the same time that she first articulated her own mystical sexuality in *Heavenly Bridegrooms*. In 1919, Aleister Crowley, then the head of the British O.T.O. and soon to become its world leader, published a favorable review of *Heavenly Bridegrooms* in the Order's journal, *The Equinox*. This is included as an appendix to the present work. The American branch of the O.T.O. has continued to support the propagation of Ida's legacy, formally recognizing her contribution to the principles for which it stands by inducting her into its honorary Order of the Eagle in 1999. The organization also maintains a website, *www.idacraddock.org*, which makes available electronic versions of her most important works.

Ida's influence can also be discerned in Louis Culling's book, *Sex Magick*.[264] In fact, Culling borrowed heavily from *Heavenly Bridegrooms* to create his three-degree system. The first two degrees, called "Alphaism" and "Dianism," are, for the most part, identical to Ida's formulation. Although Culling briefly mentioned Ida in his introduction, he failed to credit her as a major source for his ideas. Another work that bears the unattributed imprint of Ida's teachings is *Inner Studies: A Course of Twelve Lessons* by the Zoroastrian guru Otoman Zar-Adusht Hanish, of whom Ida was briefly a disciple in 1899.

In addition to the specific influence of her writings, however, Ida must also be recognized for her pioneering contributions to the early history of the free speech, women's rights, and sex education movements. She was neither the first nor the last woman targeted by Comstock, but she *was* the first to outmaneuver him successfully in the end and to turn the tide toward his eventual downfall. Later crusaders for the sexual rights of women, particularly their right to control conception—women like Emma Goldman and Margaret Sanger—owe a debt to Craddock for paving the way with both her innovative clinical work and her courageous publishing efforts. Although there are significant ideological differences between Ida's advocacy and that of later reformers, she deserves credit for challenging the status quo of 19th-century American sexual repression, and paying the ultimate price for the cause of freedom.

264 First published as *A Manual of Sex Magick* (St. Paul, MN: Llewellyn Publications, 1971). Louis Turley Culling (1894–1973) was a senior member of both O.T.O. and C. F. Russell's magical order G.B.G. ("Great Brotherhood of God" or "Gnostic Body of God").

Appendix

Although it attracted little attention in the mainstream press, *Heavenly Bridegrooms* did catch the eye of the famed British occultist Aleister Crowley. Crowley had been introduced via correspondence to Theodore Schroeder through the American poet Harry Kemp.[265] When Crowley came to America in 1914, one of the first things he did was to write Schroeder and arrange a meeting. Crowley wanted Schroeder to organize public lectures for him in America, and Schroeder was interested in Crowley's writings on sex and religion. Crowley eventually sold him a copy of his *Bagh-i-muattar: The Scented Garden of Abdullah the Satirist of Shiraz* (1910), and even offered Schroeder access to proprietary O.T.O. documents on sexual mysticism if he would agree to join the Order and swear not to reveal its secrets. Schroeder never took him up on the offer.

It was through Schroeder that Crowley became acquainted with the ideas of Ida Craddock, with whom he was unabashedly impressed. He wrote a glowing review of *Heavenly Bridegrooms* for his occult periodical *The Equinox*. It is significant that he signed the review as "Baphomet," using his name as head of the O.T.O. in the English-speaking world, thus implicitly affirming the relevance of Craddock's work to the O.T.O.'s mysteries. (Crowley regularly wrote reviews in *The Equinox* under several different names, depending on the subject.) One of his most famous quotes also came from this review: "When you have proved that God is merely a name for the sex instinct, it appears to me not far to the perception that the sex instinct is God."

---

265 Harry Kemp (1883–1960), well known as "America's tramp poet," met Crowley in London and subsequently wrote a sensationalist account of his activities for the *New York World* in 1914.

Crowley also took issue with the skepticism expressed by Schroeder in his introduction to the book, seeing no reason not to take Ida's claims at face value rather than assuming they were hallucinations. After all, Crowley was a practicing occultist who knew very well the power of the subconscious mind to communicate through visions and other mystical states. In one of his books of magical instruction, he wrote: "In this book it is spoken of the Sephiroth and the Paths; of Spirits and Conjurations; of Gods, Spheres, Planes, and many other things which may or may not exist. It is immaterial whether these exist or not. By doing certain things certain results will follow; students are most earnestly warned against attributing objective reality or philosophic validity to any of them."[266] In other words, whether or not the existence of a spirit guide or Borderland husband can be proven objectively, the important measure is the value of the experience to the mystic. In Ida Craddock's case, it is hoped that this book has provided sufficient basis for the reader to judge.

Aleister Crowley's Review of Heavenly Bridegrooms[267]

***Heavenly Bridegrooms*. By Theodore Schroeder and Ida Craddock. Reprinted from *The Alienist and Neurologist*.**

This book has been left entirely unedited by Mr. Theodore Schroeder, with the exception of a very brief explanatory note. I may say that it is one of the most remarkable human documents ever produced, and it should certainly find a regular publisher in book form. The authoress of the MS. claims that she was the wife of an angel. She expounds at the greatest length the philosophy connected with this thesis. Her learning is enormous. She finds traces of similar beliefs in every country in the world, and (having a similar experience of her own) she can hardly be blamed for arguing that one thing confirms the other. Mr. Schroeder is quite logical in calling her paper *An Unintentional Contribution to the Erotogenic Interpretation of Religion*, but commits the errors of *petitio principii*[268] and *non distributio medii*[269] with the most exquisite nonchalance. Only a lawyer could be so shameless. He begs the question with regard to this particular case, assuming

266 Aleister Crowley, "Liber O vel Manus et Sagittae," *The Equinox*, vol. 1, no. 2 (1909), p. 13.

267 Published in *The Equinox*, vol. 3, no. 1 (1919), pp. 280–281.

268 "Assuming the initial point," Latin phrase for the logical fallacy of "begging the question."

269 "Undistributed middle," referring to a type of syllogistic fallacy.

that her relation with the angel was pure hallucination, of which he has no evidence whatsoever. He argues that, since one person both loves and is religious, religion is nothing but a morbid manifestation of the sexual instinct. One does not have even to disagree with him to see how worthless is his reasoning. As a matter of fact, I do half agree with him in my calmer moments in a general way, but the conclusion can be carried a step further. When you have proved that God is merely a name for the sex instinct, it appears to me not far to the perception that the sex instinct is God.

This particular MS. is absolutely sane in every line. The fact that the woman committed suicide twelve or fifteen years afterwards is no more against the sanity of the MS. than the suicide of Socrates proves that the *Republic* is merely the lucubration of a lunatic. I am very far from agreeing with all that this most talented woman sets forth in her paper, but she certainly obtained initiated knowledge of extraordinary depth. She seems to have had access to certain most concealed sanctuaries. I should personally be inclined to attribute her suicide rather to the vengeance of the guardians of those palaces than to any more obvious cause. She has put down statements in plain English which are positively staggering. This book is of incalculable value to every student of occult matters. No Magick library is complete without it.

Baphomet

References

Anon. [Robert Willis.] *The Serpent in Mythology: A Contribution to Comparative Mythology. The Serpent in Paradise, and the Fable of the Fall of Man from a State of Perfection, which Never Existed*. London: Thomas Scott, 1876.

Asprem, Egil. "Magic 'Naturalized'? Negotiating Science and Occult Experience in Crowley's Scientific Illuminism." *Aries*, vol. 8, no. 2, 2008.

Avrich, Paul. *An American Anarchist: The Life of Voltairine de Cleyre*. Princeton, NJ: Princeton University Press, 1978.

Bancroft, Hubert H. *The Book of the Fair*. Chicago: Bancroft, 1893.

Barker-Benfield, G. J. *The Horrors of the Half-Known Life: Male Attitudes Toward Women and Sexuality in Nineteenth-Century America*. New York: Routledge, 2000.

Bastian, Adolf. *Die Völker des östlichen Asien*, vol. 1. Jena: 1866.

Bates, Anna L. *Weeder in the Garden of the Lord*. Lanham, MD: University Press of America, 1993.

Bose, Rajnarain. *The Religion of Love, Intended for All Sects and Churches*. Calcutta: B.M. Press, 1894.

Broun, Heywood, and Margaret Leech. *Anthony Comstock: Roundsman of the Lord*. New York: Albert and Charles Boni, 1927.

Bucks, Richard M. *Cosmic Consciousness: A Study in the Evolution of the Human Mind*. Philadelphia: Innes and Sons, 1905.

Bullough, Vern L. *Continence Redux: The 1880 Version of an Ongoing Debate.* The Journal of Sex Research, 31(2), 1994.

Burton, Richard F. *A Plain and Literal Translation of the Arabian Nights' Entertainments, now Entitled the Book of the Thousand Nights and a Night*, vol. 1. Benares: Kama Shastra Society, 1885.

Burton, Robert. *The Anatomy of Melancholy*. London: Chatto and Windus, 1883.

Burton, Shirley J. "Obscene, Lewd, and Lascivious: Ida Craddock and the Criminally Obscene Women of Chicago, 1873 - 1913" in *The Michigan Historical Review*, 19:1, Spring 1993.

Bush, David V. *Practical Psychology and Sex Life.* (Reprinted by Huron Press, Chicago, 1922.)

Butler, Hiram E. *Practical Methods to Insure Success*. Applegate, CA: Esoteric Publishing Co., 1893.

Cadi [Ida Craddock]. *Spiritual Joys*. Reprinted from *Azoth*, vol. 2, no. 3, March 1918.

Carlton, Donna. *Looking for Little Egypt.* Bloomington, IN: IDD Books, 1994.

Chappell, Vere. "Ida Craddock: Sexual Mystic and Martyr for Freedom." In Richard Metzger, ed. *Book of Lies: The Disinformation Guide to Magick and the Occult*. New York: The Disinformation Company Ltd., 2003.

Charles, Robert Henry. *The Book of Enoch, Translated from Professor Dillmann's Ethiopic Text*. Oxford: Clarendon Press, 1893.

Chavannes, Albert. "Magnetation," 1899. Unpublished TS, Ida Craddock Papers, 1877-1936. Southern Illinois University, Carbondale.

__________. *Magnetation, and Its Relation to Health and Character.* Knoxville, TN: privately printed, 1899.

__________. *Vital Force and Magnetic Exchange.* Knoxville, TN: privately printed, 1888.

Chevallier, Temple. *Translation of the Epistles of Clement of Rome, Polycarp, and Ignatius, and of the First Apology of Justin Martyr*. New York: Henry M. Onderdonk and Co., 1846.

Chia, Mantak and Douglas Abrams. *The Multi-Orgasmic Man.* San Francisco: HarperCollins, 1997.

Clark, William R., James B. H. Hawkins, B. L. Pratten, and S. D. Salmond. *The Writings of Methodius, Alexander of Lycopolis, Peter of Alexandria, and Several Fragments. ANCL*, vol. 14. Edinburgh: T. and T. Clark, 1869.

Conway, Moncure Daniel. *Demonology and Devil-Lore*, 2 vols. New York: Henry Holt and Company, 1881.

Coxe, Cleveland, ed. *Fathers of the Third Century. The Ante-Nicene Fathers, Translations of the Writings of the Fathers down to AD 325*, vol. 6. New York: Christian Literature Company, 1890.

Craddock, Ida C. "The Danse du Ventre," 1893. Unpublished TS, Ida Craddock Papers, 1877-1936. Southern Illinois University, Carbondale.

__________. *Heavenly Bridegrooms: An Unintentional Contribution to the Erotogenetic Interpretation of Religion*. New York: privately printed, 1918.

__________. "The Marriage Relation," 1900. Unpublished TS, Ida Craddock Papers, 1877-1936. Southern Illinois University, Carbondale.

__________. "Lunar and Sex Worship," 1902. In Vere Chappell, ed. *Lunar and Sex Worship*. York Beach, ME: The Teitan Press, 2010.

__________. *Primary Phonography*. Philadelphia: privately printed, 1882.

__________. "Psychic Wedlock," 1895. Unpublished TS, Ida Craddock Papers, 1877-1936. Southern Illinois University, Carbondale.

__________. "Records of Cases of Marital Reform Work," 1900. Unpublished TS, Ida Craddock Papers, 1877-1936. Southern Illinois University, Carbondale.

__________. "Regeneration and Rejuvenation of Men &Women Through the right use of the Sex Function," n.d. Unpublished TS, Ida Craddock Papers, 1877-1936. Southern Illinois University, Carbondale.

__________. *Right Marital Living*. Chicago: privately printed, 1899.

__________. "Sex Worship—Continued," n.d. In Vere Chappell, ed. *Lunar and Sex Worship*. York Beach, ME: The Teitan Press, 2010.

__________. "Telepathy Between the Sexes," 1900. Unpublished TS, Ida Craddock Papers, 1877-1936. Southern Illinois University, Carbondale.

__________. *The Wedding Night*. 3rd edition. New York: privately printed, 1902.

Crombie, Frederick. *The Writings of Origen*, vol. 2. *ANCL*, vol. 23. Edinburgh: T. and T. Clark, 1872.

Crowley, Aleister. *Bagh-i-muattar: The Scented Garden of Abdullah the Satirist of Shiraz*. London: privately printed, 1910.

__________. *The Equinox*, vol. 1, no. 2. London: privately printed, 1909. (Reprinted by Samuel Weiser, New York, 1972.)

__________. *The Equinox*, vol. 3, no. 1. Detroit: Universal Publishing Company, 1919. (Reprinted by Samuel Weiser, New York, 1972.)

__________. *Magick in Theory and Practice*. London: privately printed, 1930.

Culling, Louis T. *A Manual of Sex Magic*. St. Paul, MN: Llewellyn Publications, 1971.

De Montfaucon, Villars; John Yarker, trans. *The Count De Gabalis; Or, the Extravagant Mysteries of the Cabalists Exposed, in Five Pleasant Discourses on the Secret Sciences*, vol. 1. Subtitled *Sub-Mundanes; or, The Elementaries of the Cabala: Being the History of Spirits*. Bath: R. H. Fryar, 1886.

De Plancy, J. Collin. *Dictionnaire Infernal*, 3rd ed. Paris: Sagnier et Bray, 1853.

Deveney, John Patrick. *Paschal Beverly Randolph.* Albany, NY: SUNY Press, 1997.

Devine, Arthur. *Convent Life; or, the Duties of Sisters Dedicated in Religion to the Service of God.* London: R. Washbourne, 1897.

Doane, Thomas William. *Bible Myths and their Parallels in Other Religions*. 4th ed. New York: Commonwealth, 1882.

Dods, Marcus, George Reith, and B. P. Pratten. *The Writings of Justin Martyr and Athenagoras*. *ANCL*, vol. 2. Edinburgh: T. and T. Clark, 1867.

Du Prel, Carl. *Die Philosophie der Mystik.* Leipzig: Ernst Günthers Verlag, 1885.

Fletcher, William. *The Works of Lactantius*, vol. 1. *ANCL*, vol. 21. Edinburgh: T. and T. Clark, 1871.

__________. *The Works of Lactantius*, vol. 2. *ANCL*, vol. 22. Edinburgh: T. and T. Clark, 1871.

Fogel, Robert William. *The Fourth Great Awakening & the Future of Egalitarianism*. Chicago: University of Chicago Press, 2000.

Foote, Edward Bond. *Dr. Foote's Replies to the Alphites*. New York: Murray Hill Publishing Co., 1882.

__________. *Comstock versus Craddock*. New York: privately printed, 1902.

Godwin, Joscelyn, Christian Chanel, and John P. Deveney. *The Hermetic Brotherhood of Luxor.* York Beach, ME: Samuel Weiser, 1995.

Gordon, Ann D., ed. *The Selected Papers of Elizabeth Cady Stanton and Susan B. Anthony*, Volume 3. New York: Rutgers University Press, 2003.

Graves, Kersey. *The World's Sixteen Crucified Saviors, or, Christianity before Christ*. 4th ed. Boston: Colby and Rich, 1876.

Green, Elizabeth A. *Ida Craddock: A Religious Interpretation of Sexuality, 1877-1902*. Master's thesis, Southern Illinois University Carbondale, 1995.

Griffith, R. Marie. *Born Again Bodies: Flesh and Spirit in American Christianity*. Berkeley: University of California Press, 2004.

Gross, Joseph B. *The Heathen Religion in its Popular and Symbolical Development*. Boston: John P. Jewett and Company, 1856.

Guthrie, Kenneth Sylvan. *Regeneration: The Gate of Heaven.* Boston: L. Barta and Co., 1897.

Guyon, Jeanne Marie Bouvier de La Motte; Thomas Taylor Allen, trans. *Autobiography of Madame Guyon*, 2 vols. London: Kegan Paul, Trench, Trübner and Co., 1897.

Hanish, Otoman Zar-Adusht. *Inner Studies: A Course of Twelve Lessons.* Chicago: Sun Worshipper Publishing, 1902.

Healey, John. *The City of God (De Civitate Dei)*, vol. 2. London: Griffith, Farran, Okeden and Welsh, 1892.

Hartmann, Franz. *In the Pronaos of the Temple of Wisdom*. London: Theosophical Publishing Society, 1890.

Higgins, Godfrey. *Anacalypsis, an Attempt to Draw Aside the Veil of the Static Isis; or, an Inquiry into the Origin of Languages, Nations, and Religions*, 2 vols. London: Longman, Rees, Brown, Green, and Longman, 1836.

Holmes, Peter. *The Five Books of Quintus Sept. Flor. Tertullianus against Marcion*. *ANCL*, vol. 7. Edinburgh: T. and T. Clark, 1868.

Hughes, Thomas Patrick. *A Dictionary of Islam*. London: W. H. Allen and Co., 1885.

Inman, Thomas. *Ancient Faiths and Modern: A Dissertation upon Worships, Legends and Divinities in Central and Western Asia, Europe, and Elsewhere, Before the Christian Era*. New York: J. W. Bouton; London: Trübner and Co., 1876.

Ives, Halsey C. *The Dream City: A Portfolio of Photographic Views of the World's Columbian Exposition.* St. Louis: N. D. Thomson Co, 1893.

Jacolliot, Louis. *Occult Science in India and Among the Ancients, with an Account of their Mystic Initiations, and the History of Spiritism*. New York: John W. Lovell Company, 1884.

Kingsford, Anna Bonus and Edward Maitland. *The Perfect Way, or the Finding of Christ.* London: Hamilton, Adams and Co., 1882.

Kinsey, Alfred C., Wardell B. Pomeroy, and Clyde E. Martin. *Sexual Behavior in the Human Male.* Philadelphia: W. B. Saunders, 1948.

Kitto, John. *An Illustrated History of the Holy Bible*. Norwich, CT: Henry Bill, 1872.

Lane, Edward William. *An Account of the Manners and Customs of the Modern Egyptians*. 5th ed., 2 vols. London: John Murray, 1871.

Lange, Andrew. *Cock Lane and Common-Sense*. London: Longmans, Green, and Co., 1894.

Larson, Erik. *The Devil in the White City.* New York: Random House, 2003.

Le Camus, Antoine. *Medecine de l'esprit*. Paris: Ganeau, 1753.

Littré, Émile. *Dictionnaire de la langue française*, 5 vols. Paris: Hachette, 1863–1877.

Lloyd, J. William. *The Karezza Method, or Magnetation: The Art of Connubial Love*. Roscoe, CA: privately printed, 1931.

Lloyd, Mark Frazier. "Timeline of Women Pioneers and Women's Achievements at the University of Pennsylvania." University of Pennsylvania University Archives and Records Center. http://www.archives.upenn.edu/histy/features/women/chron3.html (accessed January 24, 2010).

MacDonald, George E. *Fifty Years of Freethought.* New York: The Truth Seeker Company, 1931.

Mackay, Charles. *Memoirs of Extraordinary Popular Delusions*, 2 vols. Philadelphia: Lindsay and Blakiston, 1850.

Masters, R. E. L. *Eros and Evil: The Sexual Psychopathology of Witchcraft*. New York: Julian Press, 1962.

Miller, George Noyes. *After the Sex Struck; or, Zugassent's Discovery*. Boston: Arena Publishing Company, 1895.

Milman, Henry Hart. *History of Latin Christianity; including that of the Popes to the Pontificate of Nicolas V*, vol. 1. London: John Murray, 1854.

Moore, Thomas. *Lallah Rookh*. Philadelphia: Henry Altemus, 1895.

Noirot, Louis. *L'art de vivre longtemps*. Paris: E. Dentu, 1868.

Noyes, John Humphrey. *Male Continence*. Oneida, NY: Oneida Community, 1872.

Olcott, Henry Steel. *Old Diary Leaves: The True Story of the Theosophical Society*, vol. 1. New York: Putnam's; Madras: The Theosophist, 1895.

Parkhurst, Henry M. *Diana: A Psycho-Fyziological Essay on Sexual Relations, for Married Men and Women*. New York: Burnz and Co., 1882.

Pinkerton, John. *A General Collection of the Best and Most Interesting Voyages and Travels in All Parts of the World*, vol. 9. London: Longman, Hurst, Rees, Orme, and Brown, 1811.

Putnam, Samuel P. *400 Years of Freethought*. New York: The Truth Seeker Company, 1894.

Randolph, Paschal Beverly. *The Ansairetic Mystery: A New Revelation Concerning SEX!* Toldeo: 1873. Reprinted in John Patrick Deveney, *Paschal Beverly Randolph*. Albany, NY: State University of New York Press, 1997.

Reader, A. [Hargrave Jennings] *Mysteries of the Rosie Cross*. London: A. Reader, 1891.

Roberts, Alexander and W. H. Rambaut. *The Writings of Irenaeus*. *ANCL*, vol. 5. Edinburgh: T. and T. Clark, 1868.

Rydberg, Viktor. *The Magic of the Middle Ages*. New York: Henry Holt and Company, 1879.

Savile, Bourchier Wrey. *Apparitions: A Narrative of Facts*. London: Longmans and Co., 1874.

Schaechterle, Inez L. *Speaking of Sex: The Rhetorical Strategies of Francess Willard, Victoria Woodhull, and Ida Craddock.* Doctor's thesis, Bowling Green State University, 2005.

Schroeder, Theodore. "One Religio-Sexual Maniac." The Psychoanalytic Review, vol. 23, 26-45, 1936.

__________. "Puritanism through Erotomania to Nyphomania," 1930. Unpublished TS, Ida Craddock Papers, 1877-1936. Southern Illinois University, Carbondale.

__________. "The Religious Erotism of Ida C.," 1930. Unpublished TS, Ida Craddock Papers, 1877-1936. Southern Illinois University, Carbondale.

Scot, Reginald. *The Discoverie of Witchcraft, Being a Reprint of the First Edition Published in 1584.* London: Elliot Stock, 1886.

Sinker, Robert. *The Testaments of the Twelve Patriarchs. ANCL,* vol. 22. Edinburgh: T. and T. Clark, 1871.

Smith, Goldwin. *Essays on Questions of the Day Political and Social.* New York: Macmillan; Toronto: Copp, Clark, 1893.

Smith, Thomas, Peter Peterson, and James Donaldson. *The Clementine Homilies. ANCL,* vol. 17. Edinburgh: T. and T. Clark, 1870.

Starr, Martin P. *The Unkown God: W. T. Smith and the Thelemites.* Bolingbrook, IL: Teitan Press, 2003.

Stockham, Alice B. *Karezza: Ethics of Marriage.* Chicago: Stockham Publishing Co., 1896.

__________. *Tokology: A Book for Every Woman*. Chicago: Alice B. Stockham and Co., 1886.

Stoehr, Taylor. *Free Love in America.* New York: AMS Press, 1979.

Thelwall, S. *The Writings of Quintus Sept. Flor. Tertullianus*, vol. 1. *ANCL,* vol. 11. Edinburgh: T. and T. Clark, 1869.

Thelwall, S. and Robert Ernest Wallis. *The Writings of Quintus Sept. Flor. Tertullianus, vol. 3, with the Extant Works of Victorinus and Commodianus. ANCL,* vol. 18. Edinburgh: T. and T. Clark, 1870.

Thiselton-Dyer, Thomas Firminger. *The Ghost World*. London: Ward and Downey, 1893.

Tissot, Samuel Auguste David. *L'Onanisme: dissertation sur les maladies produites par la masturbation*. Lausanne: François Grasset, 1764.

Tonna, Lewis Hippolytus Joseph. *Nuns and Nunneries: Sketches Compiled Entirely from Romish Authorities*. London: Seeleys, 1852.

Trumbull, Charles Gallaudet. *Anthony Comstock, Fighter*. New York: Fleming H. Rendell Company, 1913.

Tylor, Edward B. *Primitive Culture: Researches into the Development of Mythology, Philosophy, Religion, Language, Art, and Custom*. 3rd revised ed., 2 vols. London: John Murray, 1891.

Urban, Sylvanus. *Gentleman's Magazine and Historical Chronicle*, vol. 5. London: Edward Cave, 1735.

Vivekananda, Swami. *Raja Yoga*. New York: Baker and Taylor, 1899.

Wallis, Robert Ernest. *The Writings of Cyprian, Bishop of Carthage*, vol. 1. *ANCL*, vol. 8. Edinburg: T. and T. Clark, 1868.

__________. *The Writings of Cyprian, Bishop of Carthage*, vol. 2. *ANCL*, vol. 13. Edinburg: T. and T. Clark, 1869.

Ward, William. *A View of the History, Literature, and Religion of the Hindoos: Including a Minute Description of their Manners and Customs, and Translations from their Principal Works*. 2nd ed., 2 vols. Serampore: Mission Press, 1815.

Wasyliw, Patricia Healy. *Martyrdom, Murder and Magic: Child Saints and their Cults in Medieval Europe*. New York: Peter Lang Publishing, 2008.

Westbrook, Richard B. *The Eliminator: Skeleton Keys to Sacerdotal Secrets*. Philadelphia: J. B. Lippincott, 1894.

__________. *Girard's Will and Girard College Theology*. Philadelphia: privately printed, 1888.

Wilde, Jane F. *Ancient Cures, Charms, and Usages of Ireland: Contributions to Irish Lore*. London: Ward & Downey, 1890.

Wilson, William. *The Writings of Clement of Alexandria*, vol. 1. *ANCL*, vol. 4. Edinburgh: T. and T. Clark, 1867.

__________. *The Writings of Clement of Alexandria*, vol. 2. *ANCL*, vol. 12. Edinburgh: T. and T. Clark, 1869.

Wood, Janice. *The Struggle for Free Speech in the United States, 1872–1915: Edward Bliss Foote, Edward Bond Foote, and Anti-Comstock Operations*. New York: Routledge, 2007.

Zanchius, Hieronymus. *Excellent traité du mariage spirituel entre Iésus Christ et son église*. 1594.

To Our Readers

Weiser Books, an imprint of Red Wheel/Weiser, publishes books across the entire spectrum of occult, esoteric, speculative, and New Age subjects. Our mission is to publish quality books that will make a difference in people's lives without advocating any one particular path or field of study. We value the integrity, originality, and depth of knowledge of our authors.

Our readers are our most important resource, and we appreciate your input, suggestions, and ideas about what you would like to see published.

Visit our website at *www.redwheelweiser.com,* where you can learn about our upcoming books and free downloads, and also find links to sign up for our newsletter and exclusive offers.

You can also contact us at *info@rwwbooks.com* or at
Red Wheel/Weiser, LLC
65 Parker Street, Suite 7
Newburyport, MA 01950